The United Nations Industrial Development Organization

UNIDO and Problems of International
Economic Cooperation

YOURY LAMBERT

Westport, Connecticut
London

Library of Congress Cataloging-in-Publication Data

Lambert, Youry.
    The United Nations Industrial Development Organization : UNIDO and
problems of international economic cooperation / Youry Lambert.
       p.   cm.
    Includes bibliographical references and index.
    ISBN 0-275-94496-4 (pbk. : alk. paper)
    1. United Nations Industrial Development Organization.
    2. International agencies. I. Title.
HC60.P395 1993
341.7'5061—dc20   93-2859

British Library Cataloguing in Publication Data is available.

Library of Congress Catalog Card Number: 93-2859
ISBN: 0-275-94496-4

First published in 1993

Praeger Publishers, 88 Post Road West, Westport, CT 06881
An imprint of Greenwood Publishing Group, Inc.

Printed in the United States of America

♾™

The paper used in this book complies with the Permanent
Paper Standard issued by the National Information Standards
Organization (Z39.48–1984).

10 9 8 7 6 5 4 3 2 1

The United Nations Industrial Development Organization

Contents

Introduction

Among international economic organizations, the United Nations Industrial Development Organization (UNIDO) occupies a certain place in the sphere of international industrial cooperation. Founded in 1966, UNIDO was designed to coordinate the activities of the United Nations system in this field. Taking into account the fact that economic progress is to a large extent dependent on industrial development, the general prospects for this organization seem hypothetically to be favorable. Indeed, a great many countries have been participating in the activities of UNIDO.

It was conceived, according to General Assembly Resolution 2152 (XXI), as an autonomous organ in the system of the United Nations replacing the Industrial Development Committee of the UN. UNIDO acquired a considerable, but controversial, authority in a comparatively short period of time. General Conferences of UNIDO, especially those held in Lima (1975) and Delhi (1980), focused on the problems of international economic relations by adopting general documents, some of them strongly contested afterwards. However, the ten-year-long process of reviewing the legal status of UNIDO was completed by 1985 with UNIDO's reorganization into a specialized agency of the UN.

The present work is mostly dedicated to studying the political and legal mechanism of an international organization. The notion of a "political and legal mechanism" as applied to the activities of an international organization is used in research literature, but often without having a precise definition. Since this notion concerns the object of my study, a concise definition is necessary.

I understand the political and legal mechanism in this case as a certain system that combines the normative documents created by the organization and the corresponding political interests of the groups of individual member countries. It also characterizes the methods of maintaining the political process in that international organization. The analysis of the political and legal mechanism of cooperation in an international organization brings into focus such problems as membership in its main and auxiliary bodies, correlation between their authorities and competence, aims and functions of the organization, financial support of its activities, interaction with other intergovernmental and nongovernmental organizations, methods of decision making, forms of practical cooperation of member countries, and types of legislative activities.[1]

The political and legal mechanism, as far as UNIDO is concerned, had been evolving since the time of its formation in 1966. Considerable changes have taken place in its structure, as well as the activities typical of the organization. Special emphasis is thus placed on legal questions of UNIDO's reorganization from an autonomous organ of the General Assembly into a specialized agency of the UN.

No unanimous opinion exists on whether the totality of norms, referring to international organizations, is a part of international law. More often than not researchers believe this to be so. But others believe that some norms, in particular those regulating the relations between an organization and its personnel, form a separate category and differ from the traditional norms of international law.[2] I share the point of view that the law of international organizations goes partly beyond international law.

Some lawyers suggest that the law of international organizations forms an independent system that exists parallel to general international law. Other researchers stress the groundlessness of this thought and oppose acknowledging international organizations as primary legal subjects alongside states in the system of international law. In any event, in the normative mass of international organizations, there is a large category of norms that differ from traditional norms of international law. The law of international organizations forms an autonomous system in international law and points to a further development of international law, embracing new relations.

On the other hand, the norms regulating relations between an organization and its personnel have a lot of elements in common with international public law. That is why, as I see it, it would be fair to speak about including in the substance of international law some additional elements, those connected with norms, that regulate the activities of international organizations. These norms are inseparable from norms already adopted by international law. It would not be correct to separate, for example, some elements of the internal law of an international organization from the norms that stem from its constitutive act, since any interstate agreement undoubtedly belongs to the system of international law.

Studying UNIDO's efforts in international industrial cooperation presupposes a complex choice of which methods of analysis to apply.

Purely legal methods of analysis cannot give the optimal results because the object of study is multifaceted. In such cases, it is necessary to stress a complex approach to the interdisciplinary nature of studying international organizations.[3]

Apart from international law, this study deals with problems of international economic relations and therefore utilizes economic analysis. Thus, the striving of developing countries for the establishment of a new international economic order must be considered while taking into account factors of world economics.

Finally, a historical approach to studying the activities of UNIDO is necessary. This organization, in contrast to many other worldwide institutions, has radically evolved during a short period of time from an organ of the General Assembly into a specialized agency.

Some methods of analysis in this work are largely based on theories of cooperation and international regimes developed by Stanley Hoffmann, Robert Keohane, Ernst Haas, Harold Jacobson, Stephen Krasner, Friedrich Kratochwil, Joseph Nye, John Ruggie, and Oran Young.[4] There are numerous research publications on international organizations in particular,[5] including the works on legal aspects of their structure and activities. These publications of methodological interest include works by Robert W. Cox, Harold K. Jacobson, Leo Gross, Robert Plano, and Robert Riggs (United States); George Langrod, Daniel Colard, and Antoine Zarb[6] (France); Lutz Kollner, Bernhard Doll, and Markus Timmler[7] (Germany); H. Richards (Great Britain); Sergio Marchisio and Lina Panella[8] (Italy); Otto Burri and Regina Escher[9] (Switzerland); and Francis Seierstedt (Norway).

In recent years sharp criticism of demands by developing countries for economic help and greater rights for the third world countries in the process of decision making in international organizations has been a key point in several studies. Researchers from the developing countries, in their studies on international organizations, published increasingly more often in recent years, advocate the necessity of a radical revision of voting in some organs of worldwide international organizations, including decision making in financial questions and the issues of their operational activities. The problem is expressed in this way, for example, in the studies by Khan Rahmatulla, Seerange Rajan, and Mamulla Naidu[10] (India), Antonio Pimentol,[11] (Brazil), M. Bouhassin (Algeria), and Obed Asamoah (Ghana). That kind of research was definitely influenced by political considerations and interests of the third world countries searching more active roles in international affairs.

UNIDO itself has been so far studied insufficiently in research literature. Neither lawyers nor economists have paid any considerable attention to UNIDO, partly because many researchers did not agree with that organization's involvement in advocating a new international economic order in the 1970s. UNIDO's poor reputation among economists and lawyers was, however, not quite justified later, as it started to improve its performance.

I would like to especially thank professors Stanley Hoffmann and Robert Keohane, of Harvard, who contributed greatly to this study. I wish to thank Hurst Hannum, professor of the Fletcher School of Law and Diplomacy, for his very valuable and constructive comments to this text.

NOTES

1. This definition has very much in common with the approach taken by R. Riggs, *Politics in the United Nations*, 1958.
2. A. Verdross, "The Concept of International Law," *American Journal of International Law*, 1949, p. 438.
3. V. Moravetsky, *Funkzii mezhdunarodnykh organisazii* (Functions of International Organizations), 1975, p. 21.
4. The most significant scholarly works in this field are S. Hoffman, *Janus and Minerva*, 1986; R. Keohane, *After Hegemony: Cooperation and Discord in the World Political Economy*, 1984, pp. 1–134, 243–59; O. Young, *International Cooperation: Building Regions for Natural Resources and the Environment*, 1989, pp. 1–103; S. Krasner, ed., *International Regimes*, 1983, pp. 1–22, 93–172; S. Haggard and B. Simmons, "Theories of International Regimes," *IO*, pp. 491–517.
5. Several monographs have been published on the specialized agencies of the UN, such as International Civil Aviation Organization, Universal Postal Union, International Telecommunications Union, World Health Organization, International Labor Organization (ILO), United Nations Educational, Scientific and Cultural Organization (UNESCO): T. Buergental, *Law-Making in the International Civil Aviation Organization*, 1969; G. Codding, Jr., *The Universal Postal Union*, 1964; G. Codding, Jr., and A. Rutkowski, *The International Telecommunications Union in a Changing World*, 1982; P. Corrigan, *The World Health Organization*, 1973; W. Galenson, *The International Labor Organization. An American View*, 1981; D. Morse, *The Origin and Evolution of the ILO and Its Role in the World Community*, 1969; and J. Sewell, *UNESCO and World Politics*, 1975. Specialized agencies of the UN have been studied also in Russia, and seven books on these organizations have been published there. In terms of academic efforts regarding UNIDO, two doctoral theses on some aspects of this organization were defended in France (1969 and 1980) and one in Germany (1981). I shall refer to some arguments in these dissertations.
6. D. Colard, *Le droit de la sécurité internationale*, 1987; A. Zarb, *Les institutions spécialisées du système des Nations Unies et leurs membres*, 1980.
7. M. Timmler, *Können und Wollen*, 1972.
8. S. Marchisio, *La cooperazione per lo sviluppo nel diritto delle Nazioni Unite*, 1977; L. Panella, *Gli emendementi agli atti istitutivi delle organizazzioni internazionali*, 1986.
9. O. Burri, *Für ein Menschenheitsgewissen. UNO und Menschheit*, 1969; R. Escher, *Friedliche Erledigung von Streitigkeiten nach dem System der Vereinten Nationen*, 1985.

10.   K. Rahmatulla, *Implied Powers of the United Nations*, 1970; S. Rajan, *The Expanding Jurisdiction of the United Nations*, 1982; M. Naidu, *Collective Security and the United Nations: A Definition of the U.N. Security System*, 1974.

11.   A. Pimentol, *Democratic World Government and the United Nations*, 1980.

Acronyms

ECA	Economic Commission for Africa
ECE	Economic Commission for Europe
ECOSOC	Economic and Social Council
EEC	European Economic Community
FAO	Food and Agriculture Organization
GATT	General Agreement on Tariffs and Trade
GDR	German Democratic Republic
GNP	Gross National Product
IAEA	International Atomic Energy Agency
IBRD	International Bank for Reconstruction and Development
ICAO	International Civil Aviation Organization
ICJ	International Court of Justice
ICSC	International Civil Service Commission
IDA	International Development Association
IDB	International Development Board
IDC	Industrial Development Committee
IDF	International Development Fund
IFC	International Financial Corporation
ILO	International Labor Organization
IMF	International Monetary Fund
ITU	International Telecommunications Union
NIEO	New International Economic Order
OAU	Organization of African Unity
OECD	Organization for Economic Cooperation and Development
OPEC	Organization of Petroleum Exporting Countries
PBC	Programme and Budget Committee
PRC	People's Republic of China
SWAPO	South West Africa People's Organization
UNCTAD	United Nations Conference on Trade and Development
UNDP	United Nations Development Programme

UNESCO	United Nations Educational, Scientific and Cultural Organization
UNIDO	United Nations Industrial Development Organization
UPU	Universal Postal Union
WHO	World Health Organization
WIPO	World Intellectual Property Organization
WMO	World Meteorological Organization

Setting of Operational
Space for UNIDO

INTERNATIONAL INDUSTRIAL COOPERATION IN THE FRAMEWORK OF WORLD ECONOMICS

Effective international cooperation in the field of industrial development is most urgent in view of an extremely uneven distribution of the industrial capacities of various countries in absolute and relative figures in per capita terms. Along with the industrialized North, the large majority of the countries of the world are only beginning to establish or develop an industrial sector.

This disparity has often been explained in the third world by the aftermath of the colonial policy that the Western countries had practiced in relation to dependent territories. Such a view was definitely not always accepted. Though colonial rule had evidently different consequences for the economic development of dependent countries, one of the consequences, according to some researchers from developing countries, was the inhibition of growth in the productive forces of industry in the South. However, this widely spread assertion has never been convincingly proven by economic means of analysis, and general assumptions of that kind have not been sufficiently substantiated.

The effects of the colonial regime on the economy of dependent countries were determined above all by several factors. First, the colonies were an important source of a number of agricultural products and raw materials and thus were becoming considerable suppliers of the North, especially in relation to goods produced there in inadequate quantities or not at all. Second, by means of export the North could market surpluses of some industrial products in the colonies. Third, the communities of European settlers, where they reached considerable proportions, had to be supplied with necessities produced locally.

Naturally, for these reasons investors from the colonial powers were interested primarily in developing agricultural and some raw materials sectors in dependent territories, which supplemented some economic structures in the North. At the same time, the development of local industrial output, especially manufacturing, was rarely beneficial, because local weak economies were not prepared for this. There were, however, frequent deviations from these factors resulting from the necessity of creating some infrastructure in colonies and dependent countries. Harold Jacobson in particular noticed the phenomenon of interdependence becoming a feature of the international community even at an early stage of its formation.[1]

However, even such limited contributions by the North were a great asset to most dependent territories, which would otherwise have lagged far behind, left without incentives and input from the colonial powers.

The interests of the colonial powers in dependent territories were secured mainly by the regime of free trade with their colonies. As is often emphasized by representatives of third world countries, one of the consequences of duty-free trade, which usually meets the interests of a stronger partner, is uninhibited import of industrial goods to dependent countries. Under these conditions the development of production on the spot was impeded, since, according to this point of view, protection of the domestic market was an important condition for the formation of industry.

Some economists, however, do not embrace this rather common concept and think that free trade does not necessarily create obstacles to the economic growth of a less developed partner. For instance, economist James Ingram names the aforementioned concept "the old orthodoxy" and calls for competitive pressure for the sake of development.[2] Quite a number of third world countries with a very liberal trade regime have proven that openness of the internal market can bring a strong impetus to industrial development, as has happened in Taiwan, South Korea, Singapore, and Hong Kong.

After the euphoria of the colonial systems' disintegration and the emergence of a large number of new states, the interests of Western investors with regard to economic development, and specifically industries in the South, did not change radically. As before, they were still interested mostly in developing raw material and agricultural capacities complementary to the economic potential of the North, while retaining their domination in the production and marketing of manufactured products. The real difference existed in the methods of promoting the same economic strategy, since they dealt with independent states now, sometimes with unpredictable regimes of trade and investment.

While many third world countries embarked on impeding free market economics and introduced different restrictions, many Western investors were increasingly deterred from doing business in the South, in particular in radical countries. As the Western countries shifted the emphasis in their relations with developing countries to favor purely economic methods of cooperation, including trade and investments on average world terms, internal political problems, instability, and uncertainty in local politics were on the rise in many third world countries. These new features of political economy were well shown by Stephen Gill and David Law.[3]

Due to a number of circumstances, economic policies of Western businesses regarding the third world have been gradually modified. In the North the industrial growth was particularly spectacular in new branches of manufacturing, ensuring quick turnover of capital and high profits. At the same time, there was an increasing lack of capital and qualified labor in old, low-profit branches. The overall aggravation of ecological problems induced the Western economies to encourage shifting raw materials sectors abroad. In practice such industries had received incentives in the countries of the South.

Emergence of some branches of industry in the South did not create serious problems for the interests of Western businesses, which, while retaining their position in advanced branches, continued to dominate in economic exchange. The Western economies faced probably no other viable option while investors, possessing limited natural and labor resources, could not concentrate their efforts on all sectors of ever-diversifying industry. Since an alternative approach would slow down the development of advanced branches of industry and depress dividends, it was obvious that those processes occurred not only through a free-market mechanism, but also through growing environmental concerns and governmental interference in economics.

In the turbulent early 1970s, important developments took place in international economic relations, exemplified in the growing role of the developing countries for a certain period of time, especially in the international political landscape. This resulted in attempts to establish a so-called new international economic order, strongly biased toward interests of the third world.

Some analysts associate the changed balance of forces in the world primarily with the energy and raw materials crises that, indeed, wrought havoc with the established ideas about international economic relations. The four-fold expansion of the oil prices in 1973–1975, with another doubling in 1979–1980, led to an abrupt change in distribution of income between oil exporters and importers and played a definite role in the shift of the balance of forces. Important, too, were attempts of developing countries to establish higher prices for some other raw materials with the aim, as they insisted, of getting compensation for the previously unfavorable change in the terms of international trade. Third world representatives played quite a role in those shifts, which finally brought temporary negative consequences for the world community at large.

The new stage in the development of international economic relations was not connected exclusively with the energy and raw materials crises, as can be proved by some decisions taken by developing countries even prior to the war of October 1973 in the Middle East, followed by the decision of the Organization of Petroleum Exporting Countries (OPEC) to increase the prices for exported oil. Thus, the fourth non-aligned summit in Algeria in September 1973, among other forums at the time, demonstrated that the developing countries gave top priority to revising the established world economic order and were already launching strong demands.

It would be off the mark to associate the mounting drive for the establishment of a new international economic order only with the growing might of OPEC and a temporary improvement of marketing conditions for some other developing countries producing raw materials. The consolidation of the political and, to some extent, economic positions of some developing countries was quite logical at a certain stage after the worldwide collapse of the colonial regimes. The process of decolonization, which gathered momentum after World War II, reached its definite conclusion by the 1970s. The formation of numerous new states with overall populations several times larger than those of the advanced countries was in itself a factor of strong political significance. As full members, the developing countries quickly gained an absolute majority in the UN, its specialized agencies, and many intergovernmental organizations. Gone was the majority enjoyed by the Western countries in the General Assembly and other bodies of the UN for almost twenty years, a majority that relied on a number of developing countries dependent on the United States at that time.

Definite changes were under way also in the system of international economic relations. These changes were not purely quantitative. The new subjects of international relations, the newly independent countries, were different now, too. It became very fashionable to emphasize slogans of independence used in different contexts but invariably popular in such young states. As the states' political independence was gradually filled with new content, acceptance of the belligerent slogans of economic independence and equality in economic relations with the former colonial powers and other Western countries was gaining momentum. In practice, however, many of those slogans were interpreted as a demand for a larger share of the world's income, despite a rather low contribution.

The economies in many developing countries did not remain unchanged either. Reshaping of external economic relations in the conditions of full national independence to the detriment of old patterns of trade was designed as essential for more balanced and dynamic economic growth in the young states. However, later those presumptions proved to be premature, if not erroneous.

The policy of the Western countries, aimed at conserving a stable character of economic relations, impeded unnecessary and unwanted radical changes in the situation for some time, which could endanger world economics. However, as years elapsed, gradual changes in the 1970s turned into abrupt shifts. This was expressed in an emerging new balance of forces in the international system — and a significant increase of the developing countries' activity in their thrust for stronger political and economic positions, as became very fashionable especially at that time.

Relevant studies, including those prepared in the United Nations Industrial Development Organization (UNIDO) framework, have not yet produced a sufficiently comprehensive and theoretically sound model of industrial development that could be eventually linked to slogans popular in the third world countries.[4] Naturally, this testifies to researchers' inadequate efforts to solve the problem of general macroeconomic models for industrial development incomparable to the problem's complexity. The main factor explaining the small progress made in the elaboration of the problem is the difficulty of creating an effective universal model of industrial development in view of the extreme diversity of social, economic, political, and other conditions existing in various countries. Multiple developmental paths, fully evident in the third world countries, and diverse external factors operating in national economic systems call into question the very possibility of conceiving common industrialization models. On the other hand, it could be interpreted as a reason to call UNIDO's role into question as well.

Apparently analysts usually refuse to work on global theoretical problems of industrial development in general, which might be largely a mere academic exercise, concentrating instead on the study of particular questions related frequently to the industrial development of specific countries or regions. However, a number of researchers, for instance, Robert Keohane, Joseph Nye, and John Ruggie, have tackled the problem of economic regimes in a general prospective.[5]

The absence of a unified approach to the strategy and specific questions of industrial development is also expressed by the absence of generally recognized and accepted answers regarding ways of solving a number of problems arising from the economic policies.[6] Among existing options I identify the following:

priority development of the private or state sector, or some more balanced approach;
concentration of efforts on the development of large-scale industries and medium-sized or small enterprises;

priority development of the manufacturing or extracting industries;

comprehensive but relatively slow development of branches of industry with a comparatively balanced structure or stimulated rapid development of a few sectors most optimal for the existing conditions;

orientation on the introduction of advanced technologies requiring large expenditures or renunciation of it and saving of resources for moderate programs;

financing of industrial development mostly from internal or external resources;

development of export branches of industry or sectors oriented on the domestic market;

stimulation of branches operating on internal or imported raw materials.

The enumerated problems to be solved in the process of industrial development can be continued indefinitely through further detailed fragmentation. Naturally, solving them depends largely on the concrete conditions and the existing situation. This does not mean, however, that attempts at a global approach to the solution of industrial development problems cannot be productive. Apparently, the crux of the matter is a well-based choice of the general directions for economic policies which can be relevant regardless of specifics.

Numerous conceptions of industrial development offered by economists are most often of a specific character and imply recommendations for particular countries. These conceptions often have one defect: they take little account of the developing countries' strong emphasis on ensuring their economic independence.[7] This results in the rejection by the governments of the third world countries of sound recommendations in so many cases that one could consider it almost the rule.

No industrial development will automatically lead to real relative prosperity of a third world country, and for this reason industrialization does not necessarily signify national progress. If it is carried out without linkage to internal and world market needs, without reliance on its own forces, and entailing the threat of financial bondage on the part of lending countries and institutions, the consequences of such industrialization may be contrary to the national interests, rather than in accord with them.

This has become evident from economic history in the 1970s and the 1980s, when many industrial enterprises started in the third world countries at enormous expense turned out to be hopelessly mismanaged. Pushing the issue of industrialization at any cost, without a grounded strategy of economic development and without taking full account of the multi-faceted interests of a particular developing country, may be erroneous and even harmful in practice.[8] Only by elaboration of economic strategy based on the available experience and proceeding from comprehensive analysis of concrete conditions can all possible economic options and consequences yield positive results.

Discussing optimal ways of international development is evidently very important, as evidenced by the number of negative implementations based on erroneous conceptions. Among the most controversial concepts of industrialization was the Maoist concept actively propagated by the People's Republic of China at UNIDO forums after this country joined the organization in 1973 and through the early 1980s. According to statements by Chinese representatives, to create industry it is first necessary to develop agriculture. This is the only way of "providing food for the workers' class." The emphasis of industrialization must be on light industry, and at first the development of large-scale industry should not be set as a task. This was all presumed without free-market liberalization and privatization. In part the explanation for this approach is that China, which called itself a "socialist developing country," tried to impose its experience of industrialization on the developing countries. Until China really embarked on economic liberalization, such an approach was completely fruitless.

Another controversial approach regarding industrialization was advocated in UNIDO by the former USSR and its East European allies. According to some Russian representatives, the experience of world industrial development showed that the highest rates, the scope and volume of accomplished tasks starting from a comparatively low initial level, were characteristic of industrialization in the former USSR. Those were evidently not completely void assertions; while under the czarist regime, before the revolution of 1917, Russia was a poorly developed, mostly agrarian country that accounted for less than 5 percent of world industrial production. In just thirty to forty years after the revolution, Soviet Russia became a mighty industrial power second in gross industrial output only to the United States. Few if any other countries had undergone such large-scale and comprehensive industrial development carried out in such a brief period of time. At the same time, the colossal social losses caused by such a course of development call into question the usefulness of the applied methods, though some aspects of such development are not without theoretical interest.

FIRST UN EFFORTS TO ASSIST INDUSTRIALIZING THE THIRD WORLD

Chapters IX and X of the UN Charter, its Preamble, and Article I (paragraph 3) contain the provision that this world organization must maintain conditions of an economic and social order essential for preserving stable peace. While drawing up the UN Charter, the states participating in the San Francisco Conference of 1945 could not foresee that later assistance to international cooperation in the field of industrial development would become one of directions in the activities of the UN system. The functions and powers relating to cooperation in this field were vested mainly in the General Assembly and the Economic and Social Council (ECOSOC), but in a rather general way.

One of the first steps in promoting economic development was the inauguration of an Expanded Programme of Technical Assistance in accordance with the Economic and Social Council resolution 222 A (IX) of 1949. Economic assistance provided in the framework of the UN system at that time was gradually divided into technical and financial assistance, the latter mostly advanced by the International Bank for Reconstruction and Development (IBRD) at that time. In accordance with the aforementioned resolution of the ECOSOC, the Committee on Technical Assistance formed at that time was vested with the power to make recommendations concerning the coordination of technical assistance programs of specialized agencies. Although the Committee was not the only organ responsible for implementing the Expanded Programme of Technical Assistance, it was authorized to remove disagreements between various organs of the UN system on the use of resources under the program.

The Committee, which met twice a year, included representatives of the countries that were members of the Economic and Social Council. However, at that time this could no longer be a solution to the problems of equitable representation of third world countries, since some countries that made contributions were not even UN members. In pursuit of ECOSOC resolution 1036 (XI) of 1957, the composition of the committee was broadened with due regard to geographical distribution and contributions of states.

Though the Committee supervised the Expanded Programme of Technical Assistance, it was initially practically incapable of implementing it independently. Since the Committee's control over the program was insufficient, the Committee, in accordance with ECOSOC resolution 542 B (XVIII) of 1954, was additionally authorized to examine and approve annual programs prepared by a new auxiliary organ, the Technical Assistance Bureau. The Bureau received applications from states for technical assistance, considered the projects, and allocated funds for them. The Bureau was very dependent on specialized agencies in the allocation of resources since it used the established quotas, on governments recipients of aid, for the preparation of projects. Initially decisions of the Bureau were to be adopted unanimously, but later, by ECOSOC resolution 433 (XIV), a simple majority was sufficient.

The inadequate performance of the Committee and of the Bureau was explained largely by the fact that in the setting of the Cold War the Western countries gave priority in their foreign policy to countering the growing Eastern bloc. At the same time, the third world countries could not play a substantial role in world politics partly because they were still outnumbered.

Nonetheless, the number of developing countries was on the rise as many colonies gained independence. This was one of the catalysts that led to the adoption by the General Assembly of resolution 1240 (XIII) in accordance with which a new body, a Special Fund, was formed for rendering technical assistance. To make the Fund more independent of specialized agencies, an Administrative Council was formed from representatives of eighteen states elected by the Economic and Social Council for a term of three years, half of the represented states beneficiaries of technical assistance and the other half donor countries chosen according to the principle of equitable geographic distribution. The Fund was run by a Director-General assisted by the Consultative Committee made up of the UN Secretary General, the director of the Technical Assistance Bureau, and a representative of the World Bank. The resources of the fund were made up of voluntary contributions made by members of the UN, specialized agencies, and the International Atomic Energy Agency (IAEA). By 1964, the operational budget of the Fund reached a considerable $85 million.[9]

General Assembly resolution 2029 (XX) of November 1965 envisaged merging the Special Fund and the Expanded Technical Assistance Programme and creating the UN Development Pro-gramme (UNDP), which began to operate in January 1966 and has since become the major source of financing technical assistance through UN bodies. Initially, the UNDP Board of Administrators included thirty-seven members elected by the Economic and Social Council from UN member states, specialized agencies, and the IAEA. The arrangement was made such that the majority of members should be represented by developing countries and that the principle of equitable geographical distribution should be observed. The resolution stated that nineteen members would represent developing countries (including then Yugoslavia) and seventeen members would represent developed countries.

The issue of creating yet another body, a Facilities Fund, was on the agenda in 1960. In accordance with General Assembly resolution 1521 (XV), a committee was set up for considering the matter, one of the aims being to recommend whether the Committee should deal with technical assistance or provide credits. The Fund set up in accordance with General Assembly resolution 2186 (XXI) of December 1966 was designed to contribute to the economic growth of developing countries by means of special subsidies and interest-free, or "soft," loans. Administration of the fund was vested in the Administrative Council members, who were elected by the General Assembly from UN member states, specialized agencies, and the IAEA, with due regard for equitable geographical distribution. The Fund was headed by a Director-General, appointed by the UN Secretary General for a term of four years following approval of the candidate by the General Assembly. From the very beginning, however, the operation of the Fund was not satisfactory. In accordance with General Assembly resolution 2321 (XXII) of December 1967, the UNDP Board of Administrators began to perform the functions of the Director-General and the administrative council of the Fund. At the end of the 1970s, the weakening Fund ultimately merged with the UNDP.

For the first time in the history of the UN the General Assembly clearly defined the task of combatting economic backwardness by collective actions, with a common approach applied to the group of developing countries, by resolution 1515 (XV) of 1960. A year later, in 1961, the General Assembly adopted resolution 1707 (XVI), urging the member states to launch prompt negotiations with the aim of facilitating the expansion of trade with developing countries. Industrially developed countries were urged to refrain from unfair protection of domestic production and from restrictive and discriminating measures in relation to developing countries, as well as to ensure that the capital and aid flow to such countries constituted not less than 1 percent of the developed countries' gross national product (GNP). It was one of the earliest resolutions strongly biased toward third world countries' interests. Resolution 1710 (XVI) adopted at that time proclaimed the first UN Development Decade. The resolution set the aim of accelerating the establishment of economic independence of developing countries and their social progress so that annual growth rates of their national income should reach a minimum of 5 percent by the end of the decade, which was apparently not supported by economic estimates. The General Assembly's resolution passing was thus becoming more and more separate from reality.

In the 1950s, the UN began to devote special attention to the industrial development of the South. In connection with the UN Secretary General's report "Methods and Problems of Industrialization of Underdeveloped Countries," the ECOSOC adopted resolution 560 (XIX). In this resolution the Council requested the Secretary General to prepare a survey of studies conducted in the organs of the UN system on problems of industrial development and to propose an appropriate course of action. One of the conclusions drawn in the Secretary General's note on this issue was that the implementation of the work connected with industrial development could not be fully ensured by the UN Secretariat and the ECOSOC.[10] Economic and

Social Council resolution 597 (XXI) approved the Secretary General's point of view and the relevant work. The first projects were launched in this context.

Later the ECOSOC in its resolution 674 A(XXV) gave instructions for setting up a committee of experts to consider the work and to submit proposals for expanding it. The committee of experts recommended expanding the work of the UN secretariat on this issue and aligning the projects under the program with the UN technical assistance provided through other channels. In connection with the report of the committee of experts, the Secretary General introduced some adjustments into the research, proposing in particular that more attention should be attributed to problems of national development and complex measures. The program of scholarships was broadened also.

By the mid 1960s it had become clear that UN efforts to mobilize resources for technical assistance and pump it to the third world countries were still rather chaotic, non-systemized, and poorly coordinated. Serious improvements were becoming necessary.

INDUSTRIAL DEVELOPMENT COMMITTEE

As the activity of the UN secretariat in the field of industrial development was gradually expanding, it became increasingly apparent that its possibilities were limited and that a special organ should be set up to deal with these questions. At the proposal of the then USSR, which embarked on launching a number of void and unrealistic initiatives espoused by Nikita Khrushchev, the fourteenth General Assembly session discussed forming within the ECOSOC a commission for industrial development analogous to other specialized commissions of the Council. In its resolution 1431 (XIV) of 1959 the General Assembly recommended to the ECOSOC that it should consider forming the commission for industrial development, but without detriment to the functions of regional Economic Commissions. Accordingly, in its resolution 751 (XXIX) of April 1960, the ECOSOC approved the formation of the Industrial Development Committee. This was endorsed by the General Assembly resolution 1525 (XV) in December of the same year.

Initially, the Committee was to consist of twenty-four members, including all eighteen members of the ECOSOC and six members elected for a term of three years. By the proposal of the Eastern bloc supported by developing countries the number of its members was extended to thirty to ensure better representation of the countries that had only shortly before gained independence, including many African countries. Twelve members were thus to be elected from members of the UN, specialized agencies, and the IAEA, with due regard to equitable geographical distribution, which meant mostly developing countries. If any of the twelve elected members became a member of the Economic and Social Council, another state was to be elected in its place for the term of its membership. The Industrial Development Committee (IDC) was to function with the ECOSOC's approval between its sessions. Non-affiliated states members of the UN, specialized agencies, and the IAEA could participate in the work of the Committee but did not have voting rights. The Committee had the powers to provide consulting services to developing countries and served as a forum for the exchange of views between different countries, including the entire set of problems connected with industrial development. Further, this body was empowered to review the ECOSOC's work in this field and maintain contacts with other UN organs dealing with the same issues.

However, decision making was already getting out of hand, as the new UN bureaucracy was backing self-serving expansion of its structure. Already in its first report, which focused on the results of its first session, the Committee recommended that the ECOSOC create a center for industrial development to assist the Committee in discharging its functions. ECOSOC resolution 817 (XXXI) accordingly defined the powers of the Center, which was to be set up within the limits of resources at the disposal of the UN secretariat. The Center was to receive, analyze, and disseminate the experience of industrial development and technical assistance programs and to ensure the exchange of information about the activity of various UN organs in this field.

At the first stage of its work the Center failed to establish necessary contacts with the relevant UN agencies and institutions in developing countries dealing with problems of industrial development. In connection with this the General Assembly adopted resolution 1712 (XVI) in which it recommended to the Center that it establish, as quickly as possible, cooperation with regional economic commissions and with the competent bodies of developing countries. Problems of coordination were emerging even at the very beginning.

The Center collected and processed different documentation on industrial development, maintaining relations with the governments of recipient countries, funds and scientific institutions of donor countries. In the course of consultations with some specialized agencies it was agreed that they must prepare and send to the Center reports about their activity in the field of industrial development.

Such a system of collecting and exchanging information naturally required considerable resources. Financing of the Center could not be carried out in the framework of the Special Fund or the Expanded Programme of Technical Assistance because the activity of the Center did not meet their criteria. Nor could it be financed by the regular UN budget, for then it was necessary to specially establish whether problems of industrial development cooperation were among the priorities of the UN.

As a solution, the same means was suggested: expansion. The second session of the Industrial Development Committee recognized that the Center could not belong to the industrial development division of the UN secretariat's Economic and Social Department. The revision of the established structure was already then vehemently advocated by some developing countries that proposed reinforcing the IDC by making it a part of the secretariat and forming an executive apparatus in it under the guidance of the UN Under-Secretary General. This position was reflected in the resolution of the IDC, which recommended that the Secretary General attach the necessary staff to the secretariat under the UN commissioner for industrial development in the rank of an Under-Secretary General. J. A. Maibre was appointed to this post at that time.[11]

At its third session, held in May 1963, the Industrial Development Commission submitted a draft of a new structure of the Industrial Development Center that had two services and a group of technical advisers. One of these services dealing with research and estimates included a group of estimates and sections for drafting programs in industrial policy and economics of industry. The other service dealing with technology included a documentation group and three sections: technical research and scientific services, personnel training, and administration and coordination. Following such expansion, the Center prepared annual reports in which it reviewed the entire activity in the field of industrial development in the framework of the UN system and gave recommendations to the Economic and Social Council.

The Center made it possible to ensure better coordination of the UN system's efforts in the field of industrial development. At the same time, the capabilities of the Center were considered limited in view of rather insignificant funds provided for its needs from the UN budget. Another serious impediment was the fact that the governments of developing countries were still not well aware of the possibilities offered by such a new type of cooperation. For this reason these governments made few requests for consulting services and technical assistance.

At the IDC's third session there arose the issue of interpreting a number of concepts without which it was impossible to reach common understanding of existing documents and, still more so, documents that were forthcoming, including notions of industrialization and industrial sector. For example, some delegations interpreted "industrialization" (a term I tend to use very cautiously because of sour results of massive industrialization campaigns in centrally planned economies) as a broad process of development and reorganization of the economic structure from a predominantly agrarian type into a predominantly industrial one. Other delegations implied development of the industrial sector as such. A number of delegations were in favor of interpreting the industrial sector as manufacturing only, while others saw it as a broad complex of branches, including mining, manufacturing, building, and a part of the services sector.

As a result of this discussion, the IDC came to a broad understanding that industrialization is a process of economic development that mobilizes a constantly growing part of national resources for the creation of diversified internal economic structure, with the use of modern technology. This process is characterized by a dynamic manufacturing sector and the production of capital goods and consumption commodities. The economy as a whole, then, may reach rapid growth rates and progress in the economic and social fields.[12] As for the Industrial Development Center, it was pointed out that it must carry out its mission chiefly with the aim of developing manufacturing as it is described in the international standard classification of branches of economic activities.

In its resolution 1524 (XV) of December 1960, the General Assembly pointed to the need for additional external sources for financing the development of third world economies, including state and private capital. In this connection the General Assembly urged the member states to provide financial assistance to developing countries, on a bilateral and multilateral basis, including long-term loans, subsidies, and credits interest free or with low interest and repayable in local currency.

In accordance with General Assembly resolution 1712 (XVI) and ECOSOC resolution 817 (XXXI), the Industrial Development Committee was to examine reports by the heads of secretariats of specialized agencies, the director of the Technical Assistance Bureau, and the Director-General of the Special Fund about work of the respective bodies in the field of industrial development. In its resolution 839 (XXXII) of 1961 the ECOSOC requested the UN Secretary General to submit to the IDC a report on research and operational activity in the field of industrial development conducted by all UN organs. At the same time, the reports received by the IDC differed widely due to the various methods used in their preparation and various criteria for assessing activity in the field of industrial development. The IDC carried out work to formulate a number of criteria and concepts. Thus, it was proposed that working the field of industrial development be classified into research and operational activity and to group projects by the source of financing. The report of the sixth IDC session, "Activity of U.N. Organs in the Field of Industrial Development," again pointed out insufficient coordination within the UN system in the indicated sphere and proposed to improve accountability in the reports forwarded to it by appropriate organizations.

EMERGING UN BODY

The problem of inadequate activities on the part of the IDC industrial cooperation was raised in the early 1960s. The non-aligned conference in Belgrade in 1961 and the international conference on problems of economic development held in Cairo in 1962 indicated several main tasks for the third world, controversial already at that time. Regarding the development of cooperation among countries, assistance through joint efforts to achieve industrialization of the regions, where the industrial sector was not yet created or did not meet the requirements of the time, was strongly emphasized. The third world countries started to use the term *industrialization* strongly advocated by the then Soviet Union.

At the second IDC session in 1962 the situation in industrial cooperation was considered unfavorable. In accordance with the Committee's recommendation, the ECOSOC requested in its resolution 873 (XXXIII) that the UN Secretary General create an ad hoc group of experts for exploring and identifying new organizational forms of cooperation in solving problems of industrial development. In its report submitted in March 1963, this group, made up of representatives from India, Brazil, Egypt, Mexico, Pakistan, Nigeria, the United States, Great Britain, the USSR, and Hungary, pointed out that industrial development was a field of cooperation little covered by the UN framework. In this connection the established system of cooperation was deemed to be unsatisfactory even if it were reinforced with additional financial resources. At the same time, the idea of forming a specialized agency was considered impractical since its implementation would have required too much time and would have involved considerable difficulties. The group recommended as the most rational solution establishing an auxiliary General Assembly organ as provided for in Article 22 of the UN Charter.

In accordance with the recommendations of the third IDC session, the ECOSOC in its resolution 969 (XXXVI) proposed that the Secretary General submit to the eighteenth General Assembly session his remarks on the report by the group of experts of member states and specialized agencies related to international economic cooperation. In 1963, the General Assembly session adopted resolution 1940 (XVIII) in which it recognized the need to change the system of industrial development cooperation established in the UN system. The resolution, advocated by the third world countries, stated that the IDC should consider measures for creating an appropriate organization. The General Assembly also reaffirmed the need to form within the UN framework a new specialized agency dealing with problems of assisting third world countries in industrial development, but without indicating a timetable.

The fourth IDC session, held in 1964, examined two draft resolutions. One draft, proposed by Argentina, Brazil, Colombia, Iraq, Tunisia, Chile, Ecuador, and Yugoslavia, envisaged creating a new specialized agency for industrial development in the UN framework and was adopted by nineteen votes for to nine against. In accordance with the second draft, proposed by the Unites States, the existing structure was left unchanged; however, the Industrial Development Center was to receive additional financial resources. The second draft was approved, too, by unanimous vote, for its was interpreted as a temporary decision that did not contradict the idea of forming a new specialized agency at a later date. The IDC's recommendations were approved by ECOSOC resolution 1030 (XXXVII), which recognized the necessity of forming a specialized body for industrial development and discussing this question at the General Assembly. The ECOSOC requested the UN Secretary General to explore the proposed functions, powers, and structure of such an organization in conformity with the IDC's recommendations and advised the General Assembly to examine this question.

As a result, the draft of the constitutive act of a new organization, circulated on behalf of the UN Secretary General in December 1964, lacked clear indications concerning the juridical status of the new body, which, surprisingly, still could be either a specialized agency or an autonomous organ of the UN. Membership in the Industrial Development Agency (as this organ was called in the draft) was open to any members of the UN, specialized agencies, and the IAEA. In addition, the draft allowed membership by any other state that might be admitted by the agency's General Conference. In the structure of the agency its supreme body was to become a General Conference, which represented all member countries. A council elected at the Conference was to consist of twenty to thirty members. The Council, answerable to the General Conference, would perform the tasks set by the General Conference and regularly submit reports on practical work of the agency. Lastly, the secretariat, headed by the Director-General, was to be in charge of daily work. The organization was to be financed by means of two channels. As was becoming customary in such cases, administrative expenditures were to be covered by assessments of member countries according to agreed quotas and operational expenditures were to be covered by voluntary contributions.[13]

The submitted report was examined and approved by the ECOSOC at its thirty-ninth session. ECOSOC resolution 1081F interpreted the unclear definition of the juridical status of the Industrial Development Agency in its report to mean that it was a specialized agency of the UN. At the same time, during the examination of this question by the second Committee of the General Conference in the course of the twentieth session in November–December 1965, presentation of the question concerning the formation of a specialized agency was criticized by some Western countries as premature, if unnecessary in principle.

Thus, the draft resolution moved by Great Britain, Denmark, Finland, and Sweden recognized the need to expand the functions of the IDC and provide additional financial resources for it. At the same time it made no provisions for the formation of a new agency. This approach did not lack realism, since new UN bodies were mushrooming at that time, not always with sufficient justification. However, this draft resolution did not receive unreserved support by many other Western countries. The United States, sharply criticized at that time by the majority of developing countries for its part in the Vietnam war, was ready for definite concessions. In the end the United States refused to support the draft and thus to block the creation of the new UN body.

Most of the draft's support was given by Latin American countries that envisaged the creation of a specialized agency. However, the draft was set out in very broad terms and did not contain indications concerning the structure of this agency. Following a certain revision of the draft's text, and in conformity with the objections made by some West European countries, the draft was supported by fifty countries, including the Eastern bloc countries. On December 6, 1965, this draft was adopted by the second Committee of the General Assembly.

The draft urged the General Assembly to set up an autonomous organization, the United Nations Industrial Development Organization (UNIDO), within the UN framework. The main working body of the organization was to be the Industrial Development Board. According to the draft, financing of the administrative budget was to be carried out from the UN regular budget, and specific expenditures were to be met by voluntary contributions of UN member states, members of specialized agencies, and the IAEA and by the resources of the UNDP. The draft provided for the creation of a committee of thirty-six member countries to carry out preliminary work on procedural and administrative questions and report on its progress to the IDC, to the ECOSOC, and to the twenty-first session of the UN General Assembly. The UN Secretary General was empowered to take measures leading to formation of the secretariat of the new organization without delay, using the resources of the UN secretariat for that purpose. The Executive-Director was to be appointed by the UN Secretary General and approved by the General Assembly. The draft tabled by fifty-nine countries was adopted by the General Assembly on December 20,

1965, becoming resolution 2089, and served as the foundation of the new organization.

On December 21, 1965, the General Assembly session formed an ad hoc committee for the formation of UNIDO. It included twenty-one developing countries, ten Western countries (the United States, Australia, Great Britain, Italy, Spain, the Netherlands, Finland, France, West Germany, Sweden), four Eastern bloc countries (the USSR, Rumania, Czechoslovakia, Yugoslavia), and Cuba. In the period from March 28 to May 2, 1966, the committee met in eleven sessions.

The main problem that arose while forming a coordinated decision, as the work of the committee demonstrated most vividly, was again caused by sharp disagreements over the status of the new organization. None of the previous resolutions, including General Assembly resolution 2089 (XX), settled finally the question of whether the new organization was to be a UN specialized agency or to have some other organizational form.

The majority of developing countries were apparently in favor of forming a specialized agency in the UN system, believing that this would most fully conform to the task of extracting more international assistance for their industrial development. The UN organs that discussed this issue, the ECOSOC and the IDC, declared themselves in favor of forming a specialized agency. The first United Nations Conference on Trade and Development (UNCTAD) session, which examined the IDC's recommendations, not surprisingly also supported this proposal (by eighty-one votes to twenty-three with eight abstentions). Several developing countries, among them India, Nigeria, and Senegal, however, were against defining the question exclusively as the formation of a specialized agency. Their position reflected a compromise approach. While not opposing the status of a specialized agency, these countries realistically regarded this as an aim that should not be accomplished immediately.

The Eastern bloc countries supported in principle, though reluctantly and with some reservations, the intention of the majority of developing countries to form a specialized agency. First of all, in the view of some centrally planned countries the formation of a specialized agency would be expedient only after issues of its structure and functioning were elaborated sufficiently; this would require additional work. Moreover, they questioned the financial viability of such a specialized agency that had not been studied sufficiently; they were reluctant to undertake additional expenses in hard currency necessary for a specialized agency's budget.

The Western countries that opposed creating a specialized agency included the United States, Australia, Denmark, France, Sweden, and Japan. Their argument was that organized forms of industrial development cooperation were not decisive for its successful progress. The formation of a new specialized agency would increase the danger of duplicating the functions performed in this field by the already existing organs in the UN system. Accordingly, from the standpoint of financing administrative expenditures the formation of a specialized agency was undesirable. Behind this was also the reasoning that the status of a specialized agency would give the new organization leverage to raise more insistently the issue of additional financing by Western countries of programs that would eventually assist ill-conceived industrialization projects in developing countries.

Three drafts of the tasks, structure, and financing of the new organization were submitted to the ad hoc committee for the formation of UNIDO. The draft, proposed by twenty-one developing countries, envisaged broad powers for UNIDO, which was to be an independent and autonomous organization. This required special efforts on the part of participating countries in providing its financing. All questions in the UN framework concerning industrial development were to be entrusted to UNIDO, for which clear differentiation of its functions was deemed necessary. This group of countries proposed that the board of the new organization be elected only by the General Assembly.[14]

The second draft was submitted by eleven Western countries. Defining the tasks of UNIDO, this draft placed emphasis on assisting the developing countries in working out an effective economic policy on the national level. UNIDO was assigned the central role in international industrial cooperation, but the reservation was made that the new organization should not assume the functions of already existing UN organs, with the exception of the IDC, which was to be dissolved. It was pointed out that the main operational expenditures should be met through the UNDP channels and that the board of the new organization was to be elected by the ECOSOC.[15]

The third draft, proposed by four Eastern bloc countries, offered largely different formulations and principles. Instead of the notion *assistance in the field of industrial development* to developing countries, it proposed the notion *cooperation in the field of industrial development*, which presumably meant to emphasize the quality-based character of such cooperation in the sphere of international economic relations. The Eastern bloc countries clearly wanted to benefit from such cooperation as well, in order to modernize their industries. UNIDO was to be given the task of elaborating a global strategy of cooperation and was to coordinate the efforts of different UN organs in this field. Operational expenditures could be financed by different countries in their national currency. The board was to be elected by the General Assembly.[16]

In the course of the ad hoc committee's work, contradictions in the positions of separate groups of countries were nevertheless eradicated, though some countries, among them the United States, reserved the right to defend their former position in the future. A compromise draft of the resolution was adopted by the ad hoc committee at its ninth session without a vote. It resembled to some extent all three original drafts. The tasks of the organization were outlined rather broadly, although emphasis was placed on the necessity of strictly coordinating activities with other UN organs in this and related fields of cooperation. Financing the UNIDO's operational budget was to be carried out in a way deemed most rational to member countries. Forty-five board members were to be elected by the General Assembly. The board was supposed to submit annual reports about its activities through the ECOSOC to the General Assembly.

Financing UNIDO's activities was considered by the Fifth Committee of the General Assembly. In view of financial consequences created by the formation of the new organization, in pursuit of General Assembly resolution 2089 (XX), the Committee proposed introducing a new item (No. 21) in the UN budget for 1967 and fixing it at $3.8 million. By means of an additional loan of $1.4 million, total subsidies for UNIDO in the first year of its existence were brought to $5.2 million.[17]

On October 20, 1966, the report of the ad hoc committee for the formation of UNIDO was submitted to the second Committee of the General Assembly, which adopted it with some amendments by ninety-nine votes with one abstention. The twenty-first General Assembly session adopted on November 17, 1966, a resolution that instituted UNIDO as a General Assembly organ with a view to encouraging industrial development as well as coordinating the entire activities of the UN in this field. Accordingly, the ECOSOC adopted resolution 1194 (XLI) on December 21, 1966, whereby the Industrial Development Committee was abolished.

Since many developing countries, with the support of the Eastern bloc, wanted to insure substantial autonomy of this organization, the choice of UNIDO's seat was called into question. Apart from New York and Geneva, which could be chosen automatically as a seat of the organization since both cities accommodate most of the UN organs, the capitals of India, Greece, Austria, Kenya, Peru, Turkey, Trinidad, and Tobago were proposed to host the secretariat of the organization. The UN General Assembly chose Vienna, the capital of Austria, as a city sufficiently remote from New York City, as developing countries wanted. At the same time, Vienna is located in the central part of Europe, making it convenient for many countries. The definite geographical remoteness from the seat of major UN organs was to underline UNIDO's independence.

Thus, UNIDO's foundation, as well as UNCTAD's story,[18] in the mid 1960s reflected the first serious drive of the third world for greater influence in world politics. Both institutions were looked upon as reflections of the speedily growing number of independent states and their thirst for a fair role in the world economic and political affairs.

NOTES

1. H. Jacobson, *Networks of Interdependence: International Organizations and the Global Political System*, 1986, pp. 30–58.

2. J. Ingram, *International Economic Problems*, 1986, p. 411.

3. G. Gill and D. Law, *The Global Political Economy*, 1988.

4. This is well shown for instance by S. Gantam, *The Military Origins of Industrialization and International Trade Rivalry*, 1984.

5. R. Keohane and J. Nye, eds., *Transnational Relations and World Politics*, 1972, pp. IX–XXIX, 1–22, 48–95; J. Ruggie, "International Responses to Technology; Concepts and Trends," *International Organization*, 1975, pp. 557–84.

6. See P. Drucker, "The Changed World Economy," *Foreign Affairs*, 1986, pp. 768–91.

7. See W. Nafziger, *The Economics of Developing Countries*, 1984.

8. This was well shown in W. Asher, *Schelming for the Poor: The Politics of Redistribution in Latin America*, 1984.

9. C. Colliard, *Institutions des relations internationales*, 1968, p. 790.

10. E/2832.

11. Cf. E/C.5/L.6/Rev. I

12. Cf. E/3781.

13. A/5826, Dec. 1964.

14. A/AC. 126/6.

15. A/AC. 126/7.

16. A/AC. 126/8.

17. A/6510.

18. A very good description of UNCTAD's role in the third world's political drive is in G. Mrloz, *La CNUCED: droit international du développement*, 1980.

2

Main Stages of UNIDO as an Organ of the General Assembly

DEVELOPING WORLD IN ADVANCE

Currently industrial development is one of the key factors that predetermine the social and economic life of states and create prerequisites for their influence in the international system. At the same time, in the framework of international organizations, industrial development cooperation has not yet reached a sufficiently high level. This is explained by the fact that the economic and political goals of the main groups of countries do not, to a large degree, coincide. Thus, as far as industrial development cooperation is concerned, it is possible to discern the main general positions of the key groups of countries.[1]

In spite of a great differentiation in the level of economic development of the third world countries, their positions on the questions of international industrial cooperation are rather similar. The developing countries are usually interested in receiving the largest possible help with their industrialization from the developed countries and paying as little compensation as possible. Frequently they are guided by their immediate interests and strive to implement a restricted range of projects while the cardinal questions of a long-term strategy in economic development lose priority.

In contrast, Western countries tend to maintain and preserve their superior positions in industrial production. However, in the conditions of rapid scientific and technological progress, Western countries are ready to relinquish the less profitable old industries, usually material- and energy-intensive, which sometimes present a threat to the environment. These industries require abundant low-skilled labor and could be shifted to the countries of the South. Simultaneously, Western countries are ready, on a large but nevertheless selective basis, to render assistance for industrial development in the third world, not without the purpose of further strengthening their economic and political influence.

Until Russia, its allies in the Commonwealth, and East European countries became submerged in resolving their internal problems, they proclaimed support of the aspirations of the developing countries in their efforts to industrialize. However, even then they were not prepared to help them on a large scale. This explains in part why the USSR was not inclined to consider technical assistance as the main condition regarding successful development of the third world countries, stressing instead that it depended on the choice of an economic course corresponding to their national interests.

The emergence of the United Nations Industrial Development Organization (UNIDO) was not incidental and coincided with the formation of a large group of developing countries known as the Group of 77, which started to pursue a common strategy on economic questions in the framework of the UN and its bodies.[2] The developing countries clearly succeeded in preserving an advantage in the UN Conference on Trade and Development (UNCTAD). One of the main reasons was that by the mid 1960s the third world had secured a large majority in most of the UN bodies using the "one state–one vote" principle. As a result, as Robert Gregg writes, "The group of 77 has quite literally captured the UNCTAD secretariat, the secretary general and his top directorate are frequently its spokesmen."[3]

The activity of developing countries in favor of UNCTAD, and to some extent their efforts to create a broadly empowered UN organ dealing with industrial cooperation, contributed to the formation of a bloc of those states. Industrially developed countries fell naturally into two groups: Western countries, on the one hand, and the USSR with its East European allies, on the other. Thus, from the very start of the organization's functioning, its members formed three key groups of states whose policy and balance of forces played a determining role in the work of UNIDO.

By that time the third world countries were close to a virtual control of the resolutions passed by the General Assembly. They succeeded in creating UNIDO as a General Assembly body, which was the simplest way to get an organization on its feet without preparing the statute as a kind of an international treaty, which would have taken years to negotiate. Both Western and "socialist" countries accepted that step, although without much enthusiasm.

UNIDO became a typical case of "transgovernmental coalition building" described as follows: "Transgovernmental policy cooperation shades over into transgovernmental coalition building. . . . To improve their chances of success, governmental sub-units attempt to bring actors from other governments into their own decision-making processes as allies. When such coalitions are successful, the outcomes are different than they would be if each coalition partner were limited to his own nationality."[4] Interestingly, once created, such coalitions have remained remarkably stable in UNIDO for a quarter of a century.

At the first session of the International Development Board (IDB) held in 1967 in New York (its sessions were later held in Vienna), it was pointed out that in the previous thirty years the share of developing countries in world industrial capacities remained unchanged, constituting just 5 percent. The Group of 77, supported by the East European countries, insisted, but not with proper justification, on radically reshaping world industrial production and changing the existing unfavorable situation.

The most pressing questions raised at the IDB session concerned the tasks and practical activity of UNIDO. A number of developing countries supported by the United States proposed reducing UNIDO's tasks to operational activity and advocated decentralizing the organization and setting up large operational subdivisions in various regions. The Western countries, which exerted more influence in the Economic and Social Council (ECOSOC) and the United Nations Development Programme (UNDP) than in the new UNIDO, put a narrow interpretation of the role for the latter in questions of coordination. The Eastern bloc countries, for their part, emphasized the need for a rational combination of the operational and research activities of UNIDO and opposed decentralizing the structure of the organization. They argued that it would be expedient to strengthen its working ties with regional UN economic and social commissions.

The issues of staffing the secretariat and developing UNIDO's operational activities were characterized by substantial differences in the appraisal of the work done by the executive leadership of the organization. Thus, the second IDB session, held in 1968 in Vienna, which became the seat of the secretariat, was already a disputed forum. The Eastern bloc countries criticized UNIDO's executive leadership for ignoring the principle of respecting the interests of major parties concerned in decision making, meaning, naturally, themselves. They pointed out shortcomings in the evolving organizational structure of UNIDO, including the absence of clear differentiation of functions between the departments of the secretariat and elements of duplication in their work. This was one of the issues prompting the session to form a working group on the program and for coordination as an auxiliary organ of the IDB. The third and fourth IDB sessions, held in 1969 and 1970, made decisions on UNIDO's operational activity and its role in the UN system, but the earlier disagreements between the key groups of countries remained intact.

The differing positions of the groups of countries on UNIDO's policy and many organizational matters provided the secretariat with a pretext to call a session of the plenary organ of the organization, a special international conference of member states, although such a body was not provided for by General Assembly resolution 2152 (XXI). This was just the beginning of forthcoming politicization of UNIDO.

Developing countries considered this a favorable opportunity for calling a special conference, trying to seize an initiative. Under their influence, the twenty-fifth General Assembly session adopted resolution 2626 (XXV) on the international strategy of development, and the UNDP approved new program regulations for technical assistance.

At the special conference, which met in June 1971 (it became de facto the first General Conference), the Group of 77 submitted a draft resolution, couched in forceful terms, that referred mainly to the organizational structure and financing of UNIDO. The Group proposed immediate reorganization of UNIDO at the twenty-sixth General Assembly session, including converting it into a specialized agency, forming two permanent IDB committees, and holding general conferences in the future once a year or every two years.

By consensus, the special conference passed a resolution on the long-term strategy, structure, and financing of UNIDO. The main body of the resolution (paragraphs 1–6) concentrated on the long-term strategy and orientation of UNIDO's activities. The conference recommended that the twenty-sixth General Assembly session adopt a resolution on UNIDO's operational activities. According to that proposal, UNIDO should be oriented to provide effective assistance in solving problems of industrial development, to form a center for the exchange of industrial and commercial information, and to improve coordinating activity within the procedures of programming by countries on the part of UNDP residents. Another suggestion was that the UN Secretary General should appoint a high-level group of experts from different geographical groups for formulating UNIDO's long-term strategy. The Executive-Director of UNIDO was invited to study various types of experiences in the field of industrial development of countries with different social and economic systems. This experience should be used fully and impartially to ensure UNIDO's assistance in drafting economically sound plans of industrial development, implementing economic reforms, training highly qualified personnel, and implementing measures to end the outflow of specialists from third world countries.

The special conference focused on UNIDO's organizational structure. The conference's resolution (paragraphs 7–13) recommended that the General Assembly call the next General Conference of UNIDO in 1974–1975 to consider the demand of a number of countries for setting up regional and sub-regional bureaus as bodies promoting the operational activity decentralization, and to invest the IDB with the powers to examine and supervise the structure of the UNIDO secretariat at all levels. The conference requested that the IDB replace the working group on the program and coordination as an auxiliary organ with a permanent Committee of the Board, to be convened twice a year.

Lastly, the resolution dealt with problems of financing (part III, paragraphs 14–19). The conference confirmed that the UNDP should remain the main financing source behind the operational activities of the organization. It was proposed that the annual sessions of the IDB should carry out the exchange of views on the estimates. The conference requested the UNDP Board of Administrators to keep the minimum annual level of expenditures at $2 million; UNIDO's share was to be increased in the regular program of UNDP technical assistance.

On the whole, the developing countries were disappointed with the results of the special conference, since a considerable part of their proposals, including reorganization of UNIDO, were not accepted. However, they regarded this as a temporary situation and hoped that it would be different at the forthcoming second General Conference of UNIDO. The sixth IDB session, in 1972, in pursuit of the resolution of the special conference, decided to convene the second General Conference and to institute a permanent committee as an auxiliary organ of the IDB, as well as a special committee on cooperation between the UNDP and UNIDO.

The seventh IDB session, in 1973, examined the report of the group of experts on UNIDO's long-term strategy created by a decision of the special conference. However, the report did not satisfy all the main groups of member countries; it was decided to form an ad hoc committee from representatives of twenty-seven countries to continue work on the same issue. The committee was created in Vienna and was given a one-year term. However, no decisions of substance were adopted prior to the second General Conference because many countries associated the possibility of major decisions on UNIDO precisely with this conference.

The rising political conflict on issues of international economic relations gained momentum in April 1974, when the Sixth Special Session adopted the Declaration and a Program of Action on the Establishment of a New International Economic Order. While promoting the interests of the third world and largely ignoring interests of the industrialized countries, this unrealistic and rather biased document did not propose adequate solutions to the difficulties that the global economies faced. The document, technically adopted by the majority of developing countries, was sharply criticized in the West. For instance, Clyde Ferguson, a prominent U.S. diplomat, stated at an ECOSOC session: "We are not willing to lend our support to the creation of the kind of New International and Economic Order envisaged by the Program of Action adopted by the Sixth Special Session."[5]

It was a period when "in almost all of the agencies, the United States increasingly found itself in the minority in governing bodies dominated by developing countries using their voting strength to seek support for their own national development and to promote a new economic order in the world."[6]

The major drive of the Group of 77 in trying to impose its vision of the world economic order with the means of UNIDO took place at the second General Conference, in March 1975 in Lima, Peru. Both time and place (a developing country) played some role.

In the quarter of a century prior to the second General Conference, the share of the developing countries in the world industrial production, despite comparatively high rates of development in some of them, remained at a very low level — 7 percent. In the early and mid 1970s, the situation was compounded by the termination of the Bretton Woods financial agreements, the instability of the world monetary system, and the energy crisis that struck most of the third world no less than the North. Except for future Organization of Petroleum Exporting Countries (OPEC) members, developing countries, heavily dependent on external trade, suffered considerably. After the 1972 decision to convene the second General Conference, the position of many developing countries, including the state of their economies and their industrial sectors in particular, deteriorated. The main task before the General Conference was to find ways of improving the conditions of living for the two-thirds of the world population living in the third world.

Developing countries wanted the Conference to adopt a powerful document, even attributing a strong name to it, the Declaration and Plan of Action. The basic documents for the preparation of the Declaration and Plan of Action were resolutions 3201 and 3202 of the sixth special General Assembly session, the declarations adopted by the regional conferences on questions of industrial development held in pursuit of ECOSOC resolution 1909 (LVII): in Cairo, 1973; the third conference on industrial development of Arab countries in Tripoli, 1974; the conference of ministers of industry of developing countries of Asia and the Pacific region in Bangkok, 1974; and the conference of ministers of industry of Latin American countries in Mexico, 1974.

The second General Conference was held in March 1975 in Lima. Some third world delegations drew attention to the economic situation at large, pointing out that in the middle of the 1970s about 300 million people, or nearly a quarter of the world's work force, were jobless or had only part-time work. By the end of the century the world's work force was expected to grow to one billion people. This required a new world structure of industrial capacities and a new international division of labor. The General Conference introduced a new concept — a new social accord between developed and developing countries.

The draft of the Lima Declaration and Plan of Action in the field of development and industrial cooperation, as proposed by the third world countries, was in line with the principles outlined by the Declaration and Program of Action adopted by the General Assembly a year earlier. The Western countries had their own draft. The "socialist" countries suggested only addenda and amendments to the first draft.

Some compromises were reached, but they were few; the final version contained many controversial issues. At the plenary session of the second General Conference on March 26, 1975, the United States voted against the Lima Declaration and the Plan of Action but was not supported by the rest of Western countries, which abstained. Of the developing countries, Nicaragua abstained in one case. The East European countries voted for all the indicated cases but made their separate comments on a number of issues.

The final so-called Lima Declaration and Plan of Action was close to the original draft of the Group of 77 and was hailed then as a big success for the diplomacy of the developing countries, no matter that later it might be seen an imaginary one.

The draft of the Declaration and Plan of Action proposed by the Group of 77 contained many of the provisions of the concept of a new international economic order the group actively advanced. The group was backed in this by the Eastern bloc countries, although without much enthusiasm, and was partially approved by the General Assembly and other UN organs. Moreover, compared with the decisions of the sixth special General Assembly session, the draft contained a more radical interpretation of the principles related to sovereign rights with regard to national natural resources and control over them. It also promoted more persistently the need for the industrialization of the third world countries. Finally, the draft reflected the striving of developing countries to complement and develop the already adopted UN documents on a new international economic order with reference to international industrial cooperation.[7]

Due to the initiative of the Eastern bloc countries, the draft of the Group of 77 was complemented with provisions of dubious value to the effect that it was necessary to give assistance to the state sector playing a certain role in the industrial growth of developing countries and to apply elements of planning in the economic policy. Another addition was the provision about subordination of private and foreign capital to the requirements of national economic plans.

At the same time, the Eastern bloc countries wanted to reap dividends of disunion between the North and the South without exposing themselves. They expressed disagreement with the formula about the equal responsibility of industrially developed countries for the economic backwardness of former colonies. They also disagreed with the insistence on obligatory allocation of 1 percent of the gross national product for assistance to developing countries because it was beyond their capabilities. Doubts were cast concerning the demand of direct transfer of resources from developed to less-developed countries. They also had reservations related to the description of the economy in developed countries.

In the draft of the final document submitted by Western countries, emphasis was laid on cooperation of foreign capital with national organizations. It set forth a thesis about joint management. In particular, it expressed the idea that developing countries must provide conditions for direct assistance to them by international corporations and that the principle of equality must be observed in the cooperation of developing countries with transnational corporations. In general, the Western countries demanded that developing states grant the same status to foreign capital in their territory as that enjoyed by their national entrepreneurs and reduce state control over foreign trade. But to a large extent the demands of Western countries at the General Conference were not accepted, which contributed to increasing differences of views.

I shall consider principles advanced by the Declaration and Plan of Action in Chapter 8. While promoting a new international economic order, the Lima Declaration and Plan of Action envisaged further reorganization of UNIDO and its transformation into a specialized UN agency.

EMERGING CONTROVERSY

In the latter half of the 1970s, because of the impossibility of finding working compromises, the North-South dialogue was reaching an impasse. The hopes of the developing countries for the ever-increasing aid flow from Western countries were not justified. International forums on problems of economic cooperation and assistance were not yielding tangible results. The emerging economic order, rather far removed from the principles of the new international economic order advanced in a number of resolutions of the UN bodies including UNIDO, did not benefit the interests of developing countries and did not quite suit the Western countries either.

At that time it became fashionable to criticize bad management, duplication of work, inefficiency, and waste of resources at the working level in UNIDO, among other agencies. But it served well for putting pressure on a number of the UN bodies, UNIDO included. The real reason was the dissatisfaction of the Western countries with the third world's drive to advance their unrealistic and rather aggressive demands. However, in reality resolution-passing by UNIDO General Conferences was divorced from control of resources, as will be shown, whereas most slogans remained on paper.

In the late 1970s cooperation in the field of industrial development grew, on the whole, unsatisfactorily. It frequently fell behind other areas of international economic cooperation. The world industrial objective: 25 percent share to be reached by developing countries by the year 2000 (set earlier by the Lima Declaration and Plan of Action) gradually became more and more unrealistic. Industrial development in the third world was proceeding unevenly. About three-quarters of the increase in industrial production was accounted for by only ten of them, including Brazil, Mexico, Argentina, South Korea, and Taiwan, exactly where free-market economies were unimpeded. But in the overwhelming majority of developing countries the industry developed at a very slow pace, if at all. In many least-developed countries, some with a population of less than one million, the industrial development was not started at all.

By that time it was clear that if the third world countries continued to launch unrealistic demands, this could doom the prospects of finalizing the new organizational structure for UNIDO, which was put on agenda by the Group of 77, as the Western countries would eventually withdraw from the deal. It was a typical case of a plausible "involuntary defection" noticed by S. Haggard and B. Simmons who wrote of the pressure of political constraints.[8]

After the second General Conference three basic trends took final shape in UNIDO's work: operational activity, coordination of technical assistance from UN organs in the field of industrial development, and research work. The secretariat, whose functions are determined by the directions of the work of the organization, was allocated now the following departments accordingly: the department of policy coordination, international center of industrial research, and department of operational activity. Apart from these three basic departments there were formed the department of services for conferences, information, and foreign relations and the administrative department.

Naturally, despite the decisions adopted at the second General Conference and then incorporated in the resolutions of the IDB at its tenth, eleventh, and twelfth sessions, the actual state of international industrial cooperation changed little, and the reorganization of UNIDO's work proceeded slowly.

The poor development of international industrial cooperation, which rebounds on the developing countries, is due to the low level of effectiveness concerning the struggle for a just reshaping of international economic relations. The North-South dialogue between Western and developing countries was actually reaching an impasse. The developing countries' hopes for massive aid from Western countries were not justified. International forums on problems of economic cooperation and assistance did not yield tangible results. The emerging economic order, rather far removed from the principles of the new international economic order formulated in the course of work at the UN and its organs, including UNIDO, damaged the interests of developing countries and did not completely satisfy the Western countries.

ON THE VERGE OF AN ABYSS

Growing contradictions between developing and Western countries expedited the preparations for the third UNIDO General Conference. Prior to it the developing countries held a number of forums: the ministerial level conference on the assistance to industrial cooperation (Istanbul, 1979), the fifth conference of ministers of African countries (Addis Ababa, 1979), the conference of industry ministers of Economic and Social Commission for Asia and Pacific countries (Bangkok, 1979), the fifth conference on the industrial development of Arab countries (Algiers, 1979), and the second Latin American conference on industrialization (Kali, Colombia, 1979). The developing countries, encouraged by the success of the second General Conference, wanted even more striking results and planned to gain more advantages at the forthcoming session.

At the third General Conference, held in Delhi in January and February 1980, many third world delegations pointed out that achieving the aim set in the Lima Declaration was still far off. This aim was that a 25 percent share in world industrial production was to be reached by developing countries by the year 2000; that figure could be merely 13 percent, though in the previous seven years the rates of economic growth in the developing countries were nearly two-thirds higher than in the industrialized countries. The developing states accused the West of lacking political will to implement the Lima Declaration and Plan of Action. This explained, according to them, the poor progress made in the international industrial cooperation. A more plausible explanation, however, was that the documents were ill conceived.

The third General Conference had on its agenda the draft by the Group of 77, the report of Western countries and the joint statement of a number of Eastern bloc countries. The coordinating work at the conference ended without any results, chiefly due to objections of principle made by Western countries. Nevertheless, the draft by the Group of 77 was put to the vote.

The draft of the Delhi Declaration and Plan of Action was passed by eighty-three votes for (all developing and Eastern bloc countries) to twenty-two against (all Western countries) and one abstention (Vatican City). Though this UNIDO document was adopted by a majority of its members, all the Western countries rejected it. It was evident that by that time the developing countries had distanced themselves from the realistic assumptions, misjudged the situation, and made compromises with the West practically impossible. From the point of view of reconciling different states' interests, the conference finished with a very poor performance. Since the point at issue here was above all the political and not the legal significance of obligations of member countries, the value of the Delhi Declaration and Plan of Action was nil, if not negative.

On the whole, the Delhi Declaration and Plan of Action was couched in forceful terms with regard to developed countries, meaning countries of the West. These documents indicated that "the economic crisis in the capitalist world" spread from a number of developed countries, expressed by such phenomena as the deterioration of the world monetary system, inflation, and balance of payments problems. Deep concern was expressed by the third world countries regarding assistance to them. They insisted on the unwillingness of some developed countries to cooperate, criticized the practices of transnational companies, and alleged additional restrictions on the access to Western countries of manufactured goods and semi-finished products from developing countries. It was pointed out that the majority of developed countries did not show political will in establishing a new international economic order. Concern was expressed over the unwillingness of the majority of industrialized countries to increase their state assistance to development, which, in fact, shrank in the second half of the decade. Their contributions to international organizations was also at issue. The Declaration and Plan of Action basically reproduced and elaborated the principles of a new international economic order contained in the Lima Declaration and Plan of Action.

The Eastern bloc countries, which voted for the document, although without enthusiasm, spelled out in their joint statement their attitude to some of the provisions they did not support. Specifically, they pointed out that they did not agree with some appraisals of the causes of the deterioration of the economic situation in the developing countries, with the proposal for setting up the so-called global fund, expanding financing connected with the development of some fields in UNIDO's work, and expanding structural subdivisions of the secretariat of the organization and its staff.[9]

In their report at the conference, the Western countries demanded that special note be made of the role of foreign capital, including private capital, in the industrial development of the third world and that the governments of recipient countries should be urged to create a favorable climate for foreign investors. They emphasized the positive contribution transnational corporations could make to the social and economic progress in the respective countries and the need to use the services of the International Center for the Settlement of Investment Disputes in the framework of the World Bank.

Concerning the international transfer of industry, the Western countries proposed to stress the importance of unimpeded free market and the discontinuation of state interference, including interference of any kind on the world scale. They saw international corporations as an important source of external loans and capitals for financing development in many countries. Calling into question the need for creating new institutions or funds for the needs of development, the Western countries underlined the necessity of considerably expanding the activity of the World Bank group. Lastly, they proposed concentrating UNIDO's operational activity on a number of joint investment programs with other institutions.[10]

Consensus was not reached on the Declaration and Plan of Action, and the third General Conference as a whole seemed a dismal failure. Many Western representatives considered that the Delhi documents did not have juridical and political force. The conference had, in fact, some negative consequences. More than many other large forums under UN auspices, the conference laid bare acute contradictions between developing and Western countries, which was a counterproductive approach. The Group of 77, supported mainly by the Eastern bloc, entered into an unnecessary confrontation with the Western countries on key problems of international economic relations.

The first half of the 1980s saw a lack of cooperation in the field of industrial development, which frequently fell behind other fields of international economic cooperations. The Lima objectives set for developing countries by the year 2000 were gradually becoming more and more off the mark. Industrial development in the South was proceeding most unevenly. About three-quarters of the increase in industrial production was accounted for by ten countries, including Brazil, Mexico, Argentina, and South Korea. In the overwhelming majority of developing countries, industry developed at a very slow pace, if at all. In many of the least-developed countries, some of them with a population of less than one million, the industrial sector process had not even been founded.

Contradictions between developing and Western countries on the main problems of industrial cooperation highlighted the preparations for the fourth UNIDO General Conference, which was to be the last General Conference of this organization prior to its reorganization. Before the conference the developing countries held a series of forums in 1984: the conference of industry ministers of Asian and Pacific countries (Bangkok), the seventh conference of industry ministers of African countries (Addis Ababa), the coordinating conference of Latin American countries at the summit level (Havana), and the conference of deputy industry ministers of Arab countries (Tunis). Once again, the developing countries devoted much attention to the forthcoming UNIDO forum. However, they had learned some lessons from the earlier experience and did not launch a new offensive of slogans to be incorporated in documents.

The fourth General Conference, held in Vienna in August 1984, registered again the lack of progress in the attainment of the objectives set in the documents of the second and third General Conferences. The share of developing countries in world manufacturing industry increased from 10 percent in 1975 to only 11.9 percent in 1983. If this rate of progress continued, by the year 2000 this share would not exceed 15 percent — far below the Lima Declaration's goal, which was becoming ever more unrealistic.

The range of problems and tasks set before the fourth General Conference was much narrower than at the two previous UNIDO General Conferences. However, strong political accents were made in the preamble of the General Conference report adopted by seventy-nine votes for to one against and twelve abstentions. The preamble pointed out that after the third UNIDO General Conference the economies of some Western and developing countries were in crisis and in stagnation. These factors had particularly ruinous effects on the developing countries, causing inflation, reduction of the volume of investments, sharp growth of the prices of the main imported goods, fluctuation and fall of world prices of exported raw materials, and stagnation in official aid for development. The need for further reforms of the existing systems of economic cooperation was emphasized as a way of surmounting difficulties in financing the process of development.[11]

The activity of the organization itself was reviewed in the resolution "Coordinating Role of UNIDO in the United Nations System in the Field of Industrial Development," adopted by consensus with amendments. In this resolution the General Conference recommended that UNIDO continue and enhance coordination of its cooperation with other organizations of the UN system and other organizations concerned with industrial development. The resolution recommended making optimal use of the coordinating mechanisms and agreements and developing coordinating activity on the spot in close cooperation with the UNDP.[12]

The decisions of the fourth General Conference anticipated the forthcoming reorganization of UNIDO and therefore were not designed for long-term applicability. The majority of member countries believed that in the course of work in a new UNIDO they would return to the appraisal of key problems of international economic relations, with due regard for the experience accumulated in the twenty years of the functioning of the old organization.

HOW BADLY POLITICIZATION DAMAGED
THE ORGANIZATION

Robert Keohane and Joseph Nye point out that "'politicization' is an important concept because it casts light on the process of agenda formation."[13] Naturally, the politically biased General Conferences of UNIDO were in the focus of the political process in international relations, even if it was not very much related to the practical work of the organization. At that time UNIDO got a rather poor reputation in the United States, but a more tolerant one in Western Europe. Economists and legal experts preferred to ignore that organization, referring to it as to a potential failure, though this assessment was not necessarily correct.

Another point of irritation was that the heads of the secretariat, Abdel-Rahman (Egypt, 1966–75) and Rahman Khan (Algeria, 1976–85), had dissatisfied Western countries and Eastern bloc countries because of their alleged backing of third world countries' unbalanced demands and rather authoritarian styles of managing administrative issues.

On the other hand, it was hardly possible that UNIDO would have stayed away from the politicization surrounding the passing of resolutions in the General Assembly and many UN bodies. For instance, G. Lyons, D. Baldwin, and D. McNeman identify the problem: ". . . a myth developed that economic and social programs were 'nonpolitical' and that the specialized agencies should not be 'politicized' . . . . In some respect, this thesis of 'depoliticization' is consistent with the concept of 'functionalism', that motivated many of the founders of the specialized agencies. . . . Politicization of the specialized agencies could be viewed as an attempt by frustrated and relatively powerless nations to increase their bargaining activity."[14] Another opinion, by Douglas Williams, is that "although they [specialized agencies] deal with specific functional sectors, their functions impinge so widely on the economic and social life of most states . . . that many of their activities cannot but be 'political', in the sense they are almost bound to be a source of friction from time to time between states of differing social and economic philosophies."[15]

Robert W. Cox and Harold K. Jacobson predicted in 1973 that "the current 'politicization' of various functional agencies may be part of the global process of transition incorporating Third World nations into the international decision-making system."[16] As it appears, the prediction of imminent politicization was perfectly correct for the time being but in more recent times it is not so any more.

I think that the whole venture with General Conferences, which had not been envisaged by General Assembly resolution 2152 (XXI) establishing UNIDO in 1966, was unnecessary and erroneous.

Finally, on the balance sheet, the conferences did not help build the prestige of the organization and were counterproductive for the organization as they forced dissension between countries rather than fostering increased new understanding.

I believe that it was a mistake on the part of the Western countries and probably the Eastern bloc countries to consent to holding General Conferences under those circumstances, because they could together block convening poorly prepared and unnecessary "talking shops" that permitted the Group of 77 to launch an unbalanced offensive against the North and the West in particular.

NOTES

1. See G. Abi-Saab, "Introduction," "La Notion d'organisation internationale: essai de synthèse," *Le concept d'organisation internationale*, 1980, pp. 9–28; A. Pellet, *Droit international du développement*, 1978; M. Bedjaoui, *Pour un nouvel ordre économique international*, 1979, H. Beatus, *Interessengruppen in internationalen Organisationen*, 1967.

2. See K. Sauvant, *The Group of 77: Evolution, Structure, Organization*, 1981.

3. R. Gregg, *The Changing United Nations. Options for the United States*, 1977, pp. 74–75.

4. R. Keohane and J. Nye, Jr., eds., *Transnational Relations*, pp. 46–47.

5. Statement, C. Ferguson, Jr., head, United States Delegation to the summer session of the ECOSOC, Geneva, August 1, 1975.

6. R. Gregg, *The Changing United Nations. Options for the United States*, 1977, pp. 82–83.

7. The political stand of third world countries in the mid 1970s is well reflected in R. Mortimore, *The Third World Coalition in International Politics*, 1984.

8. S. Haggard and B. Simmons, "Theories of International Regimes," *International Organization*, 1987, pp. 514–15.

9. ID/CONF. 4/CRP.14.

10. ID/CONF. 5/CRP.15.18.

11. ID/CONF. 5/46.

12. ID/CONF. Res. II.

13. R. Keohane and J. Nye, "International Interdependence and Integration," *Handbook of Political Science*, 1975, p. 397.

14. G. Lyons, D. Baldwin, and D. NcNeman, *The Changing United Nations*, p. 87.

15. W. Douglas, *The Specialized Agencies and the United Nations. The System in Crisis*, 1990, p. 29.

16. R. Cox et al., eds., *The Anatomy of Influence: Decision-Making in International Organization*, 1973, p. 248.

3

Genesis of a
Specialized Agency

PREPARATION OF UNIDO'S CONSTITUTION

One of the most important and interesting legal problems arising from the practices of the United Nations Industrial Development Organization (UNIDO) is its reorganization from the General Assembly's body into a specialized agency. Some aspects of this problem were considered in studies by D. Ait Ouyahia and K. Köppinger.[1] Both studies emphasize many political and legal difficulties interfering with the reorganization of UNIDO. Because of those problems the reorganization took place ten years after the process was initiated by developing countries.

The main issue in the reorganization process was working out UNIDO's constitution, which, as a legal basis for the organization, replaced resolution 2152 of the General Assembly of 1966. In compliance with that resolution, UNIDO had functioned as an organ of the General Assembly, but starting from the mid 1970s, the problem of working out its constituent act as a specialized agency of the UN was pushed forward very strongly by the third world countries.

Theoretical questions of constituent acts of international organizations as a variety of multilateral international treaties are sufficiently addressed in the works of some American and British scholars, for instance, Robert Riggs, Robert Plano, and Wilfred Jenks. First, many authors substantiate the extraordinary importance of the principle that strict observation of international treaties should be the main rule of international law. They further consider their action and application in time and in space, their interpretation, the provisions of their fulfillment, and their cessation and suspension.

The law of international treaties in general has been actively developed in juridical science, particularly by such scholars as Arnold McNair, Hersch Lauterpacht, and Alfred Verdross, who

were among the founders of the modern concept.[2] Of equal interest
are more recent studies by Parry Clive and Godfredas van Hoof.[3]
There are also works by the representatives of developing countries,
for example, Taslim Elias of Nigeria.[4] In the overwhelming majority
of works on this topic great attention is paid, once again, to the
principle of the strict observation of international treaties, as it is
secured in the Charter of the UN, especially in its Preamble, Article 2
(2), as well as in the 1969 Vienna Convention on the International
Treaties Law.

At the same time some scholars have certain views that are
certainly open to discussion. For example, it is impossible to consider
as legitimate the attempts to spread the action of international
treaties of former colonial powers to the territories for which they are
responsible.[5]

So, the UNIDO Constitution has an incontestable obligatory legal
power for the member countries. Not surprisingly, creating the
norms of international law by adopting UNIDO's Constitution was a
rather difficult process. Coordinating the wills of a large number of
countries and having them accept strict obligations demanded a lot of
effort and mutual concessions by the states. It was not incidental that
working out the Constitution had taken four years and its entering
into force another six years.

A possibility of major changes in the legal position of UNIDO was
possible according to resolution 2152 (XXI) of the General Assembly.
The resolution stated, in particular, that "the General Assembly will
revise in the light of the acquired experience the effectiveness and
further evolution of the above-mentioned organizational measures, in
order to decide what changes and improvements could prove to be
necessary for a fuller satisfaction of the growing needs of industrial
development" (37).

At the second General Conference of UNIDO, in 1975, developing
countries insisted that the decisions reached ten years earlier on
establishing UNIDO as an autonomous organization in the system of
the UN did not meet their economic needs.[6] That group of countries
spoke in favor of transforming the organization into a specialized
agency. Their approach was further outlined in the Lima
Declaration and Plan of Action, which contained the proposals on the
structure of the future UNIDO. According to that document, the
number of representatives of developing countries in the main organ
of the organization, the Industrial Development Board (IDB), was to
increase. This organ was responsible for acting on decisions of
another major organ of the General Conference and for considering
and approving both the program and budget of UNIDO.[7]

The seventh special session of the General Assembly evidently
endorsed the proposal on the reorganization of UNIDO. Chapter IX
(paragraph 9) of resolution 3362 (S-VII) of September 1975 stated that

the General Assembly had supported recommendation 2 of the General Conference of UNIDO: "to transform this organization into a specialized agency and decreed to establish an intergovernmental committee of full staff, including the countries, which took part in the second General Conference. The Committee was to meet in Vienna and was to work out the Constitution, which would then be presented to the Conference of plenipotentiary representatives."[8]

The Intergovernmental Committee, in which ninety-two countries and a large number of international organizations took part as observers, was created according to the resolution of the General Assembly. The Committee held five sessions from January 1976 to April 1977. The draft of the UNIDO Constitution, which was prepared by the secretariat of the UN, as well as unofficial drafts by the Group of 77 and the Western countries, were referred to the Committee. As the drafts differed significantly even in concept, the work of the Committee was difficult. It failed to work out unanimous decisions on all issues. It did, however, reach an agreement on a considerable number of the Constitution articles. It also agreed upon drafts of the resolution submitted on the approval of the organ, which was responsible for adopting the Constitution and the drafts of the resolution on the measures of the transitional period, proposed by the General Assembly. The main divergences of the draft of the Constitution follow.

In the Preamble to the Constitution the Group of 77 and the Eastern bloc countries suggested that a number of proposals be referred to; this definitely seemed to them as developing their diplomatic successes. Those provisions were proclaimed at the sixth special session of the General Assembly, the seventh special session of the General Assembly in the Charter of Economic Rights and Duties of States, and in the Lima Declaration and Plan of Action, which calls for the establishment of a new international economic order.[9] The Eastern bloc countries also insisted on three insertions in the text of the Preamble, concerning the efforts of the governments on the slogan of "maintaining durable and just peace, and security." Western countries preferred to make the provisions of the draft more vague and proposed referring to wide aims, proclaimed in the resolution of the sixth special session of the General Assembly on establishing a new international economic order, in the Lima Declaration and the Plan of Action, and also in the resolution of the seventh special session of the General Assembly on the development and international economic cooperation, but without mentioning the charter of the Economic Rights and Duties of States and without referring to the issues of international security.[10] There was also a divergence of opinions on the formulation of the article of the Constitution mentioning the new international economic order among the aims of UNIDO. Further, the Eastern bloc and the developing countries, on the one hand, and Western countries, on the other hand, adhered to opposite points of view concerning the position of UNIDO on the activities of transnational companies (Article 2).

Very serious contradictions arose in establishing the numerical composition and geographical distribution of the members of the IDB. In this regard it resembled a contradiction between the North and the South. Western countries, supported by the Eastern bloc, proposed that the Board consist of fifty members, thirty from developing countries, and five from Eastern bloc countries. Developing countries demanded increasing the number of IDB members to sixty, although the views of different countries belonging to the Group of 77 were divided. In the opinion of the developing countries the decisions of the Board were to be adopted by a simple majority of the members, who were present and voting, while the other countries proposed the formula of a simple majority of members except in cases specified otherwise (Article 9).

Concerning the Programme and Budget Committee (PBC), which was to consider in the course of its work the financial aspects of the Organization's activities, Western and East European countries suggested that it should consist of twenty-seven members, including fifteen from developing countries, nine from Western countries, and three from Eastern bloc countries. The Group of 77 suggested increasing the number of members from developing countries.

The decisions of the Committee had to be adopted by a two-thirds majority. From the point of view of Western and Eastern bloc countries, voting had to take into account the total numerical composition of the Committee, while the Group of 77 stood for counting the members who were present and took part in the voting (Article 10).

With regard to UNIDO's regular budget, positions also differed. The Eastern bloc countries proposed that only administrative and research activities and other general expenditures of the secretariat should be included in the regular budget. In contrast, Western and developing countries proposed to include as well other general expenditures of the organization. They did not consider the PBC or the IDB on which the Eastern bloc insisted. Among those disputed items of expenditure were holding sessions envisaged in the program of work and also forms of the activities, which were previously financed out of the regular budget of the UN (Chapter 15). However, the latter expenditure was limited to only 5 percent (the proviso of Western countries) of the volume of the regular budget of UNIDO (Article 13).

As far as essential amendments to the Constitution are concerned, the Western countries and the Eastern bloc stood for adopting them by a three-fourths majority of the IDB and General

Conference while developing countries voted for a two-thirds majority (Article 23).

UN CONFERENCE ON UNIDO'S TRANSFORMATION

The Conference on working out the Constitution was held in February–March 1978 in New York. One hundred twenty-three members took part in the Conference. According to the rules of procedure, approved at the second UNIDO Conference, a two-thirds majority of members present and voting was needed for adopting any parts of the Constitution and other relevant documents, including final resolution (Rule 34).

Other decisions could be reached by a simple majority of those present and voting; if the votes were distributed equally, the proposal would be declined. For the time of the Conference, according to Rule 44, a committee on negotiations, open for all countries, was established. An editorial committee and working groups were also established.[11]

The Group of 77 and the Western countries proposed two rather different drafts of the constitutive act. The Eastern bloc countries confined themselves to the editing remarks on some items of the drafts, as they did not want any particular initiatives of their own.

The practice of one state–one vote was not necessarily the only possible option for UNIDO's future decision making. The system of weighted voting, as used by the International Monetary Fund (IMF) and the World Bank group and later by the International Fund for Agricultural Development, as the simplest negation of one state–one vote was not used in UNIDO. At that time a number of special arrangements were made, in reality restricting the meaning of the one state–one vote principle in the organization's decision making. The real arrangement was that all questions regarding finance and the program of work could be decided only if there was an approval by both the Western and the "socialist" countries. It was a part of the deal in 1965, when UNIDO came to existence, and remained surprisingly similar when the organization became a specialized agency in 1986.

In connection with the Preamble of the constitutive act, which was to state the reason for the reorganization of UNIDO into a specialized agency, a lot of disagreements surfaced. Some Western countries, including the United States, Great Britain, the Netherlands, and New Zealand, repeated their previous positions that the Preamble was unnecessary. They referred in particular to the absence of preambles in the founding documents of the International Bank for Reconstruction and Development and the International Atomic Energy Agency. This position was easily explained by the fact that the Western countries wanted to avoid unproductive controversy on a number of documents concerning the establishment of a new international economic order, including the Charter of the Economic Rights and Duties of States, about which they expressed a negative attitude.[12] Western countries felt it was unnecessary to include a clause of maintaining peace and security as well as that of noninterference in the internal affairs of other countries, which was not quite the focus of UNIDO's functions. China joined the objections of the Western countries, however, with a different reasoning and stated that such references "were not connected with reality." At the same time the Group of 77 approved of these proposals of the Eastern bloc countries, trying to get them on its side in other matters. Contradictions concerning references to a new international economic order surfaced again during the discussion of the articles of the draft devoted to functions of the new organization, but in that case the Western countries preferred to make concessions.

The report on the inner structure of UNIDO, presented by the secretariat of the UN, reproduced in general the notions usual for its specialized agencies. It envisaged functioning of a plenary organ with full composition represented by the General Conference, an executive one with a narrower composition, the IDB, and the secretariat, headed by the Director-General.

In connection with the reorganization of UNIDO into a specialized agency, it could no longer be subject to General Assembly's decisions on its activities. Much greater functions were respectively delegated to the General Conference of UNIDO. The Lima Declaration and Plan of Action envisaged convening the General Conference every four years. The report of the secretariat of the UN, however, stressed the necessity of establishing a two-year term, which was supported by the majority of developing and Western countries. Other countries believed that it was necessary to call the General Conference every year (Sri Lanka) or once every three years (France). There also appeared contradictions regarding convening an extraordinary General Conference of the organization. Neither was there consensus on the majority necessary for adopting decisions on policy issues by the General Conference. The Group of 77 and the Eastern bloc countries stood for a simple majority, while the Western countries wanted a two-thirds majority in order to have a veto option for themselves.

In compliance with the idea of increasing the composition of the IDB by including more developing countries, the report of the secretariat of the UN contained a proposal on enlarging the Board from forty-five to sixty countries. In compliance with Article 9 of the UNIDO Constitution, all its member states are divided into four groups according to Annex 1 to the Constitution: A is the developing countries of Africa and Asia; B, industrially developed Western countries; C, Latin-American countries; and D, the USSR and East European countries.

The Western countries proposed that the number of the IDB members should be enlarged to fifty, their geographical distribution to be established as follows: thirty members from the developing countries, fifteen from the Western countries (group B), and five from the Eastern bloc countries (group D).[13] The USSR and the Eastern European countries advocated preserving the number of IDB members. After some intermediate proposals the Group of 77 was satisfied in having fifty-three members in the IDB's composition, among them fifteen from groups A and C, five from group B, and three from group D.

Among the principles that were put forward as the criteria for establishing the IDB composition, the developing countries stressed that it was necessary for their position to be truly reflected. Therefore, their membership numbers should correspond to their increased influence in the world, while the Western countries demanded that the amount of the countries' contributions to the regular and operative budgets of the organization should be taken into account.

The Group of 77 advanced the opinion that the IDB's sessions must be held any time it was found necessary. In contrast, group B proposed that the IDB sessions should be convened once a year and the Director-General should be given an opportunity to call an additional session at the request of not fewer than a third of the members. A compromise was adopted that stated that an additional session might be called at the request of a simple majority of the members.[14]

The objectives of the PBC envisaged in the Lima Declaration and Plan of Action were not actually made concrete in the draft of the UN secretariat. The Western countries held that the committee should be elected by the IDB from its members. The Eastern bloc countries and some developing states supposed that it was necessary to form the committee as an auxiliary organ of the IDB, with due regard to a principle of equitable geographical distribution. There were fewer differences as far as the structure of the PBC was concerned, and nearly all the countries agreed that it would comprise twenty-seven states. At the same time groups B and D proposed that the committee should be voted for by the IDB according to quotas: fifteen members from groups A and C, nine from group B, and three from group D. The Group of 77 insisted that the committee should be voted for in quotas proportional to the geographical distribution of the General Conference members, thus trying to get absolute control of decision making.

The proposal of the Western countries to introduce a system of proportional votes of member countries depending on their financial contribution caused serious contradictions at the conference in New

York. Those proposals were routinely criticized by the Eastern bloc and developing countries, which indicated that such an approach would mean a violation of the principle of sovereign equality of states and would lead to the dependence of the organization on a certain group of countries.[15]

At the same time Western countries were against the establishment of an organization in which the solution of financial problems would be imposed on them against their will. As a result, a compromise provided that the main powers in settling financial questions would be divided between the PBC and the IDB, where the Western countries had greater opportunities to influence the decision-making process. Thus, in the PBC the developing countries were to have fifteen votes out of twenty-seven; for an absolute two-thirds majority they needed another three votes. The same situation would emerge in the IDB as well. As a result the developing countries would not be able to determine the financial policy of the organization on their own.

As a reciprocal concession the Western countries agreed with the developing countries' demand, admittedly considerable, that 5 percent of the regular budget of the organization would be allocated for technical assistance. The main part of the expenses for technical assistance, however, had to be compensated for by voluntary contributions. It should be stressed that according to resolution 2152 (XXI) of the General Assembly, a part of the expenses for technical assistance of UNIDO was covered by the UN budget.

An important legal question at the conference was defining the conditions in which the amendments to the constituent act could be made. The position of the Group of 77, which in general coincided with the draft of the secretariat of the UN, was that the amendments should be adopted by a two-thirds majority of the General Conference at the recommendation of the IDB. Groups B and D proposed that a distinction be made between fundamental amendments, which envisaged additional obligations of the member states, and other amendments. Both types of amendments required for adoption a three-fourths majority of the votes of the General Conference on a recommendation of the IDB.

As far as settling legal disputes was concerned, the majority of the countries stuck to an opinion that disputes between the member countries could be passed for consideration to the International Court of Justice, whose decision should be considered final. However, the member countries did not reach a consensus on whether the decisions of the International Court of Justice would be binding upon them.

Working out compromise decisions with respect to the constituent act of UNIDO as a specialized agency was difficult because a number of Western countries were hardly interested in reorganizing that organization. On the other hand, the USSR and the Eastern European countries supported it only halfheartedly.

It was important that during the process of drafting the documents at the Conference in New York a principle of the approval by voting (not consensus) was used, which in many respects explained considerable delays at that stage of work.

The Conference in New York ended without any results because it was impossible to gain a two-thirds majority on many questions concerning the constituent act.[16] At the same time the Conference was useful because it made it possible to reveal the positions of different groups of countries and the existing contradictions.

On the whole, the Conference in New York was a step backwards compared to the results of the work of the preparatory committee of full composition. Another impediment was the rigid position of the developing countries, who went back even on some of their former concessions and resolutely intended to achieve predominant influence in the main organs of UNIDO, as well as much larger allocations from the regular budget for technical assistance. The Conference revealed the Western countries' lack of interest in compromise, their natural discontent with the attachment of the Constitution to the principles of a new international economic order, and a guarded attitude of the United States to UNIDO in general. The majority of developing countries insisted on the opinion that Western countries were not at all interested in reaching a mutually acceptable compromise and placed the responsibility for the absence of a positive change on the USSR and the Eastern European countries. The Western countries and some developing countries drew attention to the ostensibly unyielding stand of the Eastern bloc countries. There was considerable truth behind this assertion.

An impression that the attempts to reorganize UNIDO ended in failure could have been formed if one were to judge by the results of the conference session in New York.[17] This was not, however, the intention of the main groups of the countries, and that is why in a rather short period of time they reconsidered their positions in order to find new compromises.

The second session of the Conference, according to resolution 33/161 of the General Assembly of 1978, was authorized to complete the composition of the draft and adopt the Constitution of UNIDO as a specialized agency. Eighty-one states, fewer than were at the first session, were present at the second session, which took place in March and April 1979 in Vienna. An important change in procedure was that the decisions from that point on had to be adopted by consensus, which obviously facilitated negotiating. The main work on preparing the final version of the draft was carried out in the framework of the Committee on Negotiations. The Committee on Negotiations on the whole had fulfilled its task successfully. As stated in its report,[18] the Conference had regulated all except three divergences in the drafts of the Constitution and of the resolution. In its report the Editorial Committee[19] also pointed out that almost all the differences of editorial nature had been addressed.

The countries having objections to the drafts withdrew them after the discussion, opening a way for the adoption of the documents at the seventh meeting of the second session of the Conference, which was held on April 8, 1979. The Constitution of UNIDO and corresponding points of the resolution were adopted on the basis of consensus at that meeting.

The U.S. delegation relinquished its intention of changing the point concerning the promotion of the new international economic order in Article I of the Constitution. In a speech following the adoption of the Constitution, the United States representative said that joining the consensus had not changed the United States' attitude toward the new international economic order. The United States withdrew the demand of changing the formulation of Article II (5), concerning hiring the staff of the UNIDO's secretariat, though instead of "the importance of recruiting staff on a wide and equitable geographical basis," it insisted on "the possible wider and equitable geographical basis."

Next the representative of Belgium, speaking on behalf of group B, supported such an interpretation of the provisions of the Constitution, which meant that no country had the right to demand that the organization should accept its own currency as a mandatory contribution.[20] I shall come back to this question in Chapter 6.

The delegation of the USSR, speaking on behalf of eight countries of Group D, expressed once again their objections to the provision of financing the operative functions out of the regular budget (Chapter B, annex 2, of the Constitution) because, as it was stated, it contradicted the principle of voluntary contributions for those purposes. The delegation from the USSR then spoke on Article 27, with the provision that no reservations could be made concerning that document after its adoption. That point was included at the demand of developing countries, which referred to the recommendations contained in resolution 598 (VI) of the General Assembly. In compliance with the resolution, the organs of the UN, specialized agencies, and the states had to specify a possibility or an impossibility of reservations after the adoption of multilateral documents, as well as the force of reservations, if they were permissible. The Soviet delegation again criticized Article 27, saying that there were no such articles in the charters of the majority of other specialized agencies. The Soviets added that the article's absence would permit the application of the Constitution in a more flexible way. In order not to become the only country out of the deal, the USSR delegation withdrew its objection.

Resolutions concerning the members and observers of UNIDO,[21] some financial arrangements,[22] and measures to be taken in the transitional period proposed by the General Conference were also adopted then.[23] The final act of the Conference was enacted and the Constitution was opened for signing at the Conference on April 8.

In resolution 34/96 of the General Assembly of December 1979, "measures for the transitional period, concerning the institution of the United Nations Industrial Development Organization as a specialized agency" and the Constitution of UNIDO adopted on April 8, 1979, were approved. The General Assembly decided to abolish UNIDO as its body after the last day of the calendar year, in which time the first General Conference of the new specialized agency would be convened and, correspondingly, reduce the articles of the budget. The General Assembly empowered the Secretary General to request opinions of the Consultative Committee on Administrative and Budget Matters to grant loans to the new institution until it acquired sufficient contributions and advances from its members and to transfer into the new UNIDO the UN assets used by the existing organization and the assets of the UN Industrial Development Fund.

Thus, the fundamental document of UNIDO is its Constitution, adopted on April 8, 1979, by the Conference of the UN on the reorganization of UNIDO into a specialized agency. The participants in the conference, consisting of eighty-one states (at the second session in Vienna) adopted the Constitution by consensus. Before the Constitution was entered into force, sixty states that had not taken part in the Vienna session of the Conference approved the Constitution and became full members of the organization.

UNIDO's Constitution is an international multilateral agreement that participants must fulfill in compliance with the generally accepted principle of the international law, *pacta sunt servanda* — agreements must be fulfilled. Thus, the obligations of the member states as subjects of the system of international relations according to the Constitution are of unconditional juridical power for them.

The fact that the Constitution was adopted by consensus and not by voting cannot influence its legal power because the ratification, acceptance, or approval of the Constitution by a country, regardless of whether a given country participated in the conference on the reorganization of UNIDO (according to Article 24 of the Constitution), is the condition of the membership of any country. Moreover, unlike the overwhelming majority of the international intergovernmental organizations, the Constitution of UNIDO has a clause that "no reservations could be made concerning it" (Article 27).

The Constitution is a document of strong legal force, and its significance can be interpreted broadly. For instance, according to the concept of positive international law, an international treaty concluded by a majority of states including leading powers is "more important from the point of view of the systematic unity of the law of nations, which obviously requires the existence of general rules."[24] However, apart from technical issues, the Constitution was conceived in very general terms, and among disputable provisions it mentioned just twice a new international economic order without specifying how to implement this notion.

CONVERSION INTO SPECIALIZED AGENCY

Article 25 (1) stated that the Constitution would enter into force after at least eighty states "had deposited instruments of ratification, acceptance or approval, notify the Depository that they have agreed, after consultations among themselves that the Constitution shall enter into force." As it was agreed upon at the UN conference on UNIDO's reorganization, such a clause was aimed at the Constitution entering into force only after a large number of states concerned had agreed with this.

In that case the new organization had to include a sufficient number of members that met, according to the opinion of those states, the necessary requirements, which, however, were not specified in the Constitution.[25]

By the middle of 1982, the Constitution had been ratified, adopted, and approved by ninety-six states, and thirty-six states had signed it and had the right to ratify it. In this connection and the Economic and Social Council in its resolution 1982/66A asked the Secretary General to organize consultations between the representatives of all member states that had ratified the Constitution and other member states concerned with the aim of bringing the Constitution into force and to present a report to the 37th session of the UN General Assembly. In the General Assembly resolution 37/213, "The Reorganization of the United Nations Industrial Development Organization into a Specialized Agency," of 1982, it was recommended that consultations be held between the states that ratified, adopted, or approved the Constitution and other states concerned in order to fix the date for the Constitution to enter into force.

A series of conferences was held from May 16 to May 20, 1983, in Vienna. It was agreed that the reorganization must not lead to the failure of the realization of the programs during the transitional period and immediately after it.[26] As for the upcoming General Conference, a preliminary agenda was proposed, and it was decided that the work had to be divided into sections in order to reconsider different points of the agenda.[27]

An important conclusion drawn by the conferences was that the conditions necessary for an immediate reorganization of UNIDO into a specialized agency had not yet been met. At the conference an agreement was reached that the Constitution should enter into force only when it was possible to provide for the financial viability of the new organization. The UN Secretary General was asked to consult the states that had handed in their ratification instruments or documents on adoption and approval to determine when such a condition was fulfilled. The UN Secretary General later had to call a one-day conference, which consisted of a series of consultations, as stipulated in resolution 37/213 of the General Assembly.[28]

Resolution 38/193 of the General Assembly of 1983 recommended that consultations be held on UNIDO's reorganization. The consultations of the member states concerned took place in April and May 1984 in Vienna. The states reached an agreement that the decisions on the policy and structure of the new UNIDO would be adopted by the organization's competent bodies after these bodies were created. An opinion was expressed concerning the necessity of creating the new UNIDO on a universal basis, that is, of approximately the same composition already existing.[29] These consultations ended with a final meeting in New York City on June 10, 1985.

The conclusions worked out in earlier meetings were circulated, and the participating countries gave individual notifications to the Secretary General of their consent that the Constitution should enter into force. The Constitution entered into force in conformity with Article 25 (1) on June 21, 1985 with eighty countries that had handed in their ratification instruments and documents of adoption and approval informing the depository (the UN Secretary General) of their consent.

Resolution 34/96 of the General Assembly of 1979 mentioned that UNIDO, as one of the organs of the General Assembly, would be abolished on the last day of the calendar year in which the General Conference of the new organization was called. UNIDO began to function as a specialized agency on January 1, 1986.

The period from June 21 to December 31, 1985, was characterized by two features of the legal position of UNIDO. First, UNIDO's Constitution as a specialized agency came into force. At the same time UNIDO still remained an organ of the General Assembly of the UN. There is no contradiction, however, in such a dual legal position during that period. In the first place the text of the Constitution does not say that the organization from the very beginning of its existence is granted the status of a specialized agency. The status of UNIDO is mentioned in the Preamble, which says, in particular, "The States Parties to this Constitution desiring to establish, within the terms of Chapter IX of the Charter of the United Nation, the Industrial Development Organization (UNIDO) . . . by that agree to adopt this Constitution."

Second, resolution 2152 (XXI) of the General Assembly, which served as a constitutive document for the former UNIDO, pointed out that the General Assembly "shall review in the light of experience, the effectiveness and further evolution of the institutional arrangements, with a view to deciding upon such changes and improvements as might be necessary." Consequently, the resolutions of the General Assembly concerning the reorganization of UNIDO, including resolution 34/96 of December 1979, cannot be considered contradictory to resolution 2152 (XXI). The General Assembly, itself having established UNIDO, has the right to make a decision on the existence of that organization in its own institution, as well as on the question of any changes in the formulation of the constitutive document up to replacing it with another one, as might be necessary. That is why the decisions of the General Assembly, which are contained in resolution 38/193 of December 1983, on the procedure of the UNIDO Constitution could be interpreted as a continuation of the organizational arrangements up to replacing the previous constitutive document of the organization with a new one.[30]

Since the process of reorganizing UNIDO took a long time and included a transitional period, the determination of the moment when the former organization was liquidated and the new one was created acquires theoretical and practical significance.

The item of the respective resolutions of the General Assembly, including resolution 34/96 of December 1979 that UNIDO stops existing as an organ of the General Assembly at the end of the last day of the calendar year during which the first session of the General Conference was convened, means changing the status of UNIDO, but it does not indicate a transition from a former organization to a new one.

An international organization is considered to be established at the moment its constitutive act enters into force, even if in practice it can start functioning later. In cases of the reorganization of an international organization, a similar rule should apply. Establishment of a new organization and the abolition of the former one is to be considered simultaneous with the entering into force of the new constitutive act, which replaced the previous.

On June 21, 1985, the UNIDO's Constitution entered into force. It became the new constituent act and replaced in that capacity resolution 2152 (XXI) of the General Assembly. This does not mean that the liquidation of the former UNIDO and the foundation of the new one will immediately become a specialized agency of the UN. At the initial stage of its existence the new UNIDO had the status of an organ of the General Assembly, which later changed into the status of a specialized agency. The change of status was connected with two conditions: holding the first session of the new organization within three months after the Constitution entered into force, in order to settle the key questions connected with the new status, and the end of the corresponding calendar year.

DUAL STATUS AND CONTINUITY

UNIDO became a specialized agency on January 1, 1986. By that time all the necessary requirements, including convening the first session of the General Conference in the latter part of 1985, were met. Thus, UNIDO emerged as an additional member to the "big four" among the biggest specialized agencies, using the expression of Douglas Williams.[31] The "big five," as it became from now on, also includes the United Nations Educational, Scientific and Cultural Organization (UNESCO), the Food and Agricultural Organization, the World Health Organization (WHO), and the International Labor Organization.

The preservation of the former status of UNIDO as a General Assembly organ on a temporary basis after the appearance of the new organization creates an important precedent from both theoretical and practical points of view, which once again stress the necessity of ensuring a proper continuity of the organization's functioning during its transformation. The continuity of the organization's activities must be the most important consideration during its transformation.[32]

The problem of legal continuity of international organizations has not been studied at length, in spite of the fact that the problem appeared in connection with the establishment of the UN, WHO, UNESCO, and others. The difficulty is that constitutive acts of organizations rarely contain clauses concerning legal continuity, which cannot be interpreted by analogy to the legal continuity of states. There is also a generally accepted interpretation of the subject of legal continuity of organizations, which may contain its functions, resources, obligations, and in some cases property.[33]

A peculiar feature of the legal continuity of UNIDO as a specialized agency as compared to UNIDO as the General Assembly organ is that while the two organizations have a rather close correlation of their objectives and functions, we can speak of their different legal statuses. From the legal point of view the reorganized UNIDO and the former UNIDO are different organizations; the respective constitutive acts contain no clauses on the direct inter-connection or correlation between those documents. Documents of different legal character represent the constitutive acts of the former and the reorganized UNIDO. In the first case it is resolution 2152 (XXI) of the General Assembly of the UN. In the second case, it is the Constitution of UNIDO, adopted at the Conference of the UN on its reorganization into a specialized agency, in which countries took part individually. In the first case no international agreement fixing the will of the states to establish the organization was reached; their will was expressed indirectly at the session of the General Assembly. Such a way of establishing the organization also explained the fact that although UNIDO was called "to function as an autonomous organization in the framework" of the UN, it had the status of an organ derivative of that main organ of the UN, the General Assembly, which had created it. The reorganized UNIDO was established by the states — participants of the UN conference on the reorganization of that organization and who directly expressed their will by adopting the UNIDO Constitution. The fact that the Constitution of the reorganized UNIDO does not mention its interconnection with its predecessor as an organ of the General Assembly also speaks in favor of juridical independence of the reorganized UNIDO.

According to a conception that has won general recognition, the legal status of an international organization is determined by its constitutive act. If there had been a direct connection between the legal status of the new and the former UNIDO, it would have been specified in the Constitution of the new UNIDO.

One can indirectly trace a certain legal connection between the new and the former UNIDO. The Preamble of UNIDO's Constitution indicates that state participants were taking into account "the broad objectives in the resolutions adopted by the special sixth session of the General Assembly . . . establishment of the New International Economic Order" as well as "the resolution of the seventh special session of the General Assembly on Development and International Economic Cooperation." One of the notions in the resolutions mentioned was the reorganization of UNIDO. The Preamble also refers to the Lima Declaration and Plan of Action adopted at the second UNIDO General Conference. One of the central ideas developed in detail was the reorganization of UNIDO into a specialized agency. Thus, in the Preamble of the Constitution the state participants refer to the main decisions, adopted on the reorganization of UNIDO. We can trace an indirect legal connection in the decision of the state participants to preserve the former name of the organization.

Of fundamental significance also is a rather similar interpretation of the jurisdiction of the former and the new UNIDO, correspondingly in resolution 2152 (XXI) of the General Assembly and in the Constitution. In the first case it is stressed that UNIDO "plays the central role in and is responsible for reviewing and promoting the coordination of all activities of the United Nations system in the field of industrial development" (27). The Constitution in its turn states that UNIDO "shall play the central role in and be responsible for reviewing and promoting the coordination of all types of activities of the United Nations system in the field of industrial development, in conformity with the responsibilities of the Economic and Social Council under the Charter of the United Nations and with the applicable relationship agreements." Thus, it can be concluded that the former and the new UNIDO have some common features in spite of their different statuses.

The continuity of the functions of the organization in certain important spheres is the key problem of the legal continuity of the international organizations. That problem appeared to be a principal problem for UNIDO, which was rendering a great amount of technical assistance, in view of the fact that UNIDO's secretariat had a considerable number of personnel and that this organization used considerable funds and property.

The questions of financing were the most difficult ones when ensuring the continuity of the organization during the reorganization. According to Article 15 of the Constitution, the expenditures on the regular budget of the organization are covered according to the scale of obligatory payments. But that scale can be established only by the General Conference of the new institution, and it is to be convened for that purpose. Earlier those expenses of UNIDO, in accordance with paragraph 21 of resolution 2152 (XXI) of the General Assembly, were covered out of the regular budget of the UN. So, depriving UNIDO of the status of a General Assembly organ after its Constitution's entering into force would lead to a temporary absence of a source for covering the expenses from the regular budget of the organization, which could lead to financial crisis.

During the initial period of UNIDO's existence as a specialized agency, additional reserve sums were also needed to ensure the organization's financial stability. At the first session (part two) of the IDB in November 1985, it was decided and approved to create a fund of circulating assets for the two-year period of 1986–1987 amounting to $9 million. The source of the funds was advance payments of the member states according to the scale of the regular payments, which were created on the account of the member states making those payments.

Another important question connected with legal continuity of international organizations is the problem of their being legal subjects. This is to a certain degree debatable. Unlike a state, whose international legal recognition is not of great importance, for an international organization this recognition plays an essential role. The basis for the recognition by the primary members of the organization is its constitutive act, but the moment of recognition does not coincide with the moment the constitutive act is signed. Some jurists think that ratification of the constitutive act means the recognition of the international organizations as a legal subject by member countries.[34]

The experience of UNIDO's reorganization introduces a certain new element in the interpretation of the institution of reorganizing international organizations, because ratification was not of determining importance. In Article 25 (1) of UNIDO's Constitution, it is stipulated that "this Constitution shall enter into force when at least eighty states that had deposited instruments of ratification, acceptance or approval notify the Depository that they have agreed, after consultations among themselves, that this Constitution shall enter into force." According to this article, then, the moment of recognition or of the Constitution entering into force is to be considered the moment at which the states agreed during the consultations after the ratification of the Constitution by at least eighty states.

Let us suppose that the ratification of UNIDO's Constitution meant recognition that it was a legal subject. Then the organization would become a subject of international law at the moment of the ratification of its Constitution by the eightieth state and before holding the envisaged consultations. But this is not so, because theoretically those consultations could have not led to any agreement by the states on the Constitution entering into force, and its being a legal subject cannot exist abstractly, without basing it on an acting international agreement (constitutive act). That is why, in my opinion, the peculiarity of the recognition of UNIDO as a legal subject is that the states have envisaged a special moment for the constitutive act of the organization to enter into force after its ratification by the necessary number of states.

The institution of recognition presupposes the existence of two sides, the recognizing one and the recognized one, and from its legal act, based on mutual agreement of the sides, stems their obligation to establish certain relations. The recognizing side cannot consist solely of the states taking part in the adoption of the constitutive act of the organization. In Article 25 (2) of the Constitution, it is envisaged that the states that did not take part in informing the depository are able to hand in the instruments of ratification, acceptance, or approval if they had not done that already and to inform the depository that the Constitution according to them was entering into force. The latter will mean the recognition of UNIDO.

The establishment of membership in UNIDO is not the only possible form of its recognition by states. The legal forms of the recognition of UNIDO by nonparticipating states could be concluded by special individual agreements with that organization establishing certain relations with that organization in connection with that organization's fulfilling its functions or by recognizing privileges and immunities for that organization or its officials.

Other organizations besides states have the ability to appear in the role of a recognizing side in the act of recognition. Another international organization can play the role of a recognizing side when that international organization is concerned, although the recognizing of another international organization as a legal act is of a somewhat different nature. For example, recognition by the UN has the appearance of international acceptance. Naturally, recognition by the UN is of principal importance for such an organization as UNIDO.

Recognition by the UN is implied through a number of provisions in UNIDO's Constitution and stems from the name of the organization. The repeated resolutions of the UN General Assembly in connection with the reorganization of UNIDO into a specialized agency of the UN contain an element of recognition; however, this recognition cannot be considered self-explanatory and is only an additional argument.

From the legal point of view, recognition by the UN can be considered indisputable only after concluding an agreement between the two organizations stipulated in Article 18 of the UNIDO Constitution, in which they express their will toward each other and regulate their relations in the form of a treaty.

Interestingly, the organization came into existence precisely in the wave of the U.S. pressure in financial matters on the UN system. In 1983, Secretary of State George Shultz announced the decision to reconsider U.S. membership in UNESCO; actual withdrawal came on January 1, 1985. At the same time the slogan of zero growth for budgets of all international organizations in the UN system succeeded in stopping any increase in these budgets after 1982–1983. Conversion of UNIDO thus became a real exception, especially since establishment of a new specialized agency meant creating a new item of allocations.

A legitimate question that nevertheless arises is whether conversion of UNIDO into a specialized agency was useful and necessary. I believe that the usefulness of that measure was marginal and depended mostly on the premises. As it appears, the new organization reflected a far different approach from the one the third world hoped to impose.

Also, I think that in reality there was little chance to totally block the third world's drive to create another specialized agency, because they put so much emphasis on it. The realistic options were rather on what premises and when. On both accounts the West and the East European countries gained scores. The organization was born with a virtual veto rule by the West with Eastern bloc countries on important issues; thus, the procedure of transformation, realized step by step, could always be blocked for an indefinite time if the major parties concerned were not totally satisfied.

NOTES

1. D. Ait Ouyahia, *Évolution de l'Organisation des Nations Unies pour le developpement industriel /ONUDI/*, 1980; K. Köppinger, *Der Weg der UNIDO in die Selbständigkeit. Untersuchung zum Recht der internationalen Organisationen*, 1981.

2. A. McNair, *The Law of Treaties*, 1938; H. Lauterpacht, *Private Law Sources and Analogies of International Law*, 1970; A. Verdross, *Universelles Völkerrecht. Theorie und Praxis*, 1984.

3. C. Parry, *The Sources and Evidences of International Law*, 1965; G. van Hook, *Rethinking the Sources of International Law*, 1983; I. Sinclair, *The Vienna Convention on the Law of Treaties*, 1973; H. Warldlock, *Third Report on the Law of Treaties*, 1964; P. Tavernier, *Recherches sur l'application dans le temps des actes et des règles en droit international public*, 1970; P. Reteur, *Introduction au droit des traités*, 1972; A. Blackmann, "Die Nichtrückwirkung völkerrechtlicher Verträge. Kommentar zu Article 38 der Wiener Vertragrechtskonvention," *Zeitschrift für ausländsches öffentliches Recht und Völkerrecht*, 1973.

4. T. Elias, *The Modern Law of Treaties*, 1974; T. Elias, *The International Court of Justice and Some Contemporary Problems: Essays on International Law*, 1983.

5. P. Reteur, *Introduction au droit des traités*.

6. D. Ait Ouyahia, *Évolution de l'Organisation*, pp. 488–94.

7. ID/CONF. 3/31.

8. A/CONF. 90/INF.I.

9. See M. Abraham, *Perspectives on Modernization: Toward a General Theory of Third World Development*, 1980.

10. D. Ait Ouyahia, *Évolution de l'Organisation*, pp. 497–500.

11. A/CONF. 90/8.

12. M. Bedjaoui, *Pour un nouvel ordre*, pp. 61–67; D. Ait Ouyahia, *Évolution de l'Organisation*, pp. 493–96.

13. On dividing the UNIDO members into groups A (developing countries of Asia and Africa), B (developed capitalist countries), C (Latin American countries), and D (East European countries), see D. Ait Ouyahia, *Évolution de l'Organisation*, pp. 248–51.

14. For a critique of the demands of the Group of 77, see K. Köppinger, *Der Weg der UNIDO*, pp. 4–8.

15. D. Ait Ouyahia, *Évolution de l'Organisation*, pp. 111–14, J. Strossinger, *Financing the United Nations System*, 1964.

16. D. Ait Ouyahia, *Évolution de l'Organisation*, pp. 291–300.

17. German jurist K. Köppinger thinks that the conference in New York was an obvious failure. See K. Köppinger, *Der Weg der UNIDO*, p. 72.

18. A/CONF. 90/17.

19. A/CONF. 90/18.

20. A/CONF. 90/12.

21. A/CONF. 90/18, I, add.II, A/CONF. 90/18, II, add.II.

22. A/CONF. 90/18, 4.3, add.II.

23. A/CONF. 90/16, Corr. I.

24. W. Schiffer, *The Legal Community of Mankind*, 1954, pp. 85–86.

25. UNIDO/CSA/1983/2.

26. UNIDO/CSA/1983/2.

27. UNIDO/CSA/1983/3 Rev. 1.

28. UNIDO/CSA/1983/9.

29. A/39/376.

30. That is, in particular, what K. Köppinger stressed. See K. Köppinger, *Der Weg der UNIDO*, p. 62.

31. D. Williams, *Specialized Agencies*, p. 29.

32. See B. Doll, *Völkerrechtliche Kontinuitätsprobleme bei internationalen Organizationen*, 1967.

33. G. Morozov, *Mezhdunarodniye organizatii* (International Organizations . . .), 1978, p. 274.

34. E. Krivchikova, *Osnovy prava mezhdunarodnykh organizatsii* (The Basics of the Theory of Law of International Organizations), 1979, p. 56.

4

External and Internal Jurisdiction

OBJECTIVES AND FUNCTIONS OF UNIDO

The objectives of the reorganized United Nations Industrial Development Organization (UNIDO) are formulated in Article 1 of its Constitution: "The primary objective of the Organization shall be promotion and acceleration of industrial development in the developing countries with a view to assist in the establishment of New International Economic Order. The Organization shall also promote industrial development and cooperation on global, regional and national, as well as on sectoral levels."

Two main theses are apparent in the objectives of this organization. UNIDO's first objective is promoting the industrial development of third world countries in the framework of common efforts, with a view of establishing a new international economic order. The second objective is the proportion of international industrial cooperation at various levels. The dual nature of UNIDO's objectives is mainly a reflection of the bipartite approach to the orientation of its activities displayed during the period of preparing UNIDO's Constitution.

Developing countries mainly advanced the first approach. The essence of their position was the assertion that UNIDO must be in the first place an agency of technical assistance to third world countries.[1] The Eastern bloc countries were the most active supporters of the second approach and were against such a narrow interpretation of UNIDO's objectives. They believed that the organization should deal with international industrial cooperation in a wide sense, which included promoting the industrialization of developing countries. Naturally, they expected to benefit from that. The final formulation in the Constitution was a compromise and was backed by the Western countries.

The objectives of UNIDO formulated in the Constitution basically conform to the objectives of that organization when UNIDO had the status of the General Assembly's body. However, the recommendations "to promote industrial development" according to paragraph 1 of resolution 2152 (XXI) of the General Assembly took priority in the formulation of UNIDO's objectives. Secondary to that followed the objective of promoting and accelerating the industrial development of the third world countries paying special attention to manufacturing industries by means of mobilizing national and international resources.

The changes in emphasis from this resolution to formulating UNIDO's objectives in the Constitution reflect a strengthening of the developing countries' position: that technical assistance to them is the primary, if not only, task in UNIDO's activities. At the same time it is obvious that when the developing countries put forward maximalist demands and, in particular, a demand that UNIDO should turn into a pipeline rendering massive technical assistance by the rich countries, such a position is untenable.

Multilateral assistance in itself cannot solve problems of the industrial development in the South. The assistance of some Western agencies in the framework of that organization sometimes tended to resemble certain types of commercial and entrepreneurial activities. This is also not always the best solution, because it was done on the basis of governments' contributions. External assistance can be most effective and will contribute to the national interests of developing countries if it involves mobilization of their internal resources and promotes their participation in the world economic process.

UNIDO's general objectives help identify special tasks of the organization. Industrial development is a complicated process, and influencing it cannot be considered on only one level. It depends on the whole variety of factors in economic, social, and political spheres and is closely connected with the methods of management. Growth rates of industrial production are determined by a combination of many factors, which is why promoting industrial development of third world countries results from activities in various fields. Similarly, industrial cooperation embraces a rather wide range of issues related to international economic relations, including exchange of commodities, price formation on world markets, and foreign investments. In that connection a comprehensive approach to interpreting UNIDO's tasks dealing with the problems of industrial development in the third world, and probably in the international industrial community at large, is needed.

According to the Constitution, nothing precludes UNIDO from investing in the industrial sector of developing countries. This is as yet impossible on any considerable scale, due mostly to UNIDO's limited resources. UNIDO, consequently, must promote revealing unused or little-used resources to accelerate industrial development of third world countries.

A well-balanced combination of operational activities and research on a variety of problems connected with industrial development and coordination and control of activities of various UN organs connected with this field are necessary to achieve, in the most efficient way, UNIDO's assigned objectives.

UNIDO's functions are determined in detail in its Constitution. A number of scholars correctly note the diverse interpretation of the term *function* and recognize the difficulties in its uniform use both in specialized literature and in official documents. Despite the attempts to unify the terminology used in texts of international treaties and other documents of international law, the divergence in understanding this common term is rather large. I share a definition proposed by Voitzeh Moravetsky that, when speaking of functions, one "should mean the processes of the organization's activities aimed at achieving its goals."[2] Comparing similar definitions of "function" and "goal," it is necessary to note that if the goal determines what the organization should achieve, then the "function deals with the way in which the organization acts to attain the desired transformation."[3]

Various types of functions of an international organization should be singled out. Some researchers emphasize the political process and reveal overlapping interests of member states, reaching consent in the matters of common tasks corresponding to the sphere of correlating interests and in the matters of the ways of carrying out such common tasks.[4] Those are the basic functions of a present-day international organization. The classification of more specific functions of an international organization is based on the types of its activities' processes, that is, the means and methods used by the organization to carry out various tasks. Correspondingly, those functions are divided into regulating, controlling, and operational ones.

The regulating functions in accordance with the above-mentioned definition "are in establishing norms and standards of moral, political or legal nature which are to shape the behavior of the participants of international relations in proper way."[5] Developed regulating functions can be considered a feature of influential international organizations, including UNIDO, which make an essential contribution to the process of creating norms in the international system.

The regulating functions are determined in the constitutive acts of international organizations and take shape in the process of their activities. The UNIDO Constitution (Article 2), however, sets up the limits for discharging such functions; the organization is a "forum and acts as an instrument to serve . . . in . . . contacts, consultations and on request of the countries concerned, negotiations directed towards the industrialization of developing countries." Besides, as it follows from Articles 1 and 2 of the Constitution, the regulating functions of UNIDO are defined as cooperation between member states in matters of establishing a new international order, in rendering assistance to the industrial development in the third world, and in promoting multilateral concerted action of states in that field. The UNIDO constitutive act did not envisage a more detailed definition of its regulating functions. These functions were in fact not mentioned in resolution 2152 (XXI) of the General Assembly at all, though they were significantly developed in the process of UNIDO's activities.

Policies of the organization's members in the sphere of industrial cooperation are defined by the constitution as well as by corresponding documents adopted in compliance with it. This is why discharging regulating functions means working out the norms regulating the relations among member states. UNIDO discharges its regulating functions by means of adopting documents on international economic relations that are important from a political legal point of view. Among such documents were the decisions of the UNIDO General Conference, especially the Lima and the Delhi Declarations and Plans of Action.

The control functions of UNIDO are not developed enough as a result of the peculiar features of cooperation in the field of industrial cooperation, unlike, for instance, cooperation in the field of peaceful use of nuclear energy. By "control functions," or, in general, "control," I understand activities aimed at revealing the actual situation and its assessment, which proceed from the existing legal norms. This also presupposes defining the fulfillment of, or noncompliance with, obligations assumed by a subject of a certain system of relations. In international law the role of such a subject is played primarily by a state, while the control over fulfillment of the obligations may be exercised by an international organization, of which it is a member, on the basis of legal norms accepted by the member states. International intergovernmental organizations also can be subjects of international law possessing some specific features.[6] It follows that the controlling functions towards member states of the organization in question can be discharged within the limits strictly defined by corresponding legal norms.

In order to discharge its control functions, UNIDO must become informed about the real situation in the sphere of industrial development and should therefore possess a rather developed information service. Article 2 of the UNIDO Constitution says that the organization shall "collect and monitor on a selective basis, analyze and generate for the purpose of dissemination information on all aspects of industrial development on global, regional and national as well as on sectoral levels. . . ." As far as individual countries are concerned, this means that UNIDO must procure and analytically process information on the development of industry taking place in the corresponding sectors of economy, on state policy, on international cooperation in that field, and so on.

UNIDO's control functions envisage a comparison of states' practice with international legal norms established in a certain field, the source of which is often the organization itself. Thus, the assistance rendered to developing countries through UNIDO is compared with the obligations assumed by the countries providing it. Developing countries have the right, making use of such forums as the General Conference and the Industrial Development Board (IDB), to raise the issue of the correlation of assistance rendered to them by this or that industrially advanced country or group of countries to the obligations assumed by it in the framework of the organization. At the same time, in accordance with UNIDO's policies deriving from its Constitution, developing countries are charged with those obligations dealing with their governmental policy in the field of industrialization, of using the assistance, and so on.

An essential stage in the process of control is defining the responsibility of a state for departing from the obligations assumed by it in the framework of the organization. It can be considered for the time being only as a potential sphere of UNIDO's activities. Excluding the obligations dealing directly with the organization's membership, in particular, the financial ones, general obligations of states in the field of international industrial cooperation are formulated in the Constitution and in many other UNIDO documents in a rather general way. This is why in the majority of cases the question of establishing states' responsibility for breaching the obligations assumed by them can be raised in a general political sense rather than in a juridical one.

Identifying operational functions of international organizations is often recognized in the specialized literature and is secured in practice.[7] UNIDO's Constitution does not specifically define these operational functions, as in the case of resolution 2152 (XXI) of the General Assembly, but the overwhelming majority of the provisions of Article 2 of the Constitution deals with these operational functions. In that sense the UNIDO Constitution and the resolution mentioned enumerate approximately the same operational functions of the organizations. They include assisting the developing countries in accelerating their industrialization, in particular, developing and modernizing their industries; promoting selection, adaptation, transfer, and use of industrial technology; and organizing and supporting industrial training programs. Another aspect is rendering assistance in the field of the exploitation, conservation, and local transformation of natural resources in third world countries for the purpose of furthering their industrial development; providing pilot and demonstration plants; and assisting regional planning.

Developing countries have traditionally advocated giving a special place to the operational functions in UNIDO's activities that try to reduce its role to that of a technical assistance tool.[8] Such an approach on the part of developing countries concerning the functions of UNIDO is dictated by their wish to get the greatest possible amount of technical assistance during a short period of time. This does not seem to correspond to their long-term interests. The distortion in this definition of the functions would damage the regulating and control functions of the organization, which is capable of ensuring long-term objectives of third world countries in the field of industrial development. Only a balanced correlation of these functions can ensure the effectiveness of UNIDO's activities and allow it to make greater contribution to international industrial cooperation.

However, it is my belief that at this stage, among the above-mentioned functions of UNIDO, priority should be given to the development of operational functions that make it possible to exert certain indirect influence on shaping the policy of states in the field of international industrial development.

MEMBERSHIP

Some studies that interpret the institution of membership give a definition of a state's membership in an international organization. Membership, one of the institutions of law of international organizations, combines norms regulating the procedure and terms of admission, categories of members, the whole combination of their rights and duties, the matters of suspension and withdrawal from international organizations, and responsibilities as members of the organization.[9] Usually it is necessary to single out five main issues whose interpretation is necessary to characterize membership in an international organization. This will be considered in this section.

The procedure and terms of admission into UNIDO are determined in Article 3 of its Constitution. Membership in the organization is open to all states that associate themselves with its objectives and principles. Some exceptions of that general principle have been made. First of all, member states of the UN, of a specialized agency, or of the International Atomic Energy Agency (IAEA) may become members of the organization only when they ratify, accept, or approve the Constitution of the organization and, in conformity with its Article 24, instruments of ratification must be deposited to the depository, that is, the UN Secretary General. The issue of initiating membership is connected in UNIDO's Constitution with its entering into force; for that purpose, in compliance with paragraph 1 of Article 25, it is necessary "that at least eighty States that had deposited instruments of ratification, acceptance or approval notify the Depository that they have agreed, after consultations among themselves, that this Constitution shall enter into force." For such states the membership begins in conformity with paragraph 2(a) of Article 25 on the day the Constitution enters into force. From this it follows that the number of initial members in UNIDO as a specialized agency could not be fewer than eighty (actually, it was eighty). It is quite a considerable number if we take into account the fact that in 1945 there were fifty-one original members in the UN.

At the same time states that had deposited their instruments of ratification, acceptance, or approval and had not taken part in the above-mentioned consultations could join UNIDO on the day when they informed the depository that the Constitution had entered into force for them. And finally, a state member of the UN, a specialized agency, or the IAEA after the Constitution had entered into force could become a member of UNIDO on the day they deposited instruments of ratification, acceptance, or approval or by joining the organization. It is noteworthy that the UNIDO Constitution does not distinguish between the original members and those who joined later. This was envisaged in the constituent documents of the International Telecommunications Union (ITU) and Food and Agricultural Organization (FAO).

A state that is not a member of the UN, a specialized agency, or the IAEA may also become a member of UNIDO. In conformity with paragraph (b) of Article 3 of the Constitution, such states may become members of UNIDO "after their membership has been approved by the Conference by a two-thirds majority of the members present and voting, upon the recommendation of the Board." A state's application with its request to join the organization is considered by the General Conference, which, in compliance with Rule 106 of its Rules of Procedures,[10] must review it at its next regular or special session. For this it is necessary to have a recommendation of the IDB. In a case when the General Conference approves of a positive recommendation of the IDB, it then makes a decision that the state in question should be included. If the IDB does not recommend admitting the state, the General Conference, after a comprehensive discussion of the IDB report, may return the issue to the IDB for further consideration with a complete report on the appropriate debates.

The lawfulness of the membership of former Soviet republics Ukraine and Belarus in UNIDO as well as in other organs of the UN system before they proclaimed independence in 1991 was questioned, and with good reason, by some jurists.[11] The issue of sovereignty of the republics of the former Soviet Union had not been solved completely, except for the case of the Baltic republics. It is hardly conceivable that they were subjects of international relations before 1991, but the situation has changed drastically. After all, the 1945 agreements on that matter, in particular those of the Yalta Conference, had primarily an arbitrary political background and were not made on a juridical basis; they are hopelessly outdated.

A new interpretation of membership in an international organization began to be used in the activities of UNIDO in conformity with which a formative state may become a member. That would be applicable when the national liberation struggle has not yet resulted in creating a sovereign state. This provision was made as a result of the third world's pressure. Thus, the status of the Council on Namibia of the UN as a full-fledged member of UNIDO was approved by the third General Conference in compliance with General Assembly resolution 32/9 E of November 1977, despite the legitimate objections of the United States, West Germany, Great Britain, and France. UNIDO is in general characterized by a simplified procedure of admitting its members, which reflects the attempts of the organization to be worldwide, true to the objectives and tasks facing it, and evidently reflecting the pressure of third world countries to enlarge their numerical superiority in this way.

The membership of UNIDO does not envisage the status of "co-members," which exists in ITU, or "collaborating members," which is used in the constituent acts of the World Health Organization (WHO) and United Nations Educational, Scientific and Cultural Organization. However, in conformity with Article 4 (1) an observer status can be opened, upon request, to those enjoying such status in the UN General Assembly. Besides, the General Conference has the right to invite other observers to take part in the work of UNIDO in compliance with the articles of the Constitution and the rules of procedure of the General Conference.

The idea of associated membership was discussed at the UN Conference on the UNIDO reorganization. Thus, the draft of the constituent act presented by the UN secretariat envisaged a status of an associate member in addition to full membership. It could occur, in particular, if a state did not wish to become a full-fledged member and, correspondingly, to assume all the obligations. It would also apply to certain territories that were not independent states yet wanted to participate in the work of the organization. Such a formulation was in the interests of some Western countries that would get an opportunity to use the status of an associate member in order to have options in participating in UNIDO. The majority of the members participating in the conference, dominated by third world countries, shared the opinion that the status of an observer made the status of an associate member unnecessary.

The problem of recognizing the credentials of delegations representing member states in the work of the General Conferences is connected with the question of membership. These problems linked with various political considerations, were also raised and tackled in the framework of UNIDO's activities and were similar to the corresponding decisions of the General Assembly. For instance, the Eastern bloc countries and China declared their dissent in recognizing the credentials of the delegations sent by Taiwan (at the Special Conference),[12] the South African Republic, and the military regimes in Chile and South Vietnam (the second General Conference). In their turn, Western countries objected to accepting the credentials of the delegation of Afghanistan after the USSR placed a dependent regime in Kabul (at the second General Conference).

The rights and duties of UNIDO member states arise from the contents of the Constitution. Any member has the right to participate in the work of the General Conference and to be elected in conformity with the existing quotas and the principle of just geographical distribution in the IDB and in the Programme and Budget Committee. States that are members of the organs participate in decision making in the framework envisaged by the Constitution and in compliance with the rules on procedures. Member states, as it follows from Article 1 of the Constitution, have the right to use the results of cooperation in UNIDO including those at the global, regional, national, and sectoral levels. In addition, developing countries have the right to rely on assistance in establishing a new international economic order, although the issue was always controversial.

The duty of member states, as it follows from the Constitution's Preamble, is to observe the broad objectives of the documents mentioned in its text: the resolution adopted by the sixth Special Session of the UN General Assembly on the establishment of a new international economic order, the Lima Declaration and Plan of Action, and the resolution of the seventh Special Session of the General Assembly on Development and International Economic Cooperation. Member states should strive to establish a just and equitable economic and social order and to promote international cooperation for development; however, all those intentions are too general to be relevant for concrete obligations of states.

An essential part of the duties of member states is fulfilling their financial obligations to the organization. In the first place, in conformity with Article 15 of the Constitution, member states should bear regular budget expenditures of UNIDO as apportioned in compliance with a scale of assessment. Each member and observer, in conformity with Article 12 of the Constitution, shall bear the expenses of its participation in the work of the General Conference, the IDB, or any other organ of UNIDO.

The UNIDO Constitution does not endorse a possibility of expelling members from this organization. This is typical of the UN system, although among its specialized agencies there are three in which this measure is admissible: the International Monetary Fund, International Bank for Reconstruction and Development and International Development Association. A suspension of membership is envisaged in a number of specialized agencies, for instance, International Labor Organization (ILO), WHO, International Civil Aviation Organization, World Meteorological Organization. The suspension of membership in UNIDO is possible only when a state itself is willing, while the Constitution of the organization envisages only a suspension of such a member's rights and privileges as a maximum penalty. This is rather similar to expulsion but, nevertheless, is not expulsion.[13] In such a case the state must continue to fulfill its pledges to the organization.

Suspension of rights and privileges is supposed to be a temporary measure. A member of UNIDO may be temporarily suspended for two reasons. First, temporary suspension will automatically ensue if it is suspended from the exercise of its rights and privileges connected with its UN membership. Secondly, it is suspended from the right to take part in any voting during the work of the organization if the sum of its arrears is equal to or exceeds the sum of its mandatory contribution for two previous fiscal years. At the same time, in compliance with paragraph 2 of Article 5 of the Constitution, this rule may be not applied, and any UNIDO organ may allow such a member to participate in voting, if this body admits that the nonpayment occurred because of circumstances independent of that member. As with the UN, such a provision seems to be rather "soft" in its application.

The principle of a state's sovereignty presupposes that any UNIDO member may withdraw from the organization, and the UNIDO Constitution does not envisage its obligation to motivate it. According to Article 6, such a withdrawal shall take effect on the last day of the fiscal year following the year during which an instrument of its denunciation of the Constitution was deposited with the depository (the UN Secretary General). The withdrawing state shall pay its contributions for the fiscal year following and fulfill any pledges it had made. Unlike the FAO's constitution, UNIDO's Constitution does not envisage an initial period in the existence of the organization during which withdrawal from it is prohibited.

Since the time UNIDO was established as an autonomous organ of the UN General Assembly, there have been no cases of member states withdrawing from the organization or of states being deprived of their rights. At the same time the issue of withdrawal from UNIDO was urgent in the period when transformations of the organization were being prepared: at the end of the 1970s and in the first half of the 1980s. From the practical point of view, the refusal to notify the depository of the Constitution that the state agreed that the Constitution had entered into force would be equal to the state's withdrawal from it. This could happen even if earlier the state had deposited its instruments of ratification or acceptance of the Constitution. Such a situation allowed some countries to not bind themselves to the transformed UNIDO. Some Western countries evidently reserved this nonexpressed option when the draft of UNIDO's new Constitution was being prepared in order to exert some pressure on developing countries and make them soften their positions and withdraw a number of unrealistic demands.

From 1986 to 1988, the United States started exerting pressure on the UN and many of its agencies by reducing its contribution to the UN budget more than by 20 percent.[14] Taking into account the reserved attitude of some Western states toward UNIDO, it is possible that the problem of termination of membership might appear in the agenda of the organization's work. In that sense a precedent was created in 1987 when Australia withdrew from UNIDO.

STATUS OF A SPECIALIZED AGENCY: UNIDO AND OTHER INTERNATIONAL ORGANIZATIONS

The question of the status of a UN specialized agency has been studied enough.[15] Normally researchers single out the legal features of specialized agencies according to Article 57 of the charter of the UN. Four main features can be identified: (1) the intergovernmental nature of their constitutive acts, (2) wide international responsibility in the framework of their competence, (3) the performance of their activities in certain special spheres, which are stipulated by the UN charter, and (4) connection with the UN. It is noteworthy that the last feature is considered to be specific and is characteristic only of specialized agencies (and of the IAEA), which makes them a special group of international organizations.[16] Aside from this, some researchers treat the wide international responsibility as the basis for singling out another feature — the universal character of the specialized agencies, which distinguishes them from regional organizations engaged in similar activities.[17]

UNIDO possesses in full the above-mentioned features of a specialized agency. Its constitutive act was adopted by eighty-one states at the Vienna session of the UN conference on the reorganization of UNIDO. According to the Constitution, in particular, Articles 1 and 2, UNIDO is endowed with wide international responsibilities in the "promotion and acceleration of industrial development in the developing countries."

The functions of UNIDO belong to a special sphere of social and economic activities of the UN, international industrial cooperation, which was discussed in Chapter 1. The number of UNIDO members testifies to its universal character; at the moment of its reorganization the membership exceeded 130, in the early 1990s it surpassed 150.

The status of legal subjects characteristic of specialized agencies including UNIDO singles them out from international organizations endowing them with public legal authorities. This is determined by the UN charter, by the constitutive acts of the specialized agencies, the Conventions on Privileges and Immunities of Specialized Agencies of 1947, by agreements concluded by the UN with those specialized agencies, and by the agreements concluded by the agencies with the states or the territories where their headquarters are located.

UNIDO's international legal public credentials are determined by the fact that it can conclude agreements with states and international organizations.[18] There are foreign representatives at UNIDO (as a rule, a single representative from each country, at international organizations in Vienna). This is also an important indication of its public legal character. According to the UN Convention on Privileges and Immunities of Specialized Agencies and a Protocol to it concerning UNIDO, the organization and its personnel have certain privileges and authorities. Finally, according to Article 96 of the UN charter and Article 22 of UNIDO's Constitution, this organization has the right to make inquiries into consultative conclusions of the International Court of Justice (ICJ), as is stipulated by Article 65 of the ICJ's statute.

For the legal position of UNIDO, its relationship with the UN is of essential importance. According to Article 18 of its Constitution, UNIDO "shall be brought into relationship with the United Nations as one of the specialized agencies referred to in Article 57 of the Charter of the United Nations." Article 18 further states that any agreement concluded in accordance with Article 63 of the UN charter "shall require the approval of the Conference by a two-thirds majority of the members present and voting upon the recommendation of the IDB."

The first session (part two) of UNIDO's General Conference, in December 1985, approved the draft agreement on the mutual relations with the UN, provided it was endorsed by the General Assembly.[19] According to Articles 20 and 21 of the draft, the agreement was applied after its confirmation by the Economic and Social Council (ECOSOC) with the consent of the General Assembly and the IDB, and accordingly with the approval by the General Conference. The agreement entered into force after its subsequent confirmation by the UN General Assembly and the UNIDO General Conference.

In characterizing the relationship between the UN and UNIDO in its new status, the following features are the most essential. First of all, it is possible to speak of independent subjects of international law, that is, of international organizations that do not depend on each other and that do not report directly to other organizations.

At the same time, UNIDO, as a specialized agency, is a component of the UN system. Therefore, UNIDO enters into rather close relations with the UN and cooperates on various questions. These relations are based on the recognition of the UN's wider functions and authorities.

According to the agreement between the UN and UNIDO, the former recognized UNIDO as a specialized agency of the UN system (Article 1). For its part UNIDO recognized the coordinating role as well as the commitments of the General Assembly and the ECOSOC when promoting economic and social development in its relations with the UN. UNIDO, correspondingly, recognized the necessity of effective coordination and cooperation with the UN, its organs, and its system and agreed to take part in the UN's work with the purpose of rendering assistance with cooperation and coordination (Article 2). For that purpose representatives of the UN are invited to participate in the sessions of all the organs of UNIDO and to take part in the discussions, but they do not have the right to vote. Representatives of UNIDO are invited to participate in turn in the sessions of the General Assembly and to take part in the debates of the ECOSOC, without the right to vote on agenda issues concerning industrial development. After the consultations the UN can propose questions for the consideration of UNIDO, and the latter for the consideration of the UN, first of all in the ECOSOC (Articles 3 and 4).

UNIDO pledges to present to its corresponding organ the official recommendations of the UN and in turn consult the UN, upon its request, on eventual implementation of those recommendations (Article 5). The parties pledge to cooperate in the exchange of information and documentation and in matters of statistics (Articles 6–8).

Operational activities, or rendering technical assistance, are a very important aspect of cooperation between the UN and UNIDO. The parties pledge in accordance with the agreement to avoid undesirable duplication of their activities. Simultaneously UNIDO collaborates with the agencies of the UN in promoting and facilitating the transfer of technology to developing countries. UNIDO recognized common obligations of the coordinators of the operational activities for the purpose of development and agreed to consider common use of the services (Articles 9 and 10). The General Assembly authorized UNIDO to apply to the International Court of Justice for advisory opinions on legal questions connected with its activity, excluding issues of its relations with the UN and other agencies of the UN system (Article 12).

The UN and UNIDO pledged to cooperate in administrative matters (Article 14) with regard to the staff (Article 15). They must try to maintain close budget and financial relations; in particular, UNIDO agrees to send to the UN its proposed budgets not later than they are sent for the consideration of its members. The General Assembly is therefore able to study them and give its recommendations (Article 17).[20]

Before its reorganization UNIDO was not an independent subject of international law. However, it had some features of autonomy. UNIDO's dependence on the UN was revealed by the subordination of the IDB to the General Assembly and other organs of the UN, which were delegated the corresponding functions by the General Assembly. The General Assembly played a specific role in working out UNIDO's policies. The General Assembly's decisions exerted influence on the activities of UNIDO and its organs on practically all levels. The General Assembly elected the IDB members, determined which countries had the right to be elected to it, and determined the quotas for the groups of countries in accordance with the principle of just geographical distribution. The UNIDO Executive Director was appointed by the UN Secretary General, subject to approval by the General Assembly. The IDB was to present its annual reports to the General Assembly through the ECOSOC.

At the same time UNIDO did really enjoy certain autonomy. Thus, the countries that were not members of the UN but were members of specialized agencies or the IAEA could participate in the organization. The UNIDO Executive Director had the right to appoint independently some of the managerial staff members of the secretariat. From the very beginning of its existence UNIDO had a permanent secretariat.

The determination of the role to be played by the General Assembly and the ECOSOC in working out UNIDO policies and in controlling its activities was a serious legal problem. According to Article 60 of the UN charter, the activities connected with cooperation in economic and social fields must be carried out through the ECOSOC and in the long run should be directed by the General Assembly. This point, as well as resolutions 2089 (XX) and 2152 (XXI) of the General Assembly, envisaged a wide scope for the interpretation of UNIDO's subordination to other organs of the UN.

Developing countries traditionally stood for strengthening the autonomy of this organization.[21] That group of countries maintained the opinion that UNIDO, established in conformity with a General Assembly resolution, could report only to the General Assembly. From this was derived its essential independence as far as the ECOSOC was concerned. Some countries insisted, for instance, that the reports of the IDB should be presented directly to the General Assembly, bypassing the ECOSOC. Others were of the opinion that according to established practice, before sending the IDB report to the second Committee of the General Assembly for consideration, it was to be submitted to the ECOSOC. ECOSOC's function, however, was reduced to becoming acquainted with the report and handing it over to the second Committee.

Western countries insisted on a narrower interpretation of the rights of UNIDO as an autonomous organization. That group of countries defended the standpoint that the authorities of UNIDO must not go beyond the already defined limits of their functioning with the UN. According to that position UNIDO was to report directly to the ECOSOC. Annual reports of the IDB had to be sent to the ECOSOC, which had the right to express any remarks or recommendations before handing them to the second Committee. In reality, at practically every session of the ECOSOC the issue of "cooperation in the field of industrial development" was on the agenda. The ECOSOC did not reduce its role to considering the reports of the IDB, but it frequently gave its recommendations, which were taken into account by the second Committee of the General Assembly.

UNIDO's Constitution comments on relations with other international organizations. According to point 3 of Article 2 of the Constitution, ". . . it shall initiate, coordinate and follow up the activities of the United Nations system with a view to enabling the Organization to play the central role in the field of industrial development. . . ." This point was formulated in more detail than was a similar provision in paragraph 27 of resolution 2152 (XXI) of the General Assembly, which states, "The Organization shall play the central role in and be responsible for reviewing and promoting the coordination of all activities of the United Nations system in the field of industrial development." It should be stressed that before the reorganization of UNIDO, this function could be fulfilled only with some difficulties, including certain legal problems. Thus, the coordination of any activities of the United Nations system in the field of industrial development by UNIDO envisaged by resolution 2152 (XXI) of the General Assembly could not be implemented automatically, while the status of the organization was not sufficient.

Relations with the organizations of the UN system, acting in the field of industrial development, are built on the basis of corresponding agreements in accordance with Articles 18 and 19 (1a) of the UNIDO Constitution. The same clauses were envisaged in paragraphs 28–34 of resolution 2152 (XXI). The only difference was that there was no agreement with the UN, because UNIDO was an autonomous organ of the General Assembly and, correspondingly, reported directly to it. Besides, paragraphs 63 and 64 of the resolution specified that the IDB as the main organ of UNIDO had to take into account in its activities on coordination the authorities delegated to the ECOSOC in compliance with the UN charter.

Relations with the United Nations Development Programme (UNDP) are very important for UNIDO, which depends on that organ for financing projects, choosing and substantiating them, and implementing them. In compliance with the conclusions of the consultations on the reorganization of UNIDO, the secretariat of that organization was asked to work out an agreement between the UNDP and UNIDO and to use it on a temporary basis until such an agreement came into force.[22] This draft agreement was subsequently approved by both parties.[23]

In compliance with the above-mentioned agreement, UNIDO and the UNDP pledged to cooperate in implementing the projects of mutual interest, first of all, those in which UNIDO is an executive organ. Both sides recognize that a country's resident UNIDO representative has full responsibility and all authority to distribute and allocate the UNIDO programs in that country. The resident representative directs the activities of the group of specialists of the UN organs, including advisers on industrial development.

UNIDO recognized the central coordinating role of the UNDP resident representative in connection with the UN programs of technical cooperation and agreed to consult with the UNDP and hand over information on issues of industrial development, as well as reports on how projects are being implemented (Article III). The UNDP and UNIDO agreed to exchange opinions with each other and with the government of the state recipient of assistance on arrangements deriving from the program on development in the field of technical cooperation and from other UNIDO projects (Article V). While implementing the arrangements of the development program, UNIDO has the status of an independent contractor as far as the UNDP is concerned and reports to it when implementing such arrangements (Article VIII). The UNDP is obliged to compensate for all direct expenses of UNIDO when implementing the arrangements on coordinated projects, as well as for related expenses (Article VIII).[24]

Before UNIDO's reorganization, its operational activities depended to a greater extent on financing from the UNDP. This was essentially contradictory. Even though an autonomous organization in the UN system, UNIDO turned out to be in a dependent position as far as its operational activities were concerned.[25] This contradiction was evidenced in UNIDO's lack of fulfillment of the projects, because insufficient coordination of the functions of that organization and the UNDP constantly caused problems in practical activities. That, in particular, was stressed by K. Köppinger.[26]

Technical assistance to countries was carried out jointly by the UNDP and by the governmental bodies of the country concerned without the participation of the executive organ of UNIDO. Since UNIDO was removed from working out the prospective plans of rendering assistance, discrepancies often arose, which adversely affected the final results of the projects. Thus, local representatives of the UNDP had the right to cancel the appointments of UNIDO experts even if they had already been made. They were able to limit the deliveries of equipment or interfere with implementing the project. This was guided by financial requirements and referred to requests of a recipient country. At the same time UNIDO did not have an opportunity to coordinate the questions on the project with corresponding national bodies independently. The leadership of UNIDO's secretariat insisted that the third party, the contractor, should be involved in working out the project alongside the UNDP and the governmental bodies. During the approval of programs the obligations and authorities of all three parties had to be clearly outlined.

At the beginning of the 1990s this approach began to prevail, and, as a result, the implementation of projects started to improve. UNIDO made efforts to improve in relations with the representatives of the UNDP in the localities. The UNDP, in reply to the demands by UNIDO and a number of other institutions involved in concrete realization of projects, agreed to shorter terms for project coordinating.[27]

The policy pursued by the UNDP Board of Administrators toward UNIDO has not always met the objectives of the latter. The share of UNIDO in the aggregate expenditures of the UNDP for operative activity had been at a low level for a long time, having not exceeded 8 percent in some years. UNIDO's share of UNDP expenditures for industrial development was often less than one half. This could be considered a violation of UNIDO's central role in the activities of the UN system in the field of industrial development, which was stipulated in resolution 2152 (XXI) of the General Assembly. UNIDO used to receive from the UNDP low-cost, small-scale projects, which fragmented financial means but was probably hard to avoid in view of limited resources. The preparatory work for minor projects does not really demand less effort than that for major projects. There were constant losses as a result of delays on the part of the UNDP in approving the projects, in which UNIDO acted as an institution charged with their realization.

Insufficient coordination in the relations between the two organs of the UN was in the long run explained by the reserved attitude of Western countries in the UNDP. Western countries were not interested in strengthening UNIDO, where developing countries and Eastern bloc countries occupied relatively strong positions. Using the budget dependence of UNIDO, the UNDP Board of Administrators did not show its readiness to promote expanding the activities and strengthening the role of UNIDO in the matters of the UN system's assistance to development of the third world countries.

Before its reorganization, according to General Assembly resolution 2152, UNIDO maintained constant relations with the United Nations Conference on Trade and Development (UNCTAD), with the regional economic and social commissions, and with the Economic and Social Bureau in Beirut. After its reorganization UNIDO had no legal obligations to maintain working relations with the above-mentioned organs of the UN, but in practice they were preserved, although at the initial stage without signing agreements.

UNIDO has been exchanging information with UNCTAD since 1969. Still, there is no formal agreement between the two organizations. In practice, however, close cooperation is maintained due to working groups that consider projects of mutual interest. Usually UNIDO deals with matters of industrial production while UNCTAD attends to trade policy. As for the transfer of technology, it is very difficult to distinguish between the functions of these two organizations. Besides, industrialization cooperation depends upon conditions of trade, which can promote the industrial development or interfere with it. However, considerable overlapping of both institutions' roles was counterproductive.

The UNIDO Director-General may conclude agreements that establish corresponding relations with the organizations of the UN and with other governmental organizations, according to Article 19 of UNIDO's Constitution, with the approval of the IDB and according to instructions of the General Conference.

In the late 1980s, agreements were concluded with the IAEA and ILO in which the cooperation with these organizations was regulated. The agreements stipulate a possibility of mutual participation of their representatives in the work of the plenary organs (without the right to vote), exchange of documents and information, and cooperation between the secretariats.

Before UNIDO's reorganization its relations with the UN specialized agencies were complicated by the fact that the status of the organ of the General Assembly was not sufficient to be considered an independent partner, an independent juridical entity. The difficulties in coordinating the activities of the previous UNIDO with specialized agencies were stressed, for example, by R. Charvin.[28]

The relations of UNIDO with governmental and other international organizations that are not part of the UN system, but the activities of which are connected with UNIDO, are also regulated by Article 19 of the Constitution (before the reorganization by paragraphs 35 and 36 of resolution 2152 (XXI) of the General Assembly). UNIDO cooperates with governmental organizations that are not in the UN system, such as the Organization for Economic Cooperation and Development, the European Communities, the League of Arab States, and the Organization of Petroleum Exporting Countries. Some of these organizations are given an observer status at UNIDO forums, particularly at the General Conferences. In addition, joint projects with these organizations are sometimes carried out.

While establishing relations with nongovernmental organizations the Director-General is obliged to hold consultations with corresponding governments and may conclude working agreements with such organizations. The General Conference and the IDB consider the list of organizations that might have the status of observers at their sessions. In every single case UNIDO proceeds from a possibility of using the resources of such organizations for the fulfillment of its objectives. Organizations that maintain regular relations with UNIDO include the International Chamber of Commerce, the World Federation of Organizations in the Field of Industrial and Technical Research, and the International Organization of the Employers. Exchange of information with these organizations is common practice, as are participation of the representatives of one party at the sessions of the leading organs of the other and periodic consultations at the secretariat level. Occasionally, colloquiums and seminars are organized jointly.

INTERNAL AND EXTERNAL LAW OF AN ORGANIZATION

In international law literature a discussion is going on concerning the systematization of legal regulations of international organizations. One of the attempts to carry out such systematization with the aim of solving some methodological tasks is the introduction of the concepts of internal and external law (jurisdiction) of organizations.

The concept of the internal law of an international organization is frequently applied in research literature. However, there is no full agreement on its interpretation. One increasingly recognized point of view is that with the rise and development of an international organization, direct interstate relations become supplemented by relations in the framework of an international organization. The latter include relations of states as members of an organization between themselves, their relations with the organization, relations within the organization between its organs, relations of the organization with nonmember states, and relations with other international organizations. Elena Shibayeva qualifies as relations regulated by internal law those ties between organs of an organization, relations between states as members of an organization, and relations of member states with an organization.[29]

Some researchers are inclined to interpret internal law in a narrower context. They believe that "'internal law' includes norms regulating internal legal relations — procedural rules, financial regulations, rules for the staff."[30]

The first position, in my view, helps to create a more integrated picture of the internal organization mechanism of UNIDO than the second one and may yield more effective results when applied in practice. Indeed, the internal legal regulations do not exist in UNIDO in isolation but are the products of coordination of the will of states that together constitute an integrated unity of political and legal issues. Consequently, it would be nonproductive to exclude from the internal UNIDO regulations norms regulating relations between member states in the process of the functioning of this organization and their relations with it.

In order to outline the content of internal law with reference to UNIDO, we could be guided by three criteria, which in general help draw a line between internal and external law of an international organization. First, normative material must refer to the internal functioning of the organization and must not contain norms characterizing the role of this organization in the international system. Second, decisions of the organization serving as the source of internal jurisdiction are binding, in contrast to recommendations addressed to other subjects of international law. Third, internal law is formed on the basis of relations of member states with the organization and relations between the organs of the given organization.

Of methodological interest is the concept of specific jurisdiction of an international organization formulated by a number of jurists. The proponent of this concept, Wilfred Jenks, believes that an international organization develops its own specific jurisdiction, international in its character and not forming a part of national legal systems. An international organization, then, generates its own law embracing a broad spectrum of legal relations. As Jenks writes, jurisdiction referring to cooperative activity (an international organization) naturally covers such questions as membership; the conception, composition, and relations of different organs; their procedures, rights, and obligations of an organization and its members relative to one another; financial questions; procedures for adopting amendments to the Constitution; regulations for dissolution or institution of an organization; and use of its assets under such circumstances. It may also embrace relations of an organization, its members, and its different organs with third parties on various questions.[31] As follows from this definition, the specific jurisdiction of an organization embraces, apart from the sum of norms constituting internal law, relations of organizations with third parties.

At the same time, relations with third parties are often identified as external law of an international organization. The concept of external law of international organizations is also used in juridical literature. However, researchers assign different meanings to it. Georgi Morozov writes that this concept "is used to denote the legal instrument by means of which international organizations ensure their status in the concrete conditions of their existence and their ties with states or other (including governmental) organizations, etc."[32]

Narrow interpretation of this concept is offered by Shibayeva, who believes that the term *external law* "includes norms regulating above all cooperation between organizations."[33] The main difference between these two points of view is that in the former case external law is the relations of member countries with an organization and in the latter case external law is relations with an international organization.

I think that the second point of view with reference to the political and legal analysis of UNIDO is more productive. The complex of norms regulating relations of the organization with member countries is more closely related to the internal organizational mechanism of UNIDO than to its legal impact in the international system. I think this because member countries voluntarily assuming obligations under the constitutive act, and, accordingly, entering into definite legal relations with the organization, can no longer be regarded as external parties to its legal relations.

I share the second approach that distinguishes external law as a formative sub-branch of the emerging law of international organizations. Besides, evidently the future of international organizations is linked inseparably with interorganization cooperation. Thus, the external law of UNIDO includes above all the sum of norms regulating its relations with other international organizations, both governmental and nongovernmental.

NOTES

1. D. Ait Ouyahia, *Évolution de l'Organisation*, pp. 182–87.

2. V. Moravetsky, *Funkzii mezhdunarodnykh organizaii* (Functions of International Organizations), 1975, p. 88.

3. Ibid.

4. Ibid.

5. V. Moravetsky, *Funkzii*, p. 91.

6. G. Tunkin, *Pravo i sila v mezhdunarodnoy sisteme* (Law and Power in the International System), 1983.

7. R. Keohane and J. Nye, *Transnational Relations and World Politics*, 1972, pp. 129–52, 356–98.

8. E. Luard, *International Agencies. The Emerging Framework of Interdependence*, 1977, pp. 248–50; D. Ait Ouyahia, *Évolution de l'Organisation*, pp. 249–54.

9. R. Riggs and J. Plano, *The United Nations. International Organization and World Politics*, 1988, pp. 57–63; N. Krylov, *Prinzipy uchastya gosudarstv v sisteme OON* (The Principles of the Participation of States in the UN System), 1986, p. 6. See also E. Stein, *Some Implications of Expanding UN Membership*, 1956.

10. UNIDO/CC. 1/Dec. 19.

11. See S. Olymyk, *Membership of the Soviet Ukraine in the United Nations: Background, Status and Legal Implications*, 1959.

12. See S. Bailey, *Chinese Representatives in the Security Council and the General Assembly of the United Nations*, 1970.

13. This opinion is in particular shared by H. Singh, *Termination of Membership in International Organizations*, 1958.

14. See the analytical approach to a plausible revision of the U.S. position in T. Franck, *Nation against Nation. What Happened to the UN Dream and What US*

Can DO about It, 1985; D. Pines, *A World without a UN: What Would Happen if the UN Shut Down*, 1984.

15. Interestingly, this issue was considered at length in East European literature. The characteristic features of that institution are found in studies by S. Malinin, E. Shibayeva (Russia), M. Potochny (Chechia), P. Radoinov (Bulgaria), and V. Moravetsky (Poland).

16. See, for example, E. Shibayeva, *Spezializirovannye uchrezhdenya OON (Mezhdunarodno pravovoy aspekt)* (Specialized Agencies of the UN (International Legal Aspects)), 1966, pp. 19–20.

17. K. Rubanik, *UNESCO kak spezializirovannoye uchrezhdenie OON* (UNESCO as a Specialized Agency of the UN), 1960, p. 5.

18. K. Köppinger, *Der Weg der UNIDO*, p. 116.

19. G.C. I/Dec. 38.

20. UNIDO/IDB. 1/30.

21. K. Köppinger, *Der Weg der UNIDO*, pp. 28–30.

22. UNIDO/CSA/1983/4.

23. IDS. I/Dec. 24.

24. UNIDO/IDB. I/19.

25. General Issues in J. Strossinger, *Financing the United Nations System*.

26. K. Köppinger, *Der Weg der UNIDO*, p. 107.

27. The critical assessment of previous implementing projects by the UNIDO. See E. Luard, *International Agencies*, 1977, pp. 248–50.

28. R. Charvin, *L'ONUDI. Revue génerale du droit international public*, 1969, pp. 781–83.

29. E. Shibayeva, *Spezializirovannye uchrezdenya*, p. 131.

30. E. Krivchikova, *Osnovy prava*, p. 26; E. Yemin, *Legislative Powers in the United Nations and Specialized Agencies*, 1969.

31. C. W. Jenks, *The Proper Law of International Organizations*, 1962, p. 7.

32. G. Morozov, *International Organizations*, pp. 269–70.

33. E. Shibayeva, *Spezializirovannye uchrezdenya*, p. 141; see also R. Cox and H. Jacobson, *The Anatomy of Influence*, 1973.

5

Organizational Structure of UNIDO

GENERAL CONFERENCE

A number of studies devoted to specialized agencies note that their structure is in general similar, consisting of four parts: a higher organ, an executive organ, an organizational organ, and a technical organ (secretariat, specialized commissions, and committees). According to this classification, main organs of an international organization also could be singled out, as was done in the UN charter (six main organs). The United Nations Industrial Development Organization (UNIDO) is the only specialized agency with three main organs.

In conformity with Article 7 of the Constitution, the main organs of UNIDO are the General Conference, the Industrial Development Board (IDB), and the secretariat. The order in which those organs are mentioned in Article 7 implies their significance, which is not directly stressed in the text of the Constitution but follows from their authorities as determined in Articles 8, 9, and 11.[1]

The highest UNIDO organ — the General Conference — has a name similar to the higher organs of the United Nations Educational, Scientific and Cultural Organization and the International Labor Organization. It is not, however, always imperative in specialized agencies; other names of the highest organs are Congress, Assembly, and Plenipotentiary Conference.

As the most representative organ of UNIDO, the General Conference includes representatives of all members of the organization. In compliance with Article 8 of the Constitution, regular sessions of the General Conference are convened every two years. There is, however, an important reservation: "if it does not decide otherwise." This makes it possible to convene the General Conference more often, for instance, once a year, on which developing countries insisted. In this case developing countries would have a real opportunity to impose their decisions using their preponderance in number, more than two-thirds of all the members, at plenary organs.

A term in convening regular sessions of the General Conference is important in the light of the problem of correlation between the authorities of the General Conference and the IDB. Naturally, if the General Conference were convened once a year, it would inevitably in practice perform more functions than the IDB. Special sessions of the General Conference may be convened at the IDB's request or at the request of the majority of the organization's members.

At the beginning of a regular or special session of the General Conference, in conformity with rule 28, a committee of nine members to check credentials is appointed at the proposal of the chairman. If possible, this committee should correspond in its composition to the Committee on Credentials of the UN General Assembly at its latest session. In compliance with rules 35, 36, and 40, at its next regular session the General Conference elects, according to just geographical distribution, a chairman, nine deputy chairmen, and a chairman for each of the main committees that compose the General Committee.[2] All the officials perform their duties until their successors are elected on the basis of a just geographical rotation.

Rule 90 makes a special reservation such that the General Conference "does its best to ensure the adoption of all essential decisions by consensus." This should by no means impose restrictions on the right of any member to demand a vote on a proposal. Decisions by the General Conference are taken in conformity with paragraph 6 of Article 3 of the Constitution by a simple majority of the members present and voting or by a two-thirds majority, depending on the question considered. Each member has one vote at the General Conference.[3]

For a decision to be adopted at the session of a higher organ of UNIDO it must have a majority of one half of the votes for procedural questions and a two-thirds majority for other questions. Normally, this means a majority of members present and voting.

The General Conference is authorized by Article 8 of the Constitution to approve conventions and agreements on any question within UNIDO's jurisdiction by a two-thirds majority of members present and voting and to make recommendations to the members and international organizations on issues coming under UNIDO's jurisdiction.

The General Conference may, in conformity with Article 8 of the Constitution, delegate some of its powers to the IDB, with the exception of the following: admitting new UNIDO members; working out the guiding principles and policies of the organization; considering the reports of the IDB, the Director-General, and auxiliary bodies of the General Conference; approving the work program, regular and operational budgets, and scales of mandatory contributions;

approving conventions and agreements; electing the IDB members and the Programme and Budget Committee; and appointing the Director-General.

The approval of amendments to the Constitution is very difficult — it is possible, in conformity with Article 23, for the General Conference to approve an amendment by a two-thirds majority of all members whether they take part in voting or not. The amendments must be recommended to the conference by the IDB. Unessential amendments (for instance, those not affecting the procedure of making decisions by the UNIDO bodies) must be approved by a simple majority of the IDB members, fundamental amendments, by a two-thirds majority. For such amendments to enter into force it is necessary that either two-thirds or three-fourths of the IDB members, correspondingly, should have deposited with the Depository (UN Secretary General) their instruments of ratification, acceptance, or approval of the amendment.

The General Conference as a main body in the structure of the organization was envisaged only in the UNIDO Constitution. The General Assembly resolution 2152 (XXI) did not make mention of such a body. Despite this fact, four General Conferences were convened before the transformation of UNIDO. Even prior to UNIDO's transformation, corresponding decisions of the General Assembly adopted on the recommendation of the IDB created a certain legal basis for the functioning a new main body of that organization — the General Conference. However, this could in no way be considered a binding obligation for member states.

The questions of the General Conference's authorities were only slightly touched upon in the General Assembly resolutions, and those resolutions did not reveal the correlation between the authorities of the General Conference and the IDB. Even so, the total of the General Assembly decisions on General Conferences created certain legal material. The results of the second, third, and fourth General Conferences were approved in special resolutions of the UN General Assembly. This was an indirect confirmation of the idea of regularly convening the UNIDO General Conferences once every four years, as it was approved by the second General Conference.

The UNIDO General Conferences became increasingly more representative. Thus, 108 states took part in the Special Conference, 114 in the second, 133 in the third, and 139 in the fourth. A number of states and national liberation movements were represented at the Conferences as observers; numerous UN bodies, specialized agencies, intergovernmental and nongovernmental international organizations also were represented. This was mostly the result of third world efforts to increase the emphasis on UNIDO.

Among the established regulations dealing with the work of the General Conference are the following: on the eve of convening the

General Conference the IDB was transformed into a preparatory committee; the General Conference adopted for its work, with a number of exceptions, the IDB rules of procedures as its own rules; two committees (besides the Special Conference) were formed for discussing the agenda; the Committee of Credentials had the same composition as at the latest General Conferences; and the General Assembly gave guiding instructions on the main items of the agenda.

The first session of the General Conference of the new organization, in which almost all its members participated, was convened during the transitional period of UNIDO's transformation into a specialized agency. The General Conference then functioned as the main body of the organization, in conformity with the Constitution of the organization, which had entered into force. The session was held in two parts, from August 12 to August 17 and from December 9 to December 13, 1985, and was devoted to considering the whole range of issues of UNIDO's transformation.

While the sessions of the General Conferences are of particular importance for UNIDO, I shall devote special attention to those held after the organization became a specialized agency in Chapter 10.

INDUSTRIAL DEVELOPMENT BOARD

The executive body is normally an important link in the structure of UN specialized agencies. Such a body can be named in different ways: a Board, an Executive Council, an Administrative Council, an Executive Commission, and so on. The IDB, in compliance with Article 7 of the UNIDO Constitution, is one of the three main organs of the organization. Until UNIDO had been reorganized into a specialized agency, the IDB was the only main organ of that organization.

In compliance with paragraph 1 of Article 9 of the UNIDO Constitution, the IDB is elected by the General Conference and consists of fifty-three members, in accordance with the principle of just geographical distribution. The number of IDB members is close to the maximum in the executive organs of specialized agencies, which fluctuates from eighteen to fifty-six.

The IDB members, after their election at the regular session of the General Conference, hold their office until the next General Conference session, four years later, is closed. The only exception is made for the first General Conference session, where one-half of the IDB members were elected for the term of two years. The IDB members can be elected for the next term.

The IDB was mentioned as an organ of UNIDO in resolution 2089 (XX) of the General Assembly, which laid a legal foundation for establishing that organization. The IDB membership was mentioned in detail in resolution 2152 (XXI) of the General Assembly, in particular, in Article 3. The IDB members were elected by the General Assembly from members of the UN specialized agencies and the International Atomic Energy Agency (IAEA). There were forty-five members in the IDB at the time, elected for a term of three years, and fifteen countries were to be re-elected every year. A member state could be re-elected for the next term.

The UNIDO Constitution entrusted the IDB with wide authorities. In compliance with Article 9 of the Constitution, the IDB reviews the implementation of the approved program of work, the fulfillment of the regular and operational budgets, and other decisions of the General Conference. The IDB recommends to the General Conference a scale of obligatory contributions for covering regular budget expenses, prepares a preliminary agenda for the General Conference, reports to it on the results of its activities, and requests the member states to submit information on their activities concerning UNIDO. If the post of the Director-General becomes vacant between General Conference sessions, the IDB appoints a person to discharge those duties until the next session of the IDB. In conformity with Article 8 (4) of the Constitution, the General Conference has the right to delegate some of its functions to the IDB.

The functions of the IDB are much narrower than its functions before the reorganization of UNIDO. The main powers of the IDB as set out in paragraph 7 of resolution 2152 (XXI) of the General Assembly came down to the following: to determine the political direction and the principles of the organization's activities to ensure the completion of UNIDO's tasks, to study and coordinate the activities of the UN organs dealing with the issues of industrial development, and to consider the program of work and the draft budget of UNIDO.

In compliance with Article 9 (2) of the Constitution of the IDB, members stay in office after the closing of a regular General Conference session four years later. Meanwhile, half of the members elected at the first session stay in office until the second regular session comes to an end two years later. The IDB members can be re-elected. The IDB holds its regular sessions at least once a year, on a self-determined date. A regular session of the board must be convened in accordance with rule 3 of the Rules of Procedure of the IDB[4] in order to adopt the program of work, the budget for the next fiscal period, and the report to be submitted to the General Conference. At the request of the majority of the IDB members the board may be convened by the Director-General for special sessions. Every IDB member, in compliance with rule 4 of the IDB Rules of Procedure, can express such a request. The Director-General then informs other members of that request and the questions to be discussed. If within twenty-one days the majority of the IDB members answer in the affirmative, the Director-General calls the session in compliance with rules 6 and 8 within forty-five days.[5]

In conformity with rule 23, at the beginning of its first regular session the IDB elects its chairman, three deputy chairmen, and a speaker (until then, the former chairman stays in office). The principle of fair geographical distribution is to be observed during the elections according to a five-year rotation cycle. The persons mentioned stay in office until the next ones are elected. The IDB Presidium consists of the chairman, the three deputies, and the speaker.

Each member of the IDB has one vote. When voting on fundamentally important questions concerning the activities of the organization including the approval of the program of work and the regular and operational budgets, the IDB decisions are made by a two-thirds majority of those present and voting. The IDB decisions on other issues are made by a simple majority. The IDB invites the members of the organization who do not belong to the board to take part in the debates, but they do not have the right to vote. The IDB Rules of Procedure stipulate that the board will try to create a situation such that all its decisions are made by consensus but without any restrictions on the rights of its members to demand that a vote should be arranged.[6]

The principle of equitable geographical distribution has been emphasized since UNIDO was established. According to Article 4 of resolution 2152 (XXI), all member states were divided into four groups, based on a geographical principle. The groups usually belonged to different social and economic systems, though this condition was not formally stated. That principle remained intact after the organization was reformed.

The following quotas are used when electing the IDB members: thirty-three members belonging to groups A (Africa and Asia) and C (Latin America), fifteen belonging to group B (Western countries) and five to group D (USSR and Eastern Europe). Out of the total number of the IDB members, 62.3 percent of the votes belong to the states from groups A and C, 28.3 percent to those from group B, and 9.4 percent to those from group D. This means that none of the three main groups of countries controls two-thirds of the votes at the IDB, which would enable it to make decisions on fundamental questions without an agreement by at least one other group of countries. At the same time, decisions on many nonfundamental issues (for instance, those which do not concern matters of the budget and the program of work) demand a simple majority of members present and voting. The developing countries almost always have such a majority.

Until UNIDO was reorganized there were forty-five IDB members falling into the following quota distribution: eighteen states from group A, fifteen from group B, seven from group C, and five from group D. The states from groups A and C, the developing countries, had 55.6 percent of the votes, from group B 33.3 percent, and group D 11.1 percent. A majority by the developing countries in the IDB was therefore, not as large, although in principle the situation was not different.

When the four groups of states were drawn, geographical position and political and economic regimes of corresponding countries were taken into account. The main purpose of such a division was to divide all the member states into groups, adhering, if possible, to approximately the same positions on the problems of international cooperation in the field of industrial development. The groups of states were changed from time to time, though as a rule not significantly, as new members joined the UN or specialized agencies and the IAEA.[7]

The principle of including states in these groups was subjected to criticism, since it did not always reflect the states' actual background political and economic regimes. The groups of countries are in some cases significantly oriented toward geographical position. From this it followed that within the corresponding groups there were some states that held positions on the main questions of UNIDO's activities greatly differing from those of the others.

The largest group (A) includes almost 100 developing countries of Asia, Africa, and the Middle East (as of the beginning of the 1990s). Three "socialist" countries in Asia — the People's Republic of China (PRC), Vietnam, and Mongolia — and then Yugoslavia were also included. UNIDO's experience has been that Vietnam and Mongolia do not show any initiative in the work of the organization. Yugoslavia's position did not always coincide with those of the bulk of group A countries, despite its important role in the Non-Aligned Movement. This was also explained by the fact that Yugoslavia was automatically attached to the group of states receiving assistance, though it can hardly be considered such a country. Presently, the future of Yugoslavian participation is under question as Croatia, Slovenia, and Bosnia might be considered independent states.

There is a question about the PRC that it claimed to be a developing country (often calling itself "a developing socialist state") and to dominate that group of countries.[8] In particular, the PRC was trying to be considered a member of the Group of 77, which was to play a special role in the struggle of the developing countries against two superpowers. Developing countries, however, due to political and other considerations, refused to include the PRC in their group, stating that a nuclear power cannot be considered equal to them. There was also a period during which the PRC claimed a special position among the UNIDO members and its nonattachment to any of the groups.

The main bulk of developing countries included in group A, are far from homogeneous in composition. Israel was attached to that group, though it is a rather industrially developed country that, consequently, votes in different organs of UNIDO. South Africa had belonged to group A, but its participation in the work of the organization was practically blocked by the group of African countries. Group A contains a number of states with free-market economies, including the Ivory Coast, Kenya, Morocco, Malawi, the United Arab Emirates, and Saudi Arabia. The same group also includes states with radical orientation: Laos, Kampuchea, Angola, Mozambique, and Ethiopia.

The actual subdivision of group A into two groups, Asian and African, is often used in UNIDO's practical activities. This is legally reflected in a number of the organization's documents. For instance, the adoption of two quotas in the framework of group A for elections to selected organs became an established practice at the first session of the UNIDO General Conference. This idea, however, was not legally secured in the UNIDO Constitution.

Group C (Latin American countries) comprises twenty-seven countries, including Cuba. Due to its activities in UNIDO Cuba exerts a counterproductive influence on the position of that group as a whole. The countries of group C are not homogeneous enough and include, for instance, Nicaragua and Chile, espousing very different orientations.

There is a connection between the division of the countries into four groups for electing the IDB within the limits envisaged by the UNIDO Constitution and belonging to the Group of 77. As a rule, members of the Group of 77 belong to groups A and C. At the same time there is a certain discrepancy in the above-mentioned division of the countries. For instance, Malta was admitted in 1976 during the Manila session of the Group of 77, although with some reservations, whereas it would rather be included in group B (Western countries). Rumania was also admitted at this time into the Group of 77, also with some reservations; however, it belongs to group D (Eastern bloc countries). The condition that Malta and Rumania would not lay claims to elective bodies beyond their geographical regions, including those within UNIDO, was specified at the Manila session.

Group B includes all West European industrially developed states as well as the United States, Canada, Australia, New Zealand, and Japan. It also has such developing countries as Cyprus and Turkey. This cannot be considered satisfactory even from the geographical point of view, as Cyprus is not in Europe and more than nine-tenths of Turkey is in Asia. Included are two European mini-states, Vatican City and Monaco, which are not UN members and have only observer status (beginning from 1954 and 1956, respectively). Giving them full voting rights is not quite obvious. The contribution of these two mini states in industrial development is negligible. If one takes into account a number of considerations expressed during the discussions of jurists dealing with international law on the question of a possible membership of mini-states in the UN and its bodies, these matters could be disputed.[9] One objection to including Vatican City in group B is that it cannot be considered an industrially developed country. Countries with even less economic importance in the third world (like Tuvalu) enjoy full voting rights at the plenary sessions of most UN bodies. In this sense the discussion of voting rights of small and mini-states is part of a larger problem.

If we proceed from the results of voting, group B is the least united among the main groups of countries. Differences in voting on select questions is rather common in the practice of those countries. However, such a feature of Western countries' participation does not exclude their efforts to take a unanimous stand on fundamental questions. A certain homogeneity of interests in the face of other main groups of countries makes them coordinate their efforts.

The mechanism of coordinating the positions of Western countries on fundamental questions of UNIDO's activities became noticeably formed only in the framework of the European Community. The countries that are members of that group often voted in the same way, especially during the second half of the 1970s and in the 1980s. During discussions on various questions the positions of the European Community members on their commission and on their behalf were usually expressed by one of them. There were also cases when the Northern European and Scandinavian countries expressed a unanimous position, for instance, at the UN conference on the reorganization of UNIDO.

West European countries sometimes contradicted the United States in UNIDO. It is explained by the fact that the European Community, for instance, stands for a "softer" policy toward developing countries and is ready for more compromises.

Group D included until 1992 nine Eastern bloc states: Bulgaria, Hungary, the German Democratic Republic, Poland, Rumania, Czechoslovakia, and the USSR and two of its republics, the Ukraine and Belarus.[10] In view of the dissolution of the Soviet Union, its seat is automatically inherited by Russia. Albania also belonged to that group for some time but in the 1970s it curtailed its participation in the work of UNIDO; however, it was de facto reinstated in 1991. Group D is definitely going to be renegotiated while up to twelve former republics of the dissolved Soviet Union are likely to apply individually for membership in UNIDO and will probably claim to be part of group D.

The states from group D were characterized until the 1990s by the greatest unanimity and coordination of their positions and, with the exception of Rumania before 1990, had always proposed joint documents to UNIDO. Actually all the questions of their participation in UNIDO had been settled by this group of countries in a coordinated fashion, one that promoted the effectiveness of their initiatives. As for Rumania, its joining the Group of 77 in 1976 influenced to an extent its activities in UNIDO. However, coordinating the activities of the countries belonging to group D will probably cease, beginning in the early 1990s, and this will demand a new approach to the future of that group.

The division of member states into four groups, despite some considerations mentioned, had traditionally exerted a positive influence on the functioning of various bodies of UNIDO. Coordinating the positions of the groups of countries and working out unified platforms on important questions in the work of the organization is an essential stage of the political process in the framework of UNIDO, making it possible to look for mutually acceptable decisions. In actuality, individual approaches of different countries to the questions of UNIDO's functioning would greatly hamper decision making.

First, the principle of dividing all member states into groups in the Annex to resolution 2152 (XXI) of the General Assembly and then in the Annex to the UNIDO Constitution has remained mainly uncontested, with some exceptions. Second, the groups of countries depending on their position on the major questions of UNIDO's activities coincided in general with the above-mentioned divisions into groups of countries, with the only correction being that groups A and C usually acted as a unified bloc, as members of the Group of 77. Third, mutually coordinated distribution of the member quotas of the groups of countries mentioned (often groups A and C were considered together) in the IDB, the Programme and Budget Committee (PBC), and other UNIDO bodies made it possible to reach acceptable decisions on the range of authorities of each of these bodies and the correlation of these powers, without which the viability of the organization would be undermined.

SECRETARIAT

In accordance with Article 7 of the UNIDO Constitution, the secretariat is one of the organization's main bodies, with its General Conference and the Industrial Development Board. The notion of a main body of an international organization was first used in the UN charter, which envisaged six main bodies of the UN.[11] However, a main organ as a rule was used then only when a plenary body of international organization was concerned. The equal status of the three bodies mentioned means that an administrative body (secretariat) is to some extent levelled to a plenary body (General Conference) and an executive body (Industrial Development Board).

Alfred Verdross thinks that the key criterion in defining the notion of a main organ of an international organization is "the degree of its independence" as far as other bodies are concerned.[12] In accepting that definition the UNIDO secretariat must be independent of the General Conference and the IDB, and vice versa, or the very sense of the standard structure of the organization would be lost.

Verdross's definition cannot fully apply as far as the main UNIDO organs are concerned. The relative independence of the main organs in the framework of the organization can be recognized. Other criteria are no less important, for instance, subject competence and the nature of the functions as considered in the context of purposes and tasks of an international organization. Attributing to the secretariat of UNIDO the status of a main organ of the organization underlines its greater independence than that of the overwhelming majority of other international organizations. It is worth noting that until UNIDO's reorganization, its secretariat, in compliance with paragraph 17 of resolution 2152 (XXI) of the General Assembly, was not given any special status as compared with, say, the IDB, which got powers as a main UNIDO organ.

There have been two major approaches to creating the authorities of secretariats. Some scholars tend to treat the powers of international organizations' secretariats, including the UN and specialized agencies, in a broad sense. Thus, a concept of "wide rights" of secretariats was put forward by A. Claude (United States), Wilfred Jenks (Great Britain), and George Langrod (France).[13] Other jurists, for instance, R. McLaren (United States) and Georgi Morozov (Russia), wrote about the groundlessness of the attempts to justify greater independence of administrative bodies of international organizations.[14] According to the second viewpoint, secretariats of international organizations, including the UN, are executive bodies possessing administrative and limited political powers in the framework of the charters of their respective organizations.[15]

It is noteworthy that when the UNIDO Constitution was being worked out, developing countries generally supported the concept of wide powers of the secretariat, since it was implied that the secretariat would be headed by a representative of the Group of 77. This is why an alternative position supported by Eastern bloc and some Western countries regarding the secretariat's authority was not sufficiently taken into consideration.

UNIDO's secretariat is headed by the Director-General who, in compliance with Article 11 (3) of the Constitution, is "the chief administrative officer of the Organization." Subject to general or specific directives of the conference or the board, the Director-General "shall have the over-all responsibility and authority to direct the work" of UNIDO. The Constitution stipulates that the

Director-General report to the IDB and be responsible to it in the matters of the appointment, organization, and functioning of the staff.

The authorities of the Director-General are defined rather vaguely in the Constitution and may be interpreted in a broad sense. One cannot but admit that "full responsibility and authority in directing the work of the Organization," but not of the secretariat, which would be more logical, could be interpreted contradictory to the authorities of the General Conference and the IDB as they are defined in Articles 8 and 9 of the Constitution. For instance, it is rather difficult to find a fundamental difference between the definition of the authorities of the Director-General and those of the General Conference, which, according to paragraph 3 (a) of Article 8 of the Constitution, "defines the leading principles and the policy of the Organization." Judging by the practices of the UN and other international organizations, a possibility of a broad interpretation of the authorities of the chief executive officer under certain conditions may lead to a bias in directing the organization. It may also lead to appropriation of the unreasonably wide functions by the executive chief, which has more than once led to critical situations in the organization in question.[16]

Resolution 2152 (XXI) of the General Assembly stipulates much narrower authorities for the head of the UNIDO secretariat, the Executive Director, and were defined in more detail. In compliance with paragraph 19 of the resolution, the Executive Director "shall have over-all responsibility for the administrative and research activities of the Organization. He shall also be responsible for all operational activities of the Organization."

When the General Conference appoints the Director-General, any candidate, upon the recommendation of the IDB, may be considered. The decision is made by secret ballot by a simple majority of those present and voting, but not by less than two-fifths of the number of members participating in the current session. If the candidate recommended by the IDB does not receive the necessary number of votes, the IDB considers this question again and submits a new recommendation to the General Conference. The discussion of the candidates was usually quite shielded from the media.

The Director-General is appointed for four years, may be appointed for a further term of four years, and then will not be eligible for reappointment. This provision differs from the one stipulated by resolution 2152 (XXI) of the General Assembly, which envisaged that the Director-General would be appointed by the UN Secretary General and confirmed by the General Assembly for a term of four years, eligible for reappointment after the term expired. This right was exercised in the case of UNIDO's Executive Director Rahman Khan, whose term was extended twice.

The issue of the appointment of the Director-General of the new UNIDO was considered during the first session (part one) of the IDB in August 1985. At its closed sessions, out of three candidates recommended (all from developing countries), the IDB elected Domingo Season, Jr. (of the Philippines) for the period expiring on the day fixed by the third session of the General Conference.[17] The decision was then confirmed by the first session (part two) of the General Conference.[18]

Since UNIDO was established, the post of the Executive Director had been occupied by Abdel-Rahman (Egypt), the former UN commissioner on industrial development. In 1975 Rahman Khan (Algeria), the former secretary general of the Organization of Petroleum Exporting Countries, was appointed to that post. The latter had remained the chief executive officer of UNIDO until the organization was reorganized in 1985.

During a considerable part of their terms the activities of these two UNIDO Executive Directors had been criticized by many member states because they sometimes ignored the balance of interests and tried to interpret the authorities of the Executive Director in a broad sense, contrary to what was stipulated in resolution 2152 (XXI) of the General Assembly.[19] Frequently, the representatives of the USSR and the Eastern European countries had repeatedly claimed the necessity of observing the principle of collective decision making, including the appointment of a Deputy Executive Director from those countries, but they did not avail.

The appointment of Deputy Executive Directors is within the authority of the Director-General, who must act in compliance with the provisions adopted by the General Conference on the recommendations of the IDB. But unlike other appointments, the appointments at the level of Deputy Director-General shall be subject to approval by the IDB.

The question of the number and geographical distribution of the posts of Deputy Directors-General was considered at the first session (part two) of the IDB in 1985. In compliance with the decision taken by the IDB, the number of Deputy Directors-General was established at five. Two of them must be citizens of the states belonging to group B, one to group D, and two to groups A and C. One out of the latter two must be a citizen of African countries or an Asian state but if the Director-General is a citizen of one of those groups of states, a Deputy Director-General representing that group may not be appointed.[20]

The first special session of the IDB, which had the task of considering the appointments of Deputy Directors-General, was convened on May 15, 1986. Beginning July 1986, it confirmed for a period of two years the following appointments to the posts of Deputy Directors-General: L. Alexandrenne (Senegal), who headed the Department of External Relations, Public Information, Language and

Documentation; C. Warner (United States), who headed the Department of the Administration; H. Wiesenbach (West Germany), who headed the Department of Programmes and Projects Development; A. Vasilyev (Russia), who headed the Department of Industrial Operations; and F. Suto (Brazil), who headed the Department of Industrial Development, Consultations and Technology.[21] In 1988 Warner and Suto were replaced by, respectively, L. Foro and A. Araoz. The terms of others were extended.

Until UNIDO was reorganized, the introduction of the post of a Deputy Executive Director was also an issue of dispute. Paragraph 17 of resolution 2152 (XXI) of the General Assembly did not stipulate anything to that effect. Western countries insisted that such a post should be established, referring to the necessity of concentrating the efforts of the Executive Director on the questions connected with working out policy in the field of industrialization, while the questions of administrative and financial nature should be delegated to his deputies. This was explained by their fear that the Executive Director, as a representative of developing countries, would have substantial opportunities to orient the work of the secretariat in a way contradictory to the interests of Western countries. In their turn, developing countries considered that the Executive Director could direct the work of the secretariat independently and effectively with close cooperation with the directors of the departments. Nevertheless, after long discussions of this matter and under the pressure of Western countries, a representative of France, to the disappointment of the Eastern bloc countries, was appointed to the post of the Deputy Executive Director, which was established in 1978.

The UNIDO secretariat comprises officials whose legal status is determined in Article VI of the Convention on Privileges and Immunities of Specialized Agencies of 1947. The Director-General and his deputies automatically and fully enjoy the privileges, immunities, exemptions, and benefits granted to diplomatic representatives (this applies to their spouses and minor children as well). In conformity with the convention, UNIDO itself defines the categories of other officials to whom the privileges and immunities should be applied.

Structurally the UNIDO secretariat comprises five departments. The largest of them, the Department of Industrial Operations, carries out programs of technical assistance and implements its projects in cooperation with other bodies of the UN. The department is entrusted with general control over implementation of programs and projects while the direct activities are carried out by a staff of technical advisers, whose assignments are selected by this department and other departments of the secretariat.

The second most important department is the Department for Programme and Project Development. It is responsible for carrying out the bulk of the research in UNIDO's framework. The Department for Industrial Promotion, Consultations and Technologies deals mainly with questions of technology transfer. The Department of External Relations, Public Information, Language and Documentation convenes conferences, publishes public information, and handles relations with governmental and intergovernmental organizations. The Department of Administration's structure includes financial services, personnel, recruiting, and legal departments.

Article 11 (5) of the Constitution stipulates that the function of appointing the secretariat staff is entrusted to the Director-General, who acts in compliance with the instructions given by the General Conference upon the recommendations of the IDB.[22] The UNIDO Constitution stipulates two principles of recruiting staff to the secretariat, while from the formulations given it follows that the first has some priority over the second. Article 11 (5) of the Constitution says that the "paramount consideration in the employment of the staff and in determining the conditions of service shall be the necessity of securing the highest standards of efficiency, competence and integrity." The second principle states that "due regard shall be paid to the importance of recruiting staff on a wide and equitable geographical basis."

The second point repeats Article 101 (3) of the UN charter, which contains criteria to be observed when recruiting staff. The point was later reproduced in the charters of most specialized agencies. The UNIDO Constitution introduced a new interpretation of the principle of "a wide and equitable geographical basis," as the key word *possible*, in Article 101 of the UN charter, was omitted. The new interpretation of that principle was in the UNIDO Constitution due to the pressure of the Group of 77.

The Western countries expressed their discontent over such an interpretation of the principle of recruiting staff on an equitable geographical basis and tried to reduce its observance for the purpose of increasing efficiency of the secretariat. Thus, at the final session of the conference on the reorganization of UNIDO just prior to the Constitution's adoption the representative of the United States again proposed an amendment to Article 11 (5) by introducing the formula "on a possibly wider geographical basis." Immediately after the Constitution was adopted the representative of the United States stated that the formula "wide geographical basis" should be interpreted as meaning that factors of secondary consideration, such as geographical distribution and the amount of the contributions, were to be taken into account.

For the first time independent authority in appointing the staff and in particular the managerial staff was delegated to UNIDO in the person of its Executive Director in the mid 1970s. Its framework included measures aimed at preparing to reorganize the body into a specialized agency.[23] Making appointments previously was a prerogative of the UN Secretary General, who received guidance from the decisions of the General Assembly on the geographical distribution of the posts of the professional staff of the UN bodies. The UNIDO Executive Director thus became less dependent on the corresponding decisions of the General Assembly. A commission on appointments and promotions was established within UNIDO. A parity commission of complaints and a parity disciplinary committee were established in cooperation with the IAEA.

During UNIDO's reorganization the question of staff succession arose. The first session (part one) of the General Conference proposed that the Director-General should properly observe paragraph 4 of resolution 34/96 of the General Assembly of December 1979. In the resolution the General Assembly called for granting posts with all the rights and status acquired by contract to all the UN staff employed in the former UNIDO in the new UNIDO.[24] Under the agreement, reached between the UN Secretary General and the UNIDO Director-General, all the employees who worked at the headquarters and the personnel of local projects outside headquarters were offered contracts on their transfer from the UN to the new UNIDO. After the reorganization of UNIDO all staff problems were to be solved only within the organization. Considerable functions of UNIDO's staff recruitment were delegated to the section of staff recruiting in the Department of Administration, which began to play a significant role at the secretariat.[25]

Article 11 of the UNIDO Constitution, which is standard for the organizations of the UN system, specifies the independence of UNIDO's staff as far as member states are concerned: "In the performance of their duties the Director-General and the staff shall not seek or receive instructions from any government or from any authority external to the Organization."

Nevertheless, practically all member states attach the greatest importance to the national distribution of the UNIDO secretariat staff, and each seeks to have a greater number of its own citizens among the officials of the organization.[26]

One can judge staff distribution by dividing employees into lists of the member states using data from the late 1980s. The employees from countries included in group B was 203 employees eligible to geographical distribution (54.7 percent), and the total number of their employees was 53.7 percent. The countries included in group D had fifty-two employees eligible to geographical distribution (14 percent) and the total number of their employees was sixty-three (13 percent). The number of posts occupied by employees from the countries belonging to group B is thirteen as compared to three occupied by employees from group D countries.[27]

The countries included in groups A and C, as well as developing countries that had not been UNIDO members at the time, had 116 employees of the professional category, including the personnel working under fixed-term contracts shorter than a year whose posts were eligible to geographic distribution (31.3 percent); their total number was 149 (32.6 percent). Directors' posts were held by eleven persons (40.7 percent of all the posts of a director category).[28] Altogether, it is possible to conclude that developing countries are well represented at the managerial level in UNIDO's secretariat.

In view of criticism of UNIDO's performance in the operational field, Director-General Domingo Siazon, Jr. announced a new series of structural changes (the second one after a considerable reshuffling immediately after the conversion of the organization). The changes were implemented step by step in 1989–1990. Among them was the creation of the Strategy, Policy and Planning Office, the Central Reference and Monitoring Unit, and the Project Personnel Recruitment and Administration Service. The changes did not promise a breakthrough, as evidenced by continuing discussion in the secretariat of its ideal structure. The General Conference at its third session requested the Director-General to present a report at its next session in 1991 on his overall vision of appropriate organizational and staff structures of UNIDO.

However, in my opinion, structural changes and reshuffling of the secretariat's departments can only marginally improve the performance of the organization. Since the establishment of the organization, its secretariat has undergone at least six major restructuring attempts, but the ideal structure is still being sought.

To improve the work of the UNIDO secretariat, I suggest the following politico-legal measures:[29]

The secretariat should be controlled to a greater extent by the IDB and the General Conference. Concrete issues concerning all aspects of the secretariat's functions should be included in the agenda of the IDB sessions.

The principle of widely supported decision making should be consistently observed when directing the work of the secretariat as well as that of its separate departments. The Deputy Directors-General, who are charged with special responsibility in that sense, should be given opportunities to ensure the observance of that principle after the UNIDO reorganization.

The rational structure of the secretariat should imply abolishing parallelism in the work of its departments and cutting expenses connected with nonproductive functions. It would be expedient to enlist groups of independent experts to analyze the activities of the secretariat and draft the necessary recommendations.

The principle of wide and equitable geographical distribution should be strictly observed when recruiting staff. At the same time the principle should take into account the contribution of groups of countries to the world industrial production.

The necessity of an equitable distribution of managerial posts, and the inadmissibility of giving posts of political significance to the representatives of one group of countries and of concentrating citizens of one group of countries within one department of the secretariat should be taken into consideration when appointing staff. For that purpose one could propose for instance, the creation of an outside inspection committee independent of UNIDO and consisting of the representatives of several international organizations who are citizens of different countries. The committee would consider complaints on disputable appointments within the secretariat and would then give conclusions on every inquiry.

SUBSIDIARY ORGANS

The work of UNIDO's subsidiary organs is of great importance to its normal functioning. Their establishment and development in the UNIDO structure reflects the process of decision making due as well to developing and expanding the range of its activities. The establishment of subsidiary organs as a necessary element in the structure of the UN specialized agencies was noted by some jurists in the 1970s.[30]

Since the reorganization of UNIDO the PBC has been its most important subsidiary organ. In accordance with Article 10 (1) of the Constitution, twenty-seven members are elected to it on the basis of equitable geographical distribution at the General Conference: fifteen members from the states belonging to groups A and C, nine from the states of group B, and three from the states of group D. The Constitution specifically stipulates that the states should appoint their representatives to the PBC by taking into consideration their personnel qualities and experience. The PBC members hold office beginning when the regular General Conference session at which they were elected is closed until the next session is over two years later, but they can be re-elected. The PBC holds at least one session a year.

The same concept of consensus of at least two major groups of states was used, with each member having one vote; decisions are made in the PBC by a two-thirds majority. Williams writes that "the new UNIDO arrangement . . . provides for a powerful Program and Budget Committee divided into various groups so that the market economy and the socialist countries . . . have veto."[31]

In compliance with Article 10 (4) of the Constitution, the PBC is entrusted with presenting its recommendations on the program of work and the estimate of the regular and operational budgets of the organization after considering the draft of the Director-General. The PBC also is charged with working out the draft for the scale of obligatory contributions of its members. The PBC reports on its activities to the IDB at every regular session and gives advice or submits proposals on financial matters on its own initiative.

In conformity with rule 4 of the draft of the Rules of Procedure, the PBC sessions are convened by the Director-General not later than thirty days after receiving the request of the IDB or of the PBC on its convening. According to rule 7, the PBC meetings are closed (members only admitted) unless the Committee decides otherwise. In accordance with rule 43, the PBC does its best to make decisions by consensus but this does not restrict the right of any member to demand a vote on a proposal.

Before UNIDO was reorganized it also possessed subsidiary organs. In accordance with paragraph 14 of resolution 2152 (XXI) of the General Assembly, the IDB could "establish subsidiary organs on a permanent or ad hoc basis as may be necessary for the effective discharge of its functions." That formula was a success for developing countries supported by the Eastern bloc countries when UNIDO was established. These countries also proposed that paragraph 16 of the resolution, which mentioned expert committees on various aspects of the IDB activities, should be included. Western countries were against the creation of subsidiary organs of the IDB at that time, referring to the undesirability of excessively expanding various subsidiary organs.

However, at the second session of the IDB (1968), a number of countries proposed a draft resolution on establishing a working group on the program and coordination. Such a group seemed to be necessary to prepare for the IDB sessions. All the IDB members could take part in the work of the group, and its meetings took place two weeks before every session of the board.[32] The working group on program and coordination functioned before the third, the fourth, and the fifth sessions of the IDB.

The Special Conference of UNIDO in 1971 decided to abolish the working group on program and coordination and to delegate its functions to a permanent committee of the IDB. The committee was to be convened twice a year: two weeks before the beginning of the IDB session and for a term of a week at the end of the year. The resolution of the Conference stated, "The purpose of that Committee shall be to ensure the Board a possibility to direct the Secretariat in implementing the decisions of the Industrial Development Board."[33] At the same time, the United States' attitude toward the establishment of the committee was negative, expressing the opinion that the committee functions could be discharged by the existing UNIDO organs.[34]

At its sixth session (1972), the IDB adopted resolution 32 (VI) on the permanent committee, which stipulated that the committee should consist of the representatives of all the countries that are members of the IDB. The permanent committee's functions, according to resolution 32 (VI) of the IDB, comprised the following: consider the implementation of the program of the organization's activities, develop a new program, assess the work done by the organization to improve the use of the resources available, and assist the IDB in coordinating its efforts with other organs of the UN system dealing with the matters of industrial development.

In accordance with resolution 38 (VII) of the IDB of May 1973, a special committee on the matters of UNIDO's long-term strategy was set up. It included representatives of twenty-seven countries elected on the basis of equitable geographical distribution. The task of the committee was to work out a program for the organization's long-term activities based on the recommendations of a group of high-ranking experts. In 1973–1974 the committee met three times and submitted its report to the eighth session of the IDB.

Ad hoc committees consisting of the IDB bureau members were also established from time to time; they included the Executive Director. The committees considered the requests of various non-governmental organizations for receiving observer status at some of the UNIDO organs.

At different stages of UNIDO's work various groups of member states put forward ideas of establishing new subsidiary or semi-autonomous bodies within the framework of the organization. In the field of legal cooperation it was proposed that a commission on industrial law and a UNIDO tribunal for settling industrial disputes should be established. In particular, they could develop a code of international industrial laws and a system of settling industrial conflicts. These proposals seem to be promising.

At the same time, occasionally the proposals put forward were unrealistic. For example, developing countries had been persistently proposing that major financial and economic branches of UNIDO should be set up. Among them was the International Foundation on Stimulating Industry, which was to grant long-term loans for financing the programs that were under way in developing countries, and the International Agency on Industrial Financing, which would direct extra financial resources of the third world countries to developing countries themselves, excluding the mediation of Western countries. The proposal on establishing the International Institute of Industrial Technology of UNIDO, which would direct the activities of the national research institutions and some international administrative organs in the corresponding fields, was more promising.

NOTES

1. The Programme and Budget Committee (PBC) is an important organ in the UNIDO structure, but it has not been granted status as a main committee.

2. For details of the procedure of elections to the session organs of the UN system, see N. Padleford, *Elections in the United Nations General Assembly: a Study in Political Behavior*, 1959; H. Ameri, *Politics and Process in the Specialized Agencies of the United Nations*, 1982.

3. For details of the theoretical questions of elections at international organizations, see W. Koo, Jr., *Voting Procedures in International Political Organizations*, 1947.

4. UNIDO/3.

5. Ibid.

6. Ibid.

7. On groups of states among members, see H. Ameri, *Politics and Process*.

8. For details of the question of the People's Republic of China participation in the UN bodies, see K. Mererik, *China Representation in the UN*, 1965.

9. J. Chappey, "Les micro-états et les Nations Unies," *Annuaire français de droit international*, 1973; M. Gunter, "The Problem of Mini-State Membership in the United Nations System," *Columbia Journal of Transnational Law*, 1977, pp. 476–77; N. Krylov, *Prinzipy uchastya*, pp. 45–49.

10. In connection with the unification of Germany in 1990, there will be changes there.

11. The analysis of the UN secretariat as a main body of that organization was made by S. Bailey, *The Secretariat of the United Nations*, 1978; T. Meron, *The United Nations Secretariat: The Rules and The Practice*, 1977.

12. A. Verdross, *Universelles Völkerrecht*, p. 523.

13. G. Langrod, *The International Civil Service*, 1963.

14. R. McLaren, *Civil Servants and Public Policy: A Comparative Study of International Secretariats*, 1980; G. Morozov, *International Organizations*.

15. See also T. Weiss, *International Bureaucracy: An Analysis of the Operation of Fundamental and Global International Secretariats*, 1975.

16. A vivid example is connected with UN Secretary General D. Hammerskjöld. See B. Urquhart, *Hammerskjöld*, 1972.

17. IDB. I/Dec. 2.

18. G.C. I/Dec. 12.

19. D. Ait Ouyahia, *Évolution de l'Organisation*, pp. 148–50.

20. IDB. I/Dec. 11.

21. IDB/S. I/Dec. 1.

22. For general questions, see H. Getz and H. Jütterer, *Personal in internationalen Organizationen*, 1972; H. Reymond and S. Mailick, *International Personnel Politics and Practices*, 1985.

23. K. Köppinger, *Der Weg der UNIDO*, p. 96.

24. G. C. I/Dec. 9.

25. D. Ait Ouyahia, *Évolution de l'Organisation*, pp. 391–94.

26. D. Ait Ouyahia, for instance, writes about it in *Évolution de l'Organisation*, pp. 388–90; G. Langrod, *The International Civil Service*, 1963; R. McLaren, *Civil Servants and Public Policy*, 1980.

27. IDB. 2/10, pp. 387–89.

28. Ibid.

29.   Some of the ideas are common with those expressed in N. Graham et al., *The International Civil Service: Changing Role and Concepts*, 1980.

30.   M. Hill, *The United Nations System: Coordinating Its Economic and Social Work*, 1978.

31.   Ibid.

32.   A/7215.

33.   ID/SCU/Res. 1.

34.   ID/SCU/4, pp. 73–74.

6

Financial and
Budgetary Issues

WHO CONTROLS FINANCIAL DECISION MAKING

A renewed interest in the United Nations Industrial Development Organization (UNIDO) came after adopting the Constitution of that organization as a specialized agency. For instance, Douglas Williams refers to UNIDO in his research on specialized agencies, noting "interesting provisions" in its Constitution. As he noticed, in UNIDO, the interests of Western countries and "socialist" countries became surprisingly very close in matters of finance and programs, as opposed to the maximalist and unrealistic demands of the third world states. Thus, Williams writes about a deal that the Western and "socialist" countries struck in managing UNIDO, indicating that both groups, "if they vote together, have a veto." He also notices that this arrangement is "likely to be vitiated in practice — ironically — only by the market economy countries not maintaining their solidarity."[1] He did not know, however, that the Eastern bloc countries might face a similar problem later, after the demise of the Communist regimes.

The issue of financing UNIDO's activities focussed one of the most acute problems connected with the coordination of positions of different groups of countries. Thus, Western countries usually adhered to the view that UNIDO financing must be carried out first of all from the UN regular budget and its other sources. They accepted the principle of voluntary contributions only for UNIDO operational expenditures. This group of countries was also emphatically against this organization's operational and administrative expenditures being financed from assessed contributions of member states. One of the problems apparent to the Western countries in UNIDO's financing was the fact that they did not enjoy any possibilities in considerably influencing the decisions of the General Conference and Industrial Development Board (IDB). The democratic principle of one country — one vote applied with some exceptions in UNIDO, as distinct from other international financial-economic organizations. It did not provide a tangible privileged status for these countries in making decisions on the use of resources, in view of the fact that third world countries largely outnumbered them and enjoyed a large majority. Financial support of such an organization on a substantial scale without a chance for playing a dominant role in decision making evidently was not a favorable prospect for the Western countries.[2]

The majority of developing countries emphatically expressed their disagreement with the position of the Western countries. Always advocating more autonomy for UNIDO, the developing countries above all desired its financial independence. It was implied that UNIDO must have its own budget independent as far as possible from UN resources and that the budget of the organization should be provided by direct contributions of member countries in accordance with the scale of assessment, taking into consideration, among other things, the sizes of their national incomes.

Developing countries were critical of the Eastern bloc countries that adhered to the position of Western countries on the issues of financing. The Eastern bloc countries emphasized, above all, financial stability of the organization, indicating that any other approach to financing could place the organization in a precarious position. The "socialist" countries advocated voluntary contributions in national currency because payments in hard currency would be a heavy burden for them. They argued that this would make effective use of the resources not only of Eastern Europe but also of developing countries, most of which could not afford to allocate funds in convertible currency.[3]

In accordance with Article 13 of the Constitution, all expenditures of UNIDO as a specialized agency are financed, firstly, from assessed contributions (regular budget) and, secondly, from voluntary contributions and such other income as may be provided for in the financial regulations (operational budget). The main difference from financing the expenditures of UNIDO prior to its reorganization consists in the transition to assessed contributions of member countries to the regular budget of the organization. Earlier, as specified in Clause 20 of resolution 2152 (XXI) of the General Conference, UNIDO's expenditures were divided, as is often the case in international organizations, into two categories: administrative and operational. Administrative expenditures were to be financed from the UN regular budget, implying in particular that UN financial regulations were applicable to this category of expenditures, including control and inspection by respective UN organs.

The procedures of drafting and approving budgets and the program of UNIDO's work as a specialized agency are rather complex.[4] The initial draft of budgets and the program for the next financial period together with the respective estimates are prepared by the secretariat. In accordance with Article 14 of the Constitution, the Director-General submits the drafts to the Programme and Budget Committee (PBC), which prepares its recommendations and corresponding estimates for the regular budget and the operational budget. PBC decisions require a two-thirds majority of the members present and voting. Then the drafts, together with any recommendations of the Programme and Budget Committee, are examined by the board, which adopts the program of work and the budgets with such modifications as it deems necessary. Such adoption requires a two-thirds majority of the members present and voting.

The General Conference considers and approves the program of work and the budgets by a two-thirds majority of the members present and voting. The Conference may make amendments in the program of work and the budgets. However, according to Article 14 of the Constitution, no amendment is approved by the Conference unless it is accompanied by an estimate of expenditures prepared by the Director-General, which is then submitted in turn to the Programme and Budget Committee and the board in conformity with the usual procedure for the consideration of the program and budgets. Only then is the matter submitted again to the Conference, whose decisions require a two-thirds majority of all UNIDO members.[5]

It may be concluded from the foregoing procedure that the board plays the decisive role in deciding program and budget questions. The drafts submitted by the Director-General and the relevant recommendations of the Programme and Budget Committee do not have binding juridical force for the board, which examines them but is in no way bound by them. Before submission to the General Conference the board "adopts" the program and the regular and operational budgets, in contrast to the General Conference, which "approves" them.

Formally the General Conference has the right to disagree with the board on the program and budgets if, for example, less than two-thirds of the members present and voting cast their votes for them. However, this would create difficulties for the normal functioning of the organization because the procedure for submitting new (modified) programs and budgets by the Director-General and their examination at a session of the Board would require much time. Considering that the General Conference must be convened comparatively shortly prior to the beginning of a new fiscal year (once in two years), rejection of the program of work and budgets would cause many difficulties, including problems of procedure. Incidentally, the UNIDO Constitution does not contain clear indications as to how such a situation could be settled at a short notice.

The right of the General Conference to make amendments to the program of work and budgets, while leaving them mainly intact, is also limited in view of the same procedural difficulties. It is possible, however, to avoid a situation when the organization would be compelled to enter a new fiscal year while the program and the budgets have not been approved. Thus, accepting the program and the budgets submitted by the board on the whole, the General Conference may make amendments that could be considered in accordance with the Constitution together with the corresponding estimates and finally approved by it later. True, the approval of such resolutions by the General Conference requires a two-thirds majority of all members of the organization, not the usual two-thirds majority of the members present and voting. A decision on the question of approval of amendments, then, would require calling a special session of the General Conference, at which the number of participants is usually smaller than at regular sessions, and the required two-thirds majority of members of the organization would pose a great problem for the group of countries seeking amendments.

The regular budget of the reorganized UNIDO includes more types of expenditures than those usually figuring in the budgets of specialized UN agencies.[6] According to Article 13 and Annex II to the Constitution, the regular budget provides for expenditures for administration, research, and other regular expenses of the organization, in particular, interregional and regional advisers. This budget also contains expenditures for short-term advisory services rendered by the staff of the organization, meetings, including technical meetings, provided for in the program of work, and program support costs arising from technical assistance projects, to the extent that these costs are not reimbursed to the organization by the source of the project financing.

The regular budget also covers other activities previously financed out of Section 15 of the UN regular budget in the amount of 6 percent of the total of the regular budget. These types of activities are treated somewhat differently compared with usual activities: they "shall strengthen the Organization's contribution to the United Nations development system taking into account the importance of utilizing the United Nations Development Programme country programming process . . . as a frame of reference for these activities."

At the UN conference on the reorganization of UNIDO, states of group D (except Rumania), until virtually the concluding session, disagreed with financing definite operational functions from the regular budget. They stressed that this was contrary to the generally recognized principle of voluntary participation, but they withdrew their objections so as not to impede the adoption of the Constitution of the organization.

The substance of the objections to utilizing the regular budget for purposes of operational activity was nevertheless confirmed at the first session of the Programme and Budget Committee in 1985, when the question of noncompliance with the 6 percent limit came up. The committee's ruling 1985/4 accepted the recommendation of the board for endowing allocations for the next year from the regular budget in the amount of $10.8 million, or about 12 percent of the regular budget, twice more than the limit. Five members of the committee (the United States, Japan, the USSR, Bulgaria, and the German Democratic Republic) voted against and five other members (Belgium, West Germany, Denmark, the Netherlands, and France) abstained in the first case and three (Belgium, West Germany, and France) in the second case. Some delegations emphatically stated that this was a violation of the Constitution. This position was taken also by the United States, the USSR, and Japan. Belgium, acting on behalf of the European Economic Community, declared that the adopted decision should not create a precedent.[7]

In accordance with Article 15 of the Constitution, the regular budget expenditures are borne by the members as apportioned in accordance with a scale of assessment established by the General Conference by a two-thirds majority of the members present and voting, upon the recommendation of the Board adopted also by a two-thirds majority of the members present and voting, and on the basis of a draft prepared by the Programme and Budget Committee. The article specifies that the scale of assessments shall be based to the extent possible on the scale most recently employed by the UN and that no one member shall be assessed more than 25 percent of the regular budget of the organization.

The status of assessed contributions to the regular budget of UNIDO, as established by the General Conference, is very similar to that of the UN. The only significant difference in correcting the UN scale of assessments was caused by the additional assessments of Switzerland (1.11 percent) and South Korea (0.2 percent), which were not members of the UN (South Korea was admitted in 1991) but were members of UNIDO. The largest contributors to the regular budget of UNIDO are therefore the United States (25 percent), Russia (until 1991 the Soviet Union) with the Ukraine and Belarus (10.1 percent, 1.27 percent, and 0.34 percent, respectively; however these figures are very likely to be revised in view of the dissolution of the USSR), Japan (10.75 percent), Germany (8.19 percent for the Federal Republic of Germany and 1.32 percent for the German Democratic Republic previously, but the united Germany assumed both parts), France (6.31 percent), and the United Kingdom (4.82 percent).[8]

VOLUNTARY CONTRIBUTIONS

Operational expenditures are met from voluntary contributions of member countries and are made up of contributions directly to UNIDO, through the United Nations Development Programme (UNDP) and other UN technical assistance programs redistributed in favor of this organization. Voluntary contributions can be divided into contributions without any limitations and special regulations; contributions to the Industrial Development Fund (IDF) in conformity with the regulations of the functioning of this fund; and other contributions linked to restrictions or conditions that may be adopted by UNIDO bodies. UNIDO's projects may be financed from different sources. Despite a certain complexity of such an approach, UNIDO enjoys definite freedom to maneuver in using resources.

The draft of the UNIDO Constitution submitted by the UN secretariat contained a provision to the effect that the organization could resort to loans. This was supported by the Group of 77. Western and Eastern bloc countries objected to the inclusion of this provision in the Constitution, considering that the use of loans by an international organization is a rare, special case that cannot be considered normal if it functions normally. As a result, the issue was dropped, and the Constitution does not mention this possibility.

Another financing channel is the special circulating resources provided by countries receiving industrial development assistance. Since in this case the developing countries themselves finance the services of the organization, such assistance differs from traditional forms of assistance and comes close to the acquisition of services on a commercial basis. Such resources can be supplied to the governments of developing countries for financing specially selected projects and other services of UNIDO, including the dispatch of experts to UNDP missions on the spot. Special circulating resources are provided by comparatively rich developing countries, such as oil-producing countries that can partially or fully finance UNIDO's projects and services on their territory, as well as consultations and scholarships for their students abroad. More rare are cases when times are financially unfavorable for UNIDO and in view of difficulties in accomplishing already launched projects, developing countries assume their partial financing. Such projects and services may be discounted by the UNDP as development assistance by countries and may, consequently, exceed their established volume.

Apart from funds that UNIDO gets directly from a number of sources and uses independently, Western countries favor allocation of the so-called associated resources. Strictly speaking, these resources are not resources of the organization; however, they cannot be used without its approval. The aim of this link-up of bilateral assistance and UNIDO activities, representatives of

Western countries say, is their mutual complementarity and interaction.[9]

A prominent role in UNIDO resources is played by the Industrial Development Fund. The Group of 77 initiated its formation, emphasizing the need for one more channel of centralizing resources used by UNIDO. This initiative was on the whole supported by the Eastern bloc countries. For their part, the Western countries had no particular interest in establishing the fund, reasonably arguing that this might lead to further dispersal of resources.[10]

The establishment of the IDF was discussed at the second UNIDO General Conference. In accordance with Articles 72 and 73 of the Plan of Action, this fund, with IDB-determined terms of reference and functioning regulations, was to assist in establishing a new international economic order, implementing field projects, and intensifying UNIDO's activities in the development and transfer of technology and its programs. In 1976, the General Conference adopted resolution 31/202 on the establishment of the fund and resolution 31/203 concerning general regulations of its functioning.

At its second session in 1977, the IDB requested the UN Secretary General to convene the first conference for raising contributions to the IDF, indicating the desirability of fixing the fund at $50 million. However, it was hardly surprising that this conference did not justify the hopes laid on it, and the mobilized resources constituted a small fraction of the recommended volume. The second conference was more successful: sixty-seven countries declared allocations of resources totalling $10.6 million.[11] The Fund began to function in 1978.

The provision of the UNIDO Constitution regarding the IDF is in rather general terms. Article 17 reads that in order to increase the resources of the organization and to enhance its ability to meet promptly and flexibly the needs of the developing countries, the organization shall have an Industrial Development Fund that will be financed through the voluntary contributions to the organization and other income as may be provided for in the financial regulations of the organization. The administration of the Fund is vested in the Director-General who has the right to administer it "in accordance with the general policy guidelines governing the operations of the Fund that are established by the Conference, or by the Board acting on behalf of the Conference, and in accordance with the financial regulations of the Organization" (Article 17).

Thus, the terms of reference of the General Conference and the IDB in respect of the IDF are confined to the elaboration of "the general policy guidelines governing the operation of the Fund." Measures of control by the General Conference and the IDB over the functioning of the Fund and procedures for approving its programs are not defined clearly enough. The absence of clear regulations for the Fund leads to the broadest interpretation of the powers of the Director-General in relation to the Fund, which damages chances to increase contributions to it.

Prior to the reorganization of UNIDO, questions of administration of the Fund were referred largely to the competence of the IDB. It was vested with the function of control over the operation of the Fund to ensure that it is consonant with the tasks imposed on it. Every year the UNIDO Executive Director submitted to the IDB a draft program of the Fund's activity for the next year with the indication of launched projects. The IDB approved the program and exercised control over the use of resources. However, the IDB could delegate a part of its powers, including the approval of particular projects, to the permanent committee and the Executive Director.

The drafting of the program and separate projects is complicated by the fact that a large part of voluntary contributions to the IDF are intended for particular purposes and earmarked countries, frequently with the indication of the field of application and characteristics of planned projects. UNIDO's possibilities for independent solution of questions connected with the implementation of such projects are limited.

The resources of the IDF and the UNDP are mutually complementary. They can be used for different purposes and as sources of financing, allowing definite freedom to maneuver for the organization.

The level of IDF financing was much lower than needed for the tasks set before it. Thus, at various UNIDO forums a concern was expressed over the fact that the annual volume of voluntary contributions to the IDF constituted less than 25 percent of the agreed level of financing at $50 million. Many developed countries made insufficient contributions, and most of their contributions were intended for specific purposes. It was stressed repeatedly that developed countries should increase their contributions to the IDF in proportion to their usual quotas.

Until the late 1980s, the fund was not very popular among the major donor countries, some of which did not participate in its financing at all, preferring the standard channel of the UNDP, which had a better established reputation in the West. Later, however, the fund increasingly won the confidence of donor countries as was consistent with the overall improvement of UNIDO's activities. For instance, between 1985 and 1989, yearly pledges rose by 144 percent to $38 million.[12] A better performance of the fund in the late 1980s is partially explained by Italy's decision to support it. This country's pledge of about $18 million in 1989 represented almost half of all contributions to the fund. Among other big donors are France, Switzerland, and the United Kingdom.

One of the important questions concerns the possibility of making voluntary contributions in national nonconvertible currencies. The Eastern bloc countries advanced this as an indispensable condition. Thus, some countries make contributions to the fund in nonconvertible currencies, either for general purposes or for special purposes; but in both cases in reality the money can be spent only in those countries. The largest contributors were regularly the Soviet Union (650 thousand rubles yearly until its dissolution in late 1991) and the East European countries of Poland, Hungary, and Bulgaria. Some developing countries, such as India and Madagascar, also contributed in their nonconvertible currencies.

The Western and also some developing countries called this principle of voluntary contributions into question. Their main argument was the impossibility of using resources for the designated purposes, in accordance with the programs of UNIDO's operational activity. This referred to the fact that in the overwhelming majority of countries with nonconvertible currency the equipment required for the projects cannot be acquired. Those countries do not have specialists with the qualifications to be employed as experts on projects and educational establishments of the appropriate level.[13]

There are more than enough reasons to criticize voluntary contributions in nonconvertible currencies. However, notwithstanding the difficulties with implementing projects on those contributions, I believe such nonconvertible allocations were a positive step. In hard currency, such voluntary contributions would not have been made at all. Besides, the experience of UNIDO in spending the Soviet rubles was rather successful until the 1990s, and the nonconvertible currency was spent on a number of comprehensive training courses and seminars in the states of the USSR.

In view of the fact that contributions in nonconvertible currency were not used fully, such arguments and their obvious harmfulness were repeatedly objected to at various levels by representatives of Eastern bloc and some developing countries. Thus, the level of development of some branches of industry in those countries, as they claimed, corresponded to the world standards. Therefore, the refusal to use the provided opportunities was, as those representatives believed, contrary to UNIDO's tasks.

Legal issues aside, there is still a question of substance, whether the above-mentioned countries were in the economic position to make considerable voluntary contributions in hard currency. In the majority of cases the answer would be no. Then the only choice left is either not to accept voluntary contributions in national currencies at all or to use them. As it appears, there are still ways to use such contributions with relative efficiency and the refusal to accept them would be to the detriment of operational activities of UNIDO.

Some difficulties arise in the provisions of voluntary contributions. States making such contributions often give rather vague recommendations for their use. UNIDO is compelled at various stages of preparation and implementation of projects to be regularly in contact with the respective governments to ensure proper utilization of such resources, including aims of projects, methods of their realization, and material resources and services.

It seems that a promising way of improving the legal regulation of UNIDO's financing would be to grant member countries the right to make a part of voluntary contributions in kind, including deliveries of equipment and services of their specialists. This would make managing such assistance much more difficult. However, such voluntary contributions could counterbalance the instability of the international financial situation, which is also a handicap for planning operational activities. It is frequently more convenient for countries, including East European countries, which have a market system with practically nonconvertible national currencies, to make voluntary contributions in kind. While at present contributions in nonconvertible currency are permitted without specification of services and commodities, granting each country the right to determine forms of assistance on its own, after appropriate consultations with the UNIDO secretariat and consent of the latter, could yield a considerable economic benefit.

The expenditures of countries providing assistance in kind could include partial compensation in the form of deliveries of raw materials and industrial output obtained through the implementation of such projects in developing countries. These additional resources could accrue to UNIDO for use in the organization's projects. Appropriate legal formalization of such regulation of voluntary contributions would impart broader scale, stability, and purposefulness to UNIDO's operations and give the recipient countries higher motivation in the economic efficiency of projects.

SURVIVING THE LACK OF FINANCIAL INPUT

In the mid 1980s, UNIDO, like many other UN-related bodies, found itself in a difficult financial situation. Since January 1, 1986, as the organization became independent in budgetary terms, many of its weaknesses became apparent. The cut in U.S. assessments and the lack of confidence in UNIDO on the part of some other Western countries contributed to this weakness. A rather considerable number of states were routinely late in paying their assessed contributions; however, this was not so different from the UN budgetary situation. To this was added an unexpected difficulty caused by the rise of the exchange rate of the Austrian schilling to the U.S. dollar, the standard currency in which the contributions were fixed originally. The secretariat's expenses in Austrian schillings were therefore significantly cut.

One of the problems in the areas of financial obligations and of voluntary contributions was partially caused by the clause in the Constitution (in its Annex II) that legally allowed using 6 percent of regular assessments for the purpose of technical assistance. As a matter of compromise, this clause was agreed upon in 1979. Ever since there has been controversy about this provision, even though Western countries approved it, partially in exchange for implicit veto together with the Eastern bloc countries in budgetary matters. An influential part of the secretariat staff, namely representatives from developing countries, tended to interpret this provision in loose terms, believing that 6 percent was just an indication and not a binding ceiling. Therefore, for several years subsequent to the conversion, this figure was routinely exceeded in draft programs of work, which met objections (but veto was not achieved in view of a "soft" position of the European Community members). This aroused the dissatisfaction of a number of Western countries, USSR and East European countries, which were from the very beginning strongly opposed to any provision permitting the use of assessed contributions for technical assistance. It appears that this provision did not prove a valuable innovation in view of restrained attitude of many countries.

Total outstanding contributions as of October 1, 1990, were $57 million, but most of this amount was due the same year and, according to the practice, usually was paid at the very end of the year, contrary to the rule to do so within thirty days after notification (usually in January). The largest single debtor was the United States with debt outstanding at $40 million, but of this 62 percent was to cover the same year; the real outstanding debt (unpaid assessments from 1986 to 1989) was only $19 million. Other Western countries were strict in executing payments, with the exception of Greece. The second largest debtor among the countries of the North was the USSR with $1.3 million outstanding, all for the same year (its debt is likely to be undertaken by Russia in 1992).

Among the countries of the South there were also relatively big debtors: Brazil ($2.5 million), Argentina ($1.4 million), and Iran ($1.2 million), which were actually in much worse position than these figures indicate because their debts had accumulated over a number of years and were considerable in terms of ratio per annual contribution.[14]

As many states continued to harbor doubts about UNIDO's efficiency, the inflow of voluntary contributions from member states was not strong, although on a steep rise. In 1989, pledges of voluntary contributions reached $39.3 million, which was roughly one-third of the technical assistance provided by the organization, the rest being covered by the UNDP, other multilateral sources, and regular assessments, as had become customary since the conversion of the organization.

According to the present system, the UNDP reimburses UNIDO at a flat rate of 13 percent of the cost of technical cooperation delivery (for example, experts' salaries, equipment, training, and fellowships). It amounts to a substantial sum, as UNIDO is expected to be reimbursed $36.7 million for the 1990–1991 budget, as compared to $32 million for 1988–1989.[15] Most of UNIDO's technical assistance is still financed from the UNDP (about 60 percent in the early 1990s). But in comparison with the 1970s, UNDP's share has steadily decreased from over 70 percent, which testifies to an increased role of its own resources. Non-UNDP-financed projects, for which delivery rose from $42 million in 1988 to $52 million in 1989, achieved higher growth rates.[16]

The late 1980s and early 1990s were marked for UNIDO by a slight easing in the financial crisis. Having overcome the most troubled financial periods of its existence, UNIDO emerged a leaner and slightly more efficient organization and, as some of the Director-General's reports said repeatedly, "more confident of its future." Because survival topics were no longer on the agenda, UNIDO got a chance to embark upon a period of more stability in implementing programs of work.

FINANCIAL REGULATIONS OF UNIDO

One of the most important outcomes of the Bangkok session of the General Conference in 1987 was the adoption of UNIDO's financial regulations. The regulations laid the ground for the subsequent financial activities of the organization, for both its internal functioning and the realization of projects. The financial regulations were adopted by General Conference decision 25, in accordance with Article 8.3(C) of the Constitution.[17] The financial regulations of the UN, which for the most part applied in UNIDO, ceased to have legal force for the organization.

The regulations stipulated the fiscal period of the organization, which consisted of two consecutive calendar years beginning with an even year. Since the regulations entered into force at the end of 1987, the beginning of their full application started in 1989. The financial regulations stipulate also that for each of the two years of the fiscal period, member states are to contribute exactly one-half of the total approved amount.

The usual procedure of considering expenditures practically excludes any possibility of expenditures not approved by all four bodies involved. The Director-General (secretariat) is to submit in the second year of each fiscal period a draft program of work and the corresponding estimates for the regular budget and the operational budget for the following fiscal period to the Programme and Budget Committee at least forty-five days prior to the opening of the session of that committee. In its turn the Programme and Budget Committee is to consider the proposals of the Director-General and submit to the Industrial Development Board its recommendations on the proposed documents, also forty-five days prior to the opening of its session. The recommendation is to be adopted by two-thirds of the members present and voting, as indicated in the Constitution.

A similar rule applies to the Industrial Development Board. It considers draft documents of the Director-General with the recommendations by the Programme and Budget Committee and makes decisions on them by a two-thirds majority of members present and voting. Contrary to the Programme and Budget Committee, the board does not adopt recommendations but may introduce whatever modifications it finds necessary. The IDB then presents its proposals to the General Conference at least forty-five days prior to the opening of the regular session of the Conference.

In practice, all the timetable requirements make it necessary for the Director-General to approve the secretariat's budget proposals for the next two-year period at least half a year before the convening of the regular session of the General Conference.

As it appears, the procedure of adopting decisions involving expenditures is rather complicated, implies the work of a number of UNIDO bodies, and requires quite a lot of time. The real work of the secretariat on the draft budgets starts more than one year before the beginning of actual expenditures. This means a certain inability of the organization to react to a speedily changing situation that might require a quick reallocation of resources, in particular in cases of emergency. The existing funds for discretionary use by the Director-General in case of emergency are rather miniscule. It is rather difficult even to cancel prospective approved expenditures if the need is fulfilled otherwise, for instance, on a bilateral basis by a country donor who is not bound by such long-standing commitments.

While developing financial provisions stated in the Constitution, the regulations make it absolutely clear that no resolution, decision, or amendment involving expenditures should normally bypass all the necessary steps, starting with a program presented by the Director-General. Each document implicating new expenditures is to be considered by the Programme and Budget Committee on the basis of the proposal by the Director-General and subsequently to be examined by the Industrial Development Board and finally by the General Conference. Many developed countries attributed importance to this since they were not very secure in financial management conducted by the executive head.

However, the regulations have a clause permitting the Director-General to submit a proposal of expenditure directly to the General

Conference if it is accompanied by a program and financial implication statement prepared by the Director-General. Both the Programme and Budget Committee and the Industrial Development Board may in any case request examination of such proposals and make decisions on them, which once again means the usual procedure of step-by-step approval of expenditures. In practice this limits the capacity of the Director-General to make independent financial decisions.

There might be a great deal of criticism regarding the very rigid procedures embodied in the financial regulations. The cumbersome, inefficient, and lengthy procedure of adopting budgetary documents for two years more or less assures that the interests of the overwhelming majority of member states are taken into account and would normally not lead to complaints about unjustified appropriation of allocations. In three bodies of UNIDO, decisions concerning financial matters are adopted by two-thirds of their members. In practice, it is rather difficult, if not impossible, to push through decisions that seem unsatisfactory to a considerable number of countries.

Similar cumbersome financial procedures were often criticized by a number of experts. However, there were other points of view. Douglas Williams writes: "The press often depicts both the budgets themselves and the waste as gigantic. This is untrue on both scores. The budgets represent a very small share of world public expenditure, and although waste and scandals occur and are to be entirely condemned, they probably occur less frequently than in most national administrations — or for that matter in many private concerns."[18]

A meticulous control over expenditures is rather important because after the budgets are approved by the General Conference, appropriations for regular budget expenditures are financed by mandatory contributions from member states according to the scale of assessments. The financial regulations determine when these payments are insufficient for the current expenditures of the organization. In this context the regulations mention the Working Capital Fund, implying that this provision might be used on a permanent basis and contrary to what had been suggested when the fund was created.

As is rather unusual in the practice of UN-related bodies, the UNIDO financial regulations indicate as a permanent provision that assessments are to be made in two components, U.S. dollars and Austrian schillings, in direct proportion to the respective shares of regular budget expenditures, as determined by the General Conference. Moreover, the initial assessment in Austrian schillings is to be established at the UN accounting rate, which is in effect at the time the regular budget is to be adopted by the Conference. This provision is very useful for the organization, while it indeed insures itself against any unfavorable change of exchange rates, which had already affected UNIDO badly in the mid 1980s.

This provision is evidently not very convenient for many countries, which accounts for their expenditures for international organizations in U.S. dollars. Many countries have operational plans of payments to international organizations in U.S. dollars, and in many cases such expenditures undergo the parliamentary procedure of approval far in advance of actual payment transactions. During the two-year financial period of UNIDO, the exchange rate of Austrian schillings to U.S. dollars can fluctuate considerably. Therefore, for many countries it is very inconvenient if, for instance, the second assessed payment during the financial period is one-third higher, as expressed in U.S. dollars, than had been foreseen. For member states with less rigid treasury practices, such a hypothetical situation might be less inconvenient, especially since the exchange rate can change either way.

According to financial regulations, after the General Conference approves the estimates for the regular budget, it establishes the scale of assessments and determines its amount. It also proposes the amount of the working capital fund. It is then the obligation of the Director-General to transmit the relevant documents to member states. These should include the information about the actual obligations of corresponding member states in respect of annual contributions to the regular budget and advances to the working capital fund and a formal request to make such payments.[19]

Member states are bound to make contributions and advances as indicated in the Director-General's request, in full, within thirty days of receiving such communication or as of the first day of the calendar year to which it relates, whichever is later. However, such a strict provision is enforced only by the statement that if, as of January 1 of the following year, the payments are not yet made, the member state is considered one year in arrears. Since arrears are formally acknowledged if they are at least one year long, it makes the provision of a thirty-day obligatory period rather soft.

The regulations fail to indicate the responsibility for noncompliance with those deadlines for payments, which permits member states to interpret this provision in a rather loose way; no effective sanctions are indeed foreseen in such a situation. In certain cases, some members of UNIDO did not find it inappropriate that they paid for the year in question a year and a half after it had ended. Many countries, especially in the third world, have had problems meeting their obligations to the organization on time, and in view of their majority, no mention of including strict deadlines for assessed payments was ever made.

As regards voluntary contributions, the financial regulations indicate two conditions when they are not accepted. First, they should be consistent with the policies of the organization. Second, if such contributions, according to their purposes, involve indirectly or directly financial liability for the organization, governing bodies of UNIDO should give their consent for accepting such contributions. The regulations, furthermore, indicate that in the case of trust funds, the purposes of such should be clearly stated.

A speedy adoption of financial regulations, including at least two special provisions, was needed because of the real financial crisis in which the organization found itself in the mid 1980s. However, it did not improve the situation substantially. As of late 1989, unpaid assessed contributions for the period from 1986 to 1988 amounted to $5.9 million and 190 million Austrian schillings. The unpaid assessed contributions for 1989 amounted to $6.3 million and 285 million Austrian schillings, which showed that most countries did not comply with the soft deadline drawn by the financial regulations and preferred to meet their obligations at the very end of the year. At any rate, the total unpaid assessed contributions to UNIDO amounted to the equivalent of $46.6 million (at an exchange rate of US $1 = AS 13.8).[20]

This was certainly a complicated situation for UNIDO and necessitated further measures. However, the situation was less serious than the state of the UN's finances during its worst cash crisis two to three years earlier. No special session of the General Conference was convened, whereas the UN General Assembly had once to dedicate a special session to resolving the UN financial matters.

NOTES

1. D. Williams, *The Specialized Agencies and the United Nations. The System in Crisis*, 1990, p. 7.

2. This was pointed out in particular by W. Ungerer, "UNIDO," *Aussenpolitik*, 1972, pp. 177–80.

3. See A. Altshuler, *Mezhdunarodnoye valutnoye pravo* (International Monetary Law), 1984.

4. The literature on this subject is scanty. See D. Singer, *Financing International Organizations: the United Nations Budget Process*, 1961; J. Strossinger, *Financing the United Nations System*, 1964.

5. See G. Tesauro, *Il finanziamento delle organizazzioni internazionali*, 1969.

6. Ibid.

7. UNIDO/IDB. 1/19.

8. GC. 3/36.

9. D. Ait Ouyahia, *Évolution de l'Organisation*, pp. 364–66.

10. For different positions on this question, see G. Abi-Saab, *La notion d'organisation internationale*, 1980.

11. UNIDO Annual Report for 1979, p. 199.

12. GC. 3/22.
13. E. Luard, *International Agencies*, pp. 246–48.
14. IDB. 7/32.
15. IDB. 6/2.
16. IDB. 7/22.
17. GC. 2/Dec. 25.
18. D. Williams, *The Specialized Agencies*, p. 239.
19. CC. 2/Dec. 25; Annex, Article V.
20. GC. 3/36.

7

Operational and Consultative Activities

RELATIONS WITH RECIPIENT COUNTRIES WITH REGARD TO PROJECTS

Until the early 1980s, the volume of the United Nations Industrial Development Organization's (UNIDO) expenditures on technical cooperation programs was rather low. For instance, from 1972 to 1976, the total spent on programs was $142 million, or about $28 million yearly. However, each year more programs were registered. In the next five years, from 1977 to 1981, the volume of programs expenditures was $334 million, or 2.5 times higher. In the mid 1980s the yearly volume of programs expenditures was close to $100 million; from 1982 to 1986, it was $451 million. Notwithstanding difficulties with the regular budget in the latter half of the 1980s, the technical cooperation expenditures increased from $98 million in 1987 to $134 million in 1989.[1]

The ever-increasing volume of operations required ever-more elaborate regulations. A standard agreement on cooperation between UNIDO and member states receiving UNIDO's assistance was approved by the first session (part two) of the General Conference in 1985. According to its Article II, forms of assistance are divided as follows: services of the staff, consulting experts, assistants of experts or consultants, and contract firms or organizations designated by UNIDO and bearing responsibility for work on implementation of projects; services of technical experts appointed by UNIDO and services of UNIDO volunteers; equipment and deliveries required for the implementation of projects; pilot projects; working expert groups; organization of seminars; and provision of scholarships.[2]

UNIDO's operational activities are carried out in conformity with a number of principles that are typical for many UN bodies providing technical assistance. UNIDO does not have the right to impose any recommendations beyond the framework of relevant projects concerning the general economic strategy of states or to propose measures affecting the foundations of the existing economic and political regimes. All questions relating to strategy in the field of industrial development and cooperation can be discussed only at the level of UNIDO's leading bodies, such as the General Conference or Industrial Development Board (IDB), for example.

UNIDO can provide assistance only in response to an official application of the government of a country. In each developing country national organs of power independently determine possible directions of assistance and concrete objects for it. However, technical advisers, including those sent by UNIDO, may provide assistance in drawing up and substantiating applications. Such applications for assistance must contain information about the aims of the projects, their cost estimate, and the method of apportioning expenditures between national state organs and UNIDO (or the United Nations Development Programme [UNDP]). All requests for assistance in industrial projects must be forwarded through resident representatives of the UNDP and then sent for examination to UNIDO or the UNDP. Preliminary talks on all questions concerning planned assistance projects are conducted by UNDP resident representatives.[3]

In accordance with Article IV of the standard agreement, in implementing a project the government must inform UNIDO about the state institution that would cooperate with it and would bear responsibility for participation in each project. However, by agreement with UNIDO, the government may vest the latter with the main responsibility in implementing the project in consultation with the cooperating institution. This institution, in consultation with UNIDO, must appoint a staff director for the project. For its part, UNIDO appoints, with the approval of the government, the chief technical adviser or coordinator of the project who bears responsibility to UNIDO. While performing their duties, UNIDO's expert advisers are obliged to act in close contact with the government.[4]

The government pledges to take the required set of measures for implementing a project. Project documents specify, as a contribution of the government in kind, obligatory services of local specialists and other personnel as well as provision of land plots, buildings, training facilities, equipment, and materials produced or available in the country. If equipment is imported from other countries, the government is obliged to reimburse import duties, expenditures for the transportation and insurance inside the country, and for its installation, operation, and maintenance. Throughout the implementation of the project the government ensures transportation inside the country, mailing and communications, and reimbursement of official trips of the project staff. The government bears general responsibility for ensuring the most effective use of assistance.[5]

The government of a recipient country applies a special regime to UNIDO and its staff. In relation to UNIDO and its organs, property, resources, financial assets, and staff, the government applies the provisions of the UN Convention on Rights and Immunities, except when the government has acceded to the Convention on Privileges and Immunities of Specialized Agencies. Benefits for UNIDO also imply prompt and free issue of visas, licenses, import permits, and so on.[6]

An important issue has always been appointing field advisers and experts for implementing UNIDO's projects. Of the total number of experts appointed by UNIDO in the 1970s and the 1980s (16.3 thousand) the biggest number fell to the share of the following countries: Great Britain (12.3 percent), Poland (9.4), the United States (8.3), France (7.6), India (6.1), West Germany (5.5), Austria (3.4), Belgium (3.1), Sweden (3.0), and Italy (2.6).

The appointment of experts has been discussed at different levels in the organization. A widespread presumption was that nationals of a number of countries had preference as compared to representatives of other countries. However, the traditional accusations that such bias was due to political consideration could not sustain criticism. For instance, in the second half of the 1980s, Poland was the single largest supplier of experts. From the total number of 8,000 in that period, the number of Polish experts was 930. Considerable numbers of experts were also provided by the United Kingdom (790), France (610), and the United States (610). Half a dozen countries presented 200 to 400 experts each: Germany, Italy, India, Hungary, Austria, and Belgium.[7]

Two major industrial countries, the Soviet Union and Japan, were constantly under-represented, but for different reasons. Cumbersome bureaucratic procedures for presenting nationals for expert vacancies in Moscow handicapped the use of Russian engineers who otherwise have high enough skills and experience. In the 1970s and the 1980s only 1.4 percent of experts were appointed from the USSR, the second largest contributor to the budget but only eighteenth among UNIDO members for contributing experts.[8] The recruitment of few Russian experts is due to shortcomings in the work of Soviet departments dealing with the selection of candidates, including a very limited number of technical specialists knowing foreign languages offered to UNIDO's secretariat, and time-consuming formalities of their registration, which frequently impede prompt provision of consultation services. In Japan's case, the bottleneck was a linguistic background that did not meet proficiency in major working languages. Both countries had only about 100 of their experts used in UNIDO projects. The Russian officials repeatedly complained about the situation at different working bodies of UNIDO, but its own internal bottlenecks were not removed.

One of the recruiting methods is to include expert candidates in the computer register, which accelerates the search for relevant data. At the close of the 1980s, of the total number of candidates in the register, the countries included in group B (excluding Greece, Cyprus, Malta, Portugal, and Turkey) accounted for 7.6 thousand (54 percent), the countries in groups A and C, including the countries indicated above, for 4.2 thousand (30 percent), and countries in group D (excluding Albania and Rumania) for 2.2 thousand (16 percent).[9]

Compared with the services of experts, the training of personnel is much less expensive but yields tangible results. The share of scholarships and other expenditures for personnel training in the total volume of UNIDO technical assistance is not high, and in the late 1980s it constituted just 15 percent.[10] Candidates for scholarships are selected by UNIDO. However, living expenses of trainees and scholarship holders throughout the scholarship term are normally assumed by the government.[11]

The terms of providing assistance are in general rather favorable to UNIDO. At its own discretion UNIDO can suspend or terminate provision of any forms of assistance.[12] According to Article XII of the agreement, this is possible if, in UNIDO's view, circumstances prevent the normal implementation of projects. This provision is formulated in the standard agreement most ambiguously and leaves room for arbitrary interpretation of the appearance of such circumstances by the UNIDO's administration for projects. Arbitration procedures are envisaged for the settlement of disputes.[13]

A substantial deficiency in UNIDO's technical assistance is the dispersal of its objects. Out of 1,900 projects that were carried out or were in the stage of implementation in the late 1980s, an overwhelming part of the projects, 1,100, were small-scale, worth less than $150,000.[14] Dispersal of resources lowers the effect of assistance. Relatively small projects require considerably larger expenditures on technical feasibility estimates and various surcharges. This expands the share of unproductive administrative expenses in total assistance.

Projects of assistance to the industrial sector are not always linked up with general plans for development of third world countries and at times do not fit organically into the economic systems of these countries. One of the ways of studying economic efficiency of industrial projects built under the auspices of UNIDO could be inspections at the request of governments with the aim of giving recommendations for their exploitation.

The discontent of developing countries is often caused by long implementation periods of UNIDO-sponsored projects due to imperfect procedures for expert recruitment, acquisition of equipment, and choice of sub-contract firms.[15]

CREDIT VERSUS TECHNICAL ASSISTANCE

UNIDO's presumed inefficiency is to some extent deduced from the achievements of Bretton Woods financial organizations, the operations of which overlap in some cases. Further, commercial credit is often regarded as a correct alternative to technical assistance. Comparing the performance of the World Bank group and of UNIDO is a part of a larger discussion of the issue: whether long-term loans are better and more useful than technical assistance.

In my view, legal regulation of operational activity requires substantial revision. Experience shows that technical assistance cannot be sufficiently closely tied to the operation of economic laws. In the field of industrial development, which largely determines economic progress, large-scale assistance on favorable commercial terms is most favorable. Project financing could be based in part on interest-free or easy credit. Even with a stagnant volume of voluntary contributions the total volume of assistance projects could be increased in a multiple proportion through credit operations on the world capital market. Despite the external similarity of conditions of assistance to the present activity of the World Bank or, in particular, its branch, the International Development Association, UNIDO would retain many of its specific principles of organization and activity in international industrial cooperation.

The operational activities of UNIDO evidently cannot compete with projects in the industrial field executed by the World Bank group. There are few doubts that the overall volume of projects and the efficiency of the World Bank group are much higher and more important than those of UNIDO. However, that does not justify embellishing the performance of the World Bank group either, which is by now overburdened by hopeless debts of the third world countries, who complain about their inability to pay the debts back.

For instance, Maurice Bertrand writes: ". . . there is . . . reason to question a World Bank which, although entrusted with contributing to the development, is continuing to increase the amount of third-world debt every year. The very principle of using credit to aid development should be reconsidered. It is true that profitable investment is still possible in the third world, but the use of credit, which remains possible in the business world, cannot be justified for development aid in the poorest areas."[16]

I think that this is an extreme position and negates the very useful contribution of the World Bank group to the developing countries, especially in providing overall economic expertise of management and creating infrastructure. But the real problem is identified: credit relations are far from being a flawless and indisputable solution for assisting developing countries. After an initial credit expansion, the time to repay the debt comes, but the loans are just consumed, and there is nothing to be paid back.

Bertrand's assertion, made in 1989, seems to be not quite correct now, as the external debt of the third world has been virtually frozen since 1987, after which it did not grow in real terms and even started to diminish slightly. If from 1982 to 1987 the external debt increased by half (from $836 billion to $1,212 billion), over the next four years it increased by only $43 billion.[17] This stop on the edge of the financial abyss, detrimental for both donees and donors, meant substantial sacrifices on the part of both the creditors and the third world countries that spend 16 to 20 percent of the exports of goods and services on servicing the indebtedness. In Africa and Latin America, this ratio is even higher: 31 percent and 35 percent, respectively, in 1990.[18]

Apart from the compensation issue, the World Bank's and UNIDO's projects differ in terms of volume. The difference between projects of UNIDO and the International Financial Corporation (IFC) (the closest competitor), as stressed in one report by the Director-General, is that "normally the minimum size of projects considered by the IFC involves investment of several million dollars, whereas UNIDO tends to focus on small- and medium-sized projects."[19]

However, presently, the real problem is the absence of coordination between the Bretton Woods institutions and the rest of the UN system, which does not allow for combined efforts. In this respect, there has been only one body designed to ensure coordination — the Administrative Committee of Coordination. But that committee never worked efficiently and is generally considered a total failure.

There is also a complete difference of approaches. In UNIDO, as in most UN bodies, there is a tendency to exaggerate the political, ideological, and juridical nature of international activities. The most technocratic approach of banking and financial world, which dominates the Bretton Woods institution, seems to overlook the political nature of many problems.

The problem in general was well identified by the research report *U.N.: A Successor Vision*, which states, "The dichotomy that exists between world financial institutions — the IMF and the World Bank — and the U.N. on economic matters is obviously detrimental to the U.N. In financial institutions, the representatives of the ministries of finance and economy make decisions that have consequences for their economic and monetary policies; in the U.N., diplomats discuss general questions and approve resolutions that have no practical consequences."[20]

This comparison sheds light on the UNIDO forums' experiences, which are common to many UN bodies and specialized agencies. Discussions of different issues in the IDB and at General Conferences are held often by diplomats who have no direct links with ministries of finance and other governmental bodies concerned with economic issues.

The difference of approaches highlights deficiencies of each of them. Some steps to fill the gap are being taken by UNIDO's secretariat. As evidenced by the reports of the present Director-General, UNIDO seeks cooperation with the World Bank group and has realized a number of projects in cooperation with the International Bank for Reconstruction and Development, the International Development Association, and the IFC in particular.

SYSTEM OF CONSULTATIONS, TRANSFER OF INFORMATION

Prior to the second General Conference, UNIDO's emphasis was on technical assistance to the industrial development of the South. After the Lima General Conference, UNIDO began to devote much more attention to consultative service and global problems of industrial development.[21]

The system of consultations was set up in pursuance of the Declaration and Plan of Action adopted by the second General Conference and in connection with General Assembly resolution 3362 (S-VIII). The establishment of this system was the consequence of the efforts of the Group of 77 during the preparation for the second General Conference. The group wanted to expand operations in all directions. At the Lima General Conference representatives of this group of countries pointed out that a system of permanent consultations on the global, regional, and sectoral levels was needed to coordinate the industrial development policy in the world.

The Lima Declaration and Plan of Action (paragraph 26) pointed out that "for assistance to the establishment of a New International Economic Order and for the attainment of the aims set in the Declaration on this question, UNIDO and other respective international bodies must have a system on consultations between the developed and developing countries." According to paragraph 61(d), consultations must be held "with due consideration for the relevant information concerning the development of demand and supply, the available production factors and their cost, potentialities and conditions for investment and the availability of appropriate equipment and types of technology." Consultations must be held, according to paragraph 60(b), also between developing countries themselves "so as to achieve . . . the best conditions for obtaining technology, providing experts, licenses, equipment, etc."[22]

The paragraphs of the Declaration and Plan of Action concerning the system of consultations were not voted upon, but this did not mean that the positions of different countries were similar on this question. The statements of the delegations of Britain and Norway at the General Conference took a negative view of the prospect for efficient implementation of the system of consultations.

In 1976, in the course of reorganizing the UNIDO secretariat, a section for negotiations was formed in the department of policy coordination, which was to deal specifically with the system of consultations. In June 1976 special UNIDO groups were formed for coordinating the preparatory work. After discussions with the interested organs in the UN system general provisions on the function of the system of consultations were worked out. The IDB adopted a decision that consultations must be held between member countries, but the delegations could include representatives from industry, trade unions, and groups of consumers as well as from the government. Subsequent decisions were to be made by consensus.[23] This provision was subsequently recorded in General Assembly resolution 33/78.

The mechanism of consultations includes consultations proper in their conventional meaning; various conferences and meetings, including meetings of working groups on procedural matters and groups of specialists in a specific branch of industry; and preliminary conferences of experts sent by governments for working out the set of questions for consultations. It also included conferences of experts on specific problems of industrial development in a particular region, as a rule in cooperation with one or several regional organizations, as well as major representative thematic conferences. The system of consultations functions under the IDB's control; the IDB approves the program of measures for a two-year period and receives the annual report on work in all branches. Reports reflect conclusions and recommendations of conferences.

The procedural regulations for the system of consultations specify that "the number of participants from each member state includes government officials and also representatives of industry, trade unions, consumer groups and other representatives."[24] The question of whether national delegations or individuals should take part in consultations has remained unsettled. At the insistence of the Eastern bloc it was agreed that a choice of participants depends mainly on the governments. UNIDO's task in this is merely organizational preparation for holding consultations.

Though paragraph 66 of the Lima Declaration and Plan of Action envisages consultations on three levels, one of them (global) has rarely been applied. Consultations were held at the sectoral level and preparatory meetings at the regional level. Consultations on the sectoral level are usually devoted to individual sectors that can contribute to the reorganization of world industrial production, conditions needed for this, and new forms of cooperation.

Yet many problems of industrial development require a global approach. According to the third world countries' viewpoint, consultations on the global level could embrace such issues as contributions to redistributing world industrial capacities in individual branches and different geographical regions and analysis of the general problems of industrial development in the third world. Some Western countries do not support holding consultations on such problems, stating that they are within the competence of other UN agencies.

Topics for consultative meetings are initially selected by the sector for negotiations; the secretariat then calls a conference of a group of experts. Selected topics are sometimes discussed at global preparatory conferences that take into account conclusions and recommendations of previous consultative conferences.

Expenditures for holding consultations are imposed on the participants only in the case of broadly representative specific conferences on problems of industrial development. In other cases expenditures connected with holding consultations are reimbursed from UNIDO's budget. In case of regional conferences of experts, part of the expenditures may be levied on the organization, which is sponsored by or is organized in cooperation with UNIDO. Sometimes part of the expenditures is borne by the host country.

Despite flexible regulation of the consultations system, only part of the initiatives for its development fostered in the IDB and in the secretariat of the organization came to function. Thus, some developing countries proposed, along with building up the system, setting up permanent committees for sectors of industry. The committees would become a link for organizing consultations on sectoral problems. The proposal included regional committees for preparing consultations on the regional level, special interregional committees to elaborate particular problems of cooperation between third world states and developed countries, and a permanent commission for industrial consultations with the aim of coordinating the entire system of consultations.

The system is moving from an experimental to an important feature of the organization's activities. Until the 1990s, forty consultations on world and regional levels have been held in different countries. In the early 1990s alone, five more consultations were held. For instance, among them were consultations on small- and medium-scale enterprises including cooperatives (Bari, Italy), on electronics (Valetta, Malta), and on rural transport equipment (Vienna). Although consultations do not provide an immediate return, they are a useful means to make third world countries more familiar with modern industrial technologies.

While expenditures for the system of consultations are reimbursed mainly from the UNIDO budget, this creates definite difficulties for the financial position of this organization. Still unresolved is the problem of financing the participation of the least developed countries in consultations, even if such participation is potentially advantageous. A number of industrialized countries oppose UNIDO's financing the participation in consultative meetings by this group of countries.

Two organizational problems were connected with holding consultative conferences: an insufficient participation of representatives from developing countries and ensuring the most optimal representation at consultations, because there must be representatives of industry and trade unions as well as competent government bodies.

In a number of working documents UNIDO's secretariat drew attention to the need of ensuring that consultations contribute to talks between their participants on various questions of cooperation, which could be held during and after consultative meetings. Developing cooperation in the industrial field on the basis of a sectoral approach, through conclusion of respective bilateral and multilateral agreements, was recognized as one of the long-term objectives of the consultations.

The system of consultations could indeed provide conditions for drafting standard agreements on sectoral cooperation of different types. These agreements could then be transformed into programs of work carried out at the national or regional level with the participation of member states and international organizations. However, in practice this function is frequently given different interpretations.

The system of consultations started to change in the middle of the 1980s, away from the model conceived originally. Many Western countries showed readiness to turn this forum into a mediating link in the conclusion of contracts with representatives of developing countries. Western firms, which have begun to use consultations for publicity and promotion of their commodities in the developing countries, have been increasingly active at consultations. There is probably nothing harmful in that, but for one consideration. The major financial burden of the system is borne by the organization that can find itself serving private business at the international assessments' expense.

The attempts to use the system of consultations for these aims are not always within the meaning of the respective resolutions of the UN General Assembly, UNIDO General Conference, and IDB, since none of them spoke of the expediency of supporting commercial talks in their framework. However, the conversion of the system of consultations into a form of mediating activity is not totally discordant with the UNIDO Constitution. Thus, the provision of Article 2 (Functions), paragraph (f) of the Constitution states that UNIDO "acts as an instrument serving the developing countries and the industrialized countries in their contacts, consultations and, at the request of the countries concerned, negotiations directed towards the industrialization of the developing countries." It could be interpreted as a ground for encouraging commercial activity, however not at the organization's expense.

Diverse approaches to the organization of consultations, including the choice of program, is explained largely by its inadequate coordination on the part of UNIDO's leading bodies. Although the item "the system of consultations" is periodically put on the IDB agenda, the decisions taken at this level are not always detailed and consequent.

Another substantial direction in UNIDO's activities since the late 1970s has been assisting in transferring information on technology to developing countries. In 1977, the Executive Director submitted to the IDB Report ID/B/183 concerning the formation of a Bank of Industrial and Technological Information. Upon the IDB's recommendation, the General Conference in its resolution 3507 (XXX) confirmed the need to create the bank within UNIDO's framework. The bank was to accumulate the broadest possible information about technology, parameters of alternative technological processes, technical data, and terms of contracts. After the formation of the bank in 1978 an agreement on the use of patents for getting technological information was concluded with the World Intellectual Property Organization. The bank began to receive all UNIDO's technical documentation on projects, according to the principle of selecting advanced technology and transferring it to developing countries at their request.

In its decisions, for example, rulings 1984/5 and 1985/6 adopted at its eighteenth and nineteenth sessions respectively, the IDB pointed out the usefulness of the bank. However, in reality the bank did not live up to the hopes laid on it. No final solution was found to the dilemma of whether the bank should perform mediating functions and search for required sources of information at the request of developing countries or become an independent supplier of industrial information with a constantly expanding and supplemented base of data. On the whole the interest of developing countries in the bank's services remains low, since they have broad opportunities of getting required information on a bilateral basis without recourse to UNIDO. As a result, the volume of the bank's operations has increased comparatively little since the end of the 1970s.

Another direction in UNIDO's activities is scientific research. It is carried out at the Department of Industrial Promotion, Consultations and Technology of the UNIDO secretariat and includes the following divisions: global issues and policy analyses, studies by regions and countries, sectoral studies and research, and industrial information and statistics.

The dual aim of global and conceptual studies, as noted in the documents of the secretariat, is: "Firstly, to lay the foundation for initiatives on questions of policy in the future and, secondly, to ensure the necessary reference material for UNIDO technical cooperation programmes."25

In these studies attempts are made to draw up short-term prognosis of industrial development in the world, as, for example, in the annual "Global Report on Questions of Industry and Development." Studies by regions and countries are intended to contribute analysis and information to framing policy in the industrial field in developing countries and to provide the needed analytical support for the preparation of the program of work and projects. There are also sectoral studies in all twenty-eight sectors of industry singled out in the international standard classification of branches of economic activity.

In its studies UNIDO must cooperate closely with many UN agencies dealing with economic questions; with governmental bodies in different countries, research centers, and institutes; and with private organizations. A considerable part of required statistical materials comes from UN statistics bureaus. More detailed information related to the development of national industry can be obtained often only in respective countries themselves. UNIDO sometimes experiences numerous difficulties since many governments, especially in developing countries, are not ready to provide sufficient operational information on particular questions. In Western countries, private companies in some cases withhold requested information about capacities and the range and volume of output. Collecting information through questionnaires is not efficient because replies are sent only by a small fraction of organizations and companies.

This direction in UNIDO's activities seems to require expert appraisal by experts from different countries who could make concrete recommendations on improving the work of the organization on these questions.

PROBLEM OF EFFICIENCY

A serious problem is connected with the fact that UNIDO's operational activities yield a rather modest economic effect on the whole, first of all because the cost of services and commodities provided as assistance frequently does not compare with the economically justified expenditures. Control on the part of the secretariat is frequently insufficient to ensure the provision of services and commodities as part of assistance at the lowest prices. Moreover, developing countries are not given enough incentives for using aid to the greatest effect and to link it up with their economic development programs.

One important reason for the organization's efficiency could be the ratio between the technical cooperation programs expenditures and expenditures on headquarters, the latter representing mostly administrative costs.

At an early stage of UNIDO's activities, from 1972 to 1976, this ratio was 58.5 percent. From 1977 to 1981, it rose to 62.3 percent, and in the next five-year period to 63.6 percent. However, the sharp increase of headquarters expenditures calculated in U.S. dollars in the latter half of the 1980s lowered this ratio to 58 percent, but most probably temporarily.[26] This ratio is approximately the same as in most UN bodies providing technical assistance, where 60 percent is considered normal.

It is important also to look into how the headquarters' expenditures are realized. Generally speaking, expenditures on UNIDO's headquarters are by no means a pure waste of resources, because a bulk of managerial work is done at the headquarters. For instance, from five departments of UNIDO's secretariat three are closely linked to projects: the department of industrial operations, the department for program and project development, and the department for industrial promotion, consultations and technology. However, from the point of view of recipients of assistance, those expenditures in Vienna headquarters are considered not so useful for them.

A relevant measure of UNIDO's performance after its conversion into a specialized agency is the relationship between the number of employees at the secretariat and the amount of assistance actually executed. In the latter half of the 1980s the number of professional posts decreased from 486 in 1986 to 466 in 1988, but came back to 486 in 1991, resulting in zero growth. The total number of posts, including technical, decreased from 1,310 to 1,290 during the same period.[27] However, in the same period technical cooperation delivery rose by 40 percent, which meant evidently an ever-growing workload for the secretariat.

From my point of view, one of the weaknesses of UNIDO's projects has always been their small size, which does not permit tackling problems of underdevelopment on a large scale. However, I believe that this is mainly unavoidable in view of the limited resources and enormous list of requests for assistance from more than 120 countries. As of 1989, the average cost of projects implemented by UNIDO was $134,000 this is very modest compared to World Bank group projects that are usually in the range of $8–25 million. Nineteen hundred technical projects under implementation in 1989 were too large for the available resources. Of that number, only 580 exceeded the costs level of $150,000 and 206 were above the level of $1 million.[28] Therefore, UNIDO cannot be reproached for not implementing large-scale projects of industrialization, such as building metallurgical plants, electric power stations, and other big enterprises, most of which turned out to be mismanaged and highly unprofitable in the third world countries.

An analysis of average project components shows that 41 percent of total investment is spent on project personnel, 28 percent on equipment, 15 percent on fellowships and training, and 14 percent on subcontracts. Even if personnel wages seem a rather high component, in real terms it averages only $54,000 per employee, or just enough to cover one year's salary for one Western engineer.[29] It is hardly possible to reduce that component.

A component spent on subcontracts, then, seems to be reasonably low, which testifies that unlike badly managed organizations, UNIDO does not pass most of its project implementation costs to third parties. There are, however, doubts that an equipment component is sufficient for a viable industrial project, which could affect the economy of a third world country. Therefore, the other options requiring less costs become viable.

The component that needs to be drastically increased is fellowships and training. Preparing national engineer cadres in a third world country is a very promising and rewarding effort. Such training is relatively cheap compared to financing services provided by Western experts. Furthermore, newly trained national cadres retain their skills and acquired qualification after a concrete project is implemented. They could contribute to national economy twenty or thirty years afterwards. In that sense placing emphasis on professional training of national cadres means contribution to the future development of a country.

Expanding the share of personnel training programs is the most effective form of assistance to developing countries in the total volume of UNIDO's technical assistance. It would be worthwhile to put personnel training programs in individual countries on a regular basis and in future to set up respective educational establishments under the aegis of the organization.

All of UNIDO's industrial projects are in the form of technical assistance, the deficiencies of which are well known and are caused by their grant nature. If assistance is received free of charge, the recipient usually has no motivation to seek economic efficiency of projects, because there is no obligation to get the return in full plus interest on the principal of the loan plus, hypothetically, profit. Given the loose terms of accepting technical assistance, the recipient has very few obligations.

On the other hand, UNIDO has rather few obligations regarding the efficiency of the projects. Therefore, the project personnel does not necessarily do its best to get equipment and materials at the cheapest prices, check the quality of services, and so on. In other words, free-market economics work here on a very limited scale.

NOTES

1. IDB. 6/10.
2. UNIDO/IDB. 1/13: GC. 1/Dec. 40.
3. Critical assessment of UNIDO's operational activity can be found in E. Luard, *International Agencies*, pp. 244–50.
4. UNIDO/IDB. 1/13.
5. Ibid.
6. UNIDO/IDB. 1/13; for a general study, see W. Jinks, *The Proper Law of International Organizations*, 1962, pp. 147–49.
7. IDB. 6/10, p. 132.
8. IDB. 4/10.
9. IDB. 3/10, p. 67.
10. Ibid., p. 42.
11. UNIDO/IDB. 1/13.
12. For fulfillment of contracts by international organizations, see W. Jenks, *The Proper Law of International Organization*, pp. 147–49; for a general approach, M. Doxey, *Economic Sanctions and International Enforcement*, 1980; K. Raman, *Dispute Settlement Through the United Nations*, 1977.
13. UNIDO/IDB. 1/13.
14. IDB. 3/10.
15. E. Luard, *International Agencies*, pp. 433–34.
16. M. Bertrand, *The Third Generation World Organization*, 1989, p. 130.
17. IMF, *World Economic Outlook*, May 1990.
18. Ibid.
19. IDB. 6/22, p. 2.
20. P. Fromuth, ed., *U.N.: Successor Vision. The United Nations of Tomorrow*, 1988, p. 138.
21. D. Ait Ouyahia, *Évolution de l'Organisation*, pp. 433–34.
22. ID/CONF. 3/31, p. 77.
23. A/32/16, pp. 162–63.
24. PI/84, Part 1, n. 23.
25. IDB. 2/10, p. 191.
26. IDB. 6/10, p. 106.
27. IDB. 7/28, p. 2.
28. IDB. 6/10, p. 2.
29. IDB. 6/10, p. 132.

8

Issues of Norm-Setting

LEGAL ACTS OF UNIDO AND THEIR JURIDICAL FORCE

When considering the juridical force of documents issued by an international organization, it is necessary to specify the object of their juridical force. Legal researchers most often concentrate attention on strengthening the activity of international organizations in respect of the states, its main subjects. As some jurists point out, the participation of international organizations in legal regulation of international relations is determined by their ability to be the subject of international law, and so create norms of international law.[1] These norms operate first in relation to states that participated in their adoption in the framework of a particular international organization.

Depending on the range of states that adopted them and the framework in which they were adopted, United Nations Industrial Development Organization (UNIDO) documents can be divided into three categories: first, the Constitution of UNIDO; second, the Declarations and Plans of Action and resolutions of UNIDO General Conference; and third, the Industrial Development Board's (IDB) resolutions and decisions.

The Constitution, as discussed in Chapter 2, is the only international legal document strictly binding for members of the organization. UNIDO member countries can create norms that are not norms of international law in the full meaning of that term but that have a certain regulating effect in the international system. This is ensured by the organization's adopting decisions, in particular in the form of the plenary organ's resolutions.

International law literature varies regarding the juridical force of resolutions adopted by different UN agencies. Usually with regard to the General Assembly, plenary organs of specialized agencies, and leading autonomous bodies of the UN, the positions of researchers come down to three basic premises. Some international law jurists believe that resolutions of the indicated organs entail juridical obligations for the states. This view is advocated above all by researchers from developing countries, which now have a considerable majority in plenary organs.[2] The opposite view is expressed most often by jurists from Western countries. In their opinion, resolutions of plenary organs have no more force than recommendations and cannot in principle entail juridical obligations for the state.[3] Finally, there is a compromise position, according to which some categories of resolutions may contain elements of a juridical obligation. Most researchers recognize the political significance of such resolutions and accept a limited norm-setting capacity of international organizations in the international system.[4] I tend to share that last point of view.

Some researchers stress the norm-setting character of international organizations. Grigori Tunkin emphasizes the boundaries of the norm-setting activity of an international organization, "which have only the force provided for them by the constitution of the respective organization."[5]

This thesis is justified for organizations whose constitutions contain sufficiently clear provisions on their norm-setting capacity in the international system. However, this is rarely stated specifically in the constitutions. In such cases some researchers advance a theory about the "presumed competence" of an international organization. The constitution may define only general provisions concerning the competence of an international organization, while concrete questions of activity may be decided only in the process of its functioning. A view was also expressed that the competence of an international organization on specific questions may be established by putting proposals to the vote to determine their correspondence to its competence. I do not share that last point of view because third world countries will always have the advantage in imposing their position.[6]

The UNIDO Constitution specifies the norm-setting capacity of the organization in the international system in very general terms. Article I of the Constitution says that the primary objective of UNIDO is "promotion and acceleration of industrial development in the developing countries with a view to assisting in the establishment of a New International Economic Order." However, the new international economic order (NIEO), when it was conceived, implied, according to third world countries, a complex of norms in the international system and, more specifically, in the sphere of international economic relations. Most arguments about a new international economic order have remained on paper and have not had serious legal impact.

Article 8 of the Constitution contains the provision that the General Conference gives recommendations to members and international organizations on questions within the competence of the organization. The same article specifies that this function of the

General Conference may be delegated to the IDB. However, the Constitution does not make further reference to the juridical force of the recommendations of the General Conference or the IDB and special differentiation of the competence of the organization. This leaves room for broad interpretations, although the term *recommendations* is itself explicit enough.

In order to establish the legal force of the resolutions of the General Conference or the IDB, member states or international organizations might determine what sanctions or other consequences of juridical nature may be taken by the organization against the subjects that do not comply with its recommendations.

As this is customary in the UN–related international organizations, the UNIDO Constitution does not provide for rescinding a state's membership. Article 5 (I) specifies that any state suspended from the exercise of the rights and privileges of membership of the United Nations is automatically suspended from the exercise of the rights and privileges of membership of the organization. Naturally, UNIDO may not strip any state of membership on its own, even if that state systematically violates UNIDO's recommendations. Equally, the Constitution does not provide for any other juridical sanctions against a member state failing to reckon with UNIDO's recommendations in its policies.[7]

Though UNIDO's recommendations do not have binding juridical force for member countries, this in no way detracts from the political significance of resolutions of the General Conference and the IDB. Since such obligations of states have a general political character, possible sanctions may imply mainly a reaction of the world public and other states, partners in cooperation. In the political field, violation of assumed obligations may lead to grave charges and the loss of prestige by the government of the respective country and worsening relations with other countries. One of the ways of exerting pressure with the aim of ensuring observance of the provisions of an approved document is informing the public and consultations on different levels.

With respect to secondary subjects of international law, such as international organizations, that fail to comply with UNIDO's recommendations, there are no sanctions envisaged on the part of the organization. Article 19 of the Constitution contains the provision that the Director-General may enter into agreements with other international organizations with the approval of the board and subject to guidelines established by the Conference. However, the Constitution states nothing about such sanctions as termination of agreements with international institutions on UNIDO's initiative. Thus, the norms established by UNIDO apply to the policy of member states in the field of international industrial cooperation, to the extent that they have assumed relevant obligations.

The most important documents adopted by UNIDO are resolutions of its General Conferences. The broader significance of such resolutions compared with the IDB's resolutions stems from the more representative composition of the General Conference and from the greater volume of powers provided for by the Constitution. Since General Assembly resolution 2152 (XXI) did not envisage holding a General Conference, prior to the entry of the Constitution into force the IDB's powers were determined mainly by analogy with other autonomous organizations and specialized agencies practicing convocation of plenary organs.[8]

Of the documents adopted by the UNIDO General Conference, the Declarations and Plans of Action, adopted at the second and third General Conferences, deserve special attention. Among different forms of international law documents, the form of a convention or international treaty on questions of industrial development in the cases cited was not convenient for a number of reasons, one being the prolonged procedure for adopting such documents and a strong possibility that the Western countries would oppose it. A more acceptable form was a solemn declaration, which could be adopted in a comparatively short period of time, convenient for Western countries. In contrast to the Charter of Economic Rights and Duties of States and the Declaration and Programme of Action for Establishing a New International Economic Order, adopted by the UN General Assembly as resolutions, the Declarations and Plans of Action for Industrial Development and Cooperation were adopted by an autonomous organ of the General Assembly, which implies that the latter documents are politically less significant than the former ones.

However, an implied indication of a certain juridical force of these documents is the formulation in the preambles of the Declarations and Plans of Action, which stress that the "States solemnly declare," not "the General Conference believes." This implies that the political obligations contained in these documents are borne by the member states. The significance attached to disagreements of states with separate provisions of these documents indirectly reflects the fact that they all recognize their certain political force. Lastly, some of the provisions in the Declarations and Plans of Action were rather specific, envisaging practical actions of states.

A number of General Assembly resolutions on social and economic questions made reference to those documents of UNIDO. At some international forums reference was made to the need to comply with the provisions of these documents. However, this is only an indirect indication.

I adhere to the understanding that the force of a resolution, even in the event of its formal adoption, depends to some extent on the results of voting. A current point of view in juridical literature is that resolutions could be divided into those adopted unanimously; those adopted by a majority with an insignificant number of votes against; those adopted by a majority but with a considerable number of votes against, including large countries; and those adopted by consensus.

Adopting UNIDO's resolutions displayed three situations. The draft of the Lima Declaration and Plan of Action in the field of development and industrial cooperation was proposed by the Group of 77 in the framework of the preparatory committee for the second UNIDO General Conference. The Western countries proposed their own draft. The Eastern bloc countries proposed addenda and amendments to the first draft with the aim of making it less controversial, but inserting dubious points of their own. The Lima Declaration and Plan of Action were not adopted at the second UNIDO General Conference by consensus as third world countries wanted it. At Great Britain's proposal it was decided that the General Conference report would include the statements of participating countries in connection with their individual opinions on separate clauses.

At the plenary session of the second UNIDO General Conference on March 26, 1975, the United States voted against the Lima Declaration and Plan of Action. A large number of other Western countries abstained: Belgium, Canada, West Germany, Italy, Japan, Great Britain, and Israel. Voting on separate clauses of these documents also showed different positions of the Western countries. The United States voted against on seven clauses and abstained on two clauses, Great Britain six and three, West Germany seven and two, and Japan four and four.

Of the developing countries, Nicaragua abstained in one case. As for the Eastern bloc countries, they voted in favor of all the indicated cases, thinking that they scored in contradictions between the West and the South.

In the end the Lima Declaration and Plan of action was adopted by eighty-two votes for with one against and seven abstentions. In other words, the document was adopted by an overwhelming majority of member countries. It is also significant that the majority of Western countries voted for the adoption of the document. From this one may conclude that practically all the main groups of member states declared in favor of the Declaration and Plan of Action and thereby assumed definite political obligations. The member country that refused to approve this document, the United States, was not supported by other Western countries. However, since the United States is the largest financial contributor to the organization, it was a very important objection.

The situation was different at the third UNIDO General Conference during the adoption of the Delhi Declaration and Plan of Action. No accord was reached on many clauses in the process of comparing different points of view on the draft Declaration and Plan of Action proposed by the developing countries. The General Conference decided to set up a committee, headed by the conference chairman, to work out a compromise on disputed clauses. However, all the efforts to achieve a compromise on the single draft text of the Declaration and Plan of Action were in vain, because the initial draft by the third world was too unrealistic. The Group of 77 proposed adopting the draft of the Declaration and Plan of Action in toto and to hold for that purpose on the text as a whole. The East European countries expressed their regret, as they routinely put it, "that the lack of political will on the part of Western countries" made it impossible to work out a coordinated text of the document. The Western countries expressed their disagreement with the draft in advance. Nevertheless, most of the document's clauses were coordinated and approved. Consensus was not reached on one of the twenty-two clauses of the preamble of the Declaration and seven of the thirty-five clauses of the Declaration, but those were important ones. No agreement was reached also on three clauses of the Plan of Action. Hard pressed for time, the participants discussed several clauses of the Plan of Action but did not vote on them. Despite political convergence it appears that the conference itself was not prepared sufficiently. The proposed draft was too long and complicated to tackle in one week of a plenary meeting.

The draft of the Delhi Declaration and Plan of Action submitted by the Group of 77 was passed by eighty-three votes for to twenty-two against and one abstention. All developing and Eastern bloc countries voted for the document, and all Western countries voted against. Vatican City abstained. Though this time, too, a directive document of UNIDO was adopted by a majority of its members, one whole group of members rejected it. In terms of reconciling different states' interests, the conference ended with a very poor performance. Since the issue involved here is the political significance of the obligations of member countries, the political significance of the Delhi Declaration and Plan of Action is without doubt less meaningful than that of the Lima Declaration and Plan of Action.

Politically significant for member countries are a number of other resolutions adopted by the UNIDO plenary organ. For example, UNIDO's Special Conference (1971) adopted by consensus a resolution on the strategy, structure, and financing of the organization. It appeared as a draft resolution with inseparable amendments.[9]

Apart from the Declarations and Plans of Action, the second and third UNIDO General Conferences adopted three and two resolutions respectively concerning the strategy of industrialization for developing countries. Of the fifteen resolutions of the fourth UNIDO General Conference, more than ten also pertained to this question. However, at the first session of the General Conference of UNIDO as a specialized agency, no decisions were made on problems of policy in the field of international industrial cooperation, since the session was fully devoted to questions of reorganizing the organization. The documents adopted by the two latest sessions of the General Conference will be considered in detail later in this chapter.

Some IDB resolutions have a small impact on UNIDO's regulating activities in the international system. Among them were resolutions 25 (third session) on international cooperation in the field of industrial development, 31 (VI), and 37 (VII) and conclusions 1984/9 (XVIII) referring to assistance to the least developed countries, 1984/3 (XVIII), and 1985/4 (XIX) on reshaping world industrial production and transferring industrial capacities.

Measures for the development and adjustment of legal cooperation in the field of industrial development were proposed. A number of documents and studies prepared by the UNIDO secretariat presented the idea of considerable activization of norm-setting work in the field of industrial cooperation. There were repeated motions for setting up a commission on industrial law. It was also proposed to forward disputes on cooperation in the field of industrial development to a special international tribunal, which could be set up within the UNIDO framework.

The difficult implementation of these proposals was due to some Western countries not finding in these measures any constructive contribution to cooperation in the field of industrial production. Real progress in this direction remains rather modest.

Still, substantial consideration should be given to the analyses of such measures. It would be worthwhile to include the question of elaboration of international law documents on cooperation in the field of industrial development as a special item into the agenda of different UNIDO organs. It would also be useful to draw up a long-term program of UNIDO work in this direction.

CONTROVERSY OVER A NEW INTERNATIONAL ECONOMIC ORDER

Attempts by UNIDO in the second half of the 1970s and the early 1980s to create norms of a new international economic order were among the most controversial matters and naturally caused a bitter resistance from the West, nearly destroying the organization. However, UNIDO was hardly responsible for that kind of crises of international confidence, because the organization's actions were only a part of the overall strategy of the third world countries, which involved the General Assembly and the United Nations Conference on Trade and Development in particular.

This wave of political belligerency from the third world caused serious concern in the West. The official U.S. diplomatic response was hard enough. For instance, C. Clyde Ferguson, Jr., head of U.S. delegations at a number of UN–sponsored conferences, stated, "What is at issue, then, in the NIEO is nothing less than an attempt to create a new world order is preeminently a political question. Hence the politics of the NIEO becomes central to the matter of the world order of the next quarter-century."[10] This prediction, dated 1977 — the height of the controversy on the question, did not prove viable, however. The demands around slogans of a new international economic order were in focus only for a couple of years, but then started to abate. I believe that the threat of the new international economic order's norms was exaggerated.

One widely accepted presumption was that UNIDO's member countries could create limited norms to regulate the international system within a specific area of cooperation. Here I understand norms as proposed by Friedrich Kratochwil and John Ruggie: "standards of behavior defined in terms of rights and obligations."[11] But this was not ensured owing to the adoption of recommendations by the organization, as most of them never had serious legal impact, particularly those to which the Western countries objected.

Most of the demands incorporated in the notion of a new international economic order appeared to be a kind of demagoguery that finally turned out to be counterproductive for the third world countries. The dispute about notions did not really change anything, as the new international economic order remained mostly on paper.

A concept of an economic regime based upon interests of the third world states vis-à-vis the industrially advanced countries did not realistically take into account the interests of the Western countries, never grew into a mature regime, and, without international consensus, was therefore doomed to remain unenforceable. However, owing to the majority of the developing countries in the bodies of the UN system, the principles of such an order found their way into many international documents. In this regard, UNIDO was one of the examples.

Some of UNIDO's documents to the principles of a new international economic order. As stated in the Preamble to the UNIDO Constitution, the "States parties to the Constitution bear in mind the broad objectives in the resolutions" adopted by the sixth Special Session of the UN General Assembly "on the establishment of a new international economic order." The states declare that it is necessary to establish a just economic and social order, to be achieved through the elimination of economic inequalities and the establishment of rational and equitable economic relations. The formulation is even more clearly defined in Article I of the Constitution, which states that the primary objective of the organization "shall be the promotion and acceleration of industrial development in the developing countries with a view to assisting in the establishment of a New International Economic Order."

This reference to a new international economic order in an interstate treaty was not supported from the very start by the Western countries.[12] When the intergovernmental committee was working on the UNIDO Constitution, the Group of 77, supported by the Eastern bloc countries, stressed the role of the organization in the establishment of a new international economic order. The Western countries favored the formula "a new and equitable international economic order," which was slightly different from the formulation in the Charter of Economic Rights and Duties of States and a number of other documents that they did not support. At the UN Conference on the reorganization of UNIDO, the Western countries, especially the United States, emphasized this. At the concluding session of the Conference, before the adoption of the Constitution, the U.S. representative proposed an amendment to Article I: to insert, before the concept "a New International Economic Order," the definition "now in the process of evolution," which would have slightly changed the meaning of the formulation of UNIDO's objective. As soon as the Constitution was adopted, the U.S. representative declared that the third clause of the preamble does not signify renouncing the position of his country with regard to a number of UN resolutions and that the new international economic order should be interpreted as an economic order established as a result of the efforts of all states.

The Western countries were naturally against any reference to the new international economic order in the Lima Declaration and Plan of Action, even though this had been suggested by the resolution of the UN General Assembly.[13] General Assembly resolution 3306 (XXIX) of December 1974 stated that one of the primary objectives of the second UNIDO General Conference should be assistance in the establishment of a new international economic order through the adoption of an international declaration and plan of action. The Western countries refused to accept the principle of assistance in establishing a new international economic order, contained in paragraph 76 of the Declaration and Plan of Action. The United States and West Germany voted against this paragraph, and seventeen Western countries abstained.

Thus, the Western countries meant to stress that they continued to regard the respective provisions of the Charter of Economic Rights and Duties of States as ineffective. Had they agreed fully with this principle, they would have had to revise some other recognized principles concerning economic relations, including probably a voluntary character of assistance for the needs of development and the possibility of arbitrary changes of economically viable terms of trade. The Delhi Declaration and Plan of Action, adopted at the third UNIDO General Conference, included in the section "Survey and Appraisal" a statement that the majority of developed countries did not exhibit the political will for the establishment of a new international economic order.

One of the main principles of this order recorded in the UNIDO Constitution is the principle of sovereign equality of the states in their economic relations. This provision of the Preamble to the Constitution basically reiterates the respective clauses of resolutions 3201 and 3202 (S-VI), 3281 (XXIX), and 3362 (S-VII), which laid down principles of a new international economic order. This principle signifies the democratization of international relations and presupposes the establishment of more equitable relations between different groups of countries.[14] However, interpretation of this principle can be led to a bias. Developing countries, supported by the Eastern bloc, insisted on genuine equality, distinct from formal, "declarative equality which does not have a sufficient real content."[15]

One of the consequences of consistent application of the principle of national sovereignty is the right to freely dispose of the natural riches on the territory of a respective state. The right to use one's own natural resources as an inalienable element of national sovereignty was recognized long ago. General Assembly resolutions 626 (VII) in 1952 and 1803 (XVII) in 1962 actually contained the formulation of this principle. It was set out most consistently in the Charter of Economic Rights and Duties of States. In the Lima Declaration and Plan of Action it was stated in paragraph 29.

Developing countries adhere to the view that one of the main causes of their economic backwardness is the almost uncontrolled exploitation of their natural resources by Western countries, which in some periods of the colonial regime bordered on outright appropriation of those resources. According to such claims, developing countries could not put an end to the uncontrolled operation of transnational corporations that exploit their natural resources in new conditions.[16] According to that view, the Western countries, represented by transnational corporations, continue to draw unjustifiably huge profits from exploiting natural resources of developing countries. The latter must thus receive at least partial compensation for the losses suffered in the past.[17] Such claims are usually not well explained economically and tend to be considerably biased.

The right of states to dispose of their natural resources cannot be discontinued, even during a change of the political regime in a country. In practice this is true when foreign companies get concessions for developing national natural resources. Despite the temporary granting of a concession, the right of a state to dispose of its natural riches can never be transferred in full. Since the 1970s this argument has been accepted by most lawyers who researched it, for instance, Pierre Vellas and Antonio Cassese.[18]

Another specific feature of this right is that it cannot be restricted; however, this is sometimes disputed. Some jurists stress that there is a need for compromise between the sovereign right to develop national resources and supranational interests. In some cases, according to this concept, considerations of reliable supply of important strategic commodities may justify the restriction of the right of states to dispose of their own resources. It was proposed to delegate a part of these powers of states to some international organ, such as the Economic and Social Council.[19] In the future, globalization of all international issues and the rise of interde-pendence could give more credence to this proposal.

An important but controversial application of the right to dispose of one's own resources is the right of states to nationalize foreign property on their territory, to regulate foreign investments, and to control the activity of foreign companies. This is a major issue, and interests of different groups of states differ. The Lima Declaration and Plan of Action noted the right of states to nationalize foreign property, an impermissibility of any economic and political pressure that impedes the exercise of this right (paragraph 32), and the renunciation of discriminatory measures against any state making a decision on the exercise of sovereignty over its natural resources (paragraph 59j).

While the right of states to nationalize foreign property on their territory is no longer questioned in principle, the question of compensation has become a major issue.[20] The majority of developing countries do not dispute the obligation to provide compensation for nationalized foreign property.[21] However, the views of developing countries and different groups of countries diverge rather substantially regarding the volume and conditions of such compensations. Some conceptions of developing countries supported by the Eastern bloc postulated that the state inde-pendently determine the volume and conditions of compensation.[22] In this case, however, there is a strong probability of arbitrary decisions.

Some jurists, for example, J. Tumblir (Germany) and G. Gallais-Hamonno (France), put forward a well-grounded view that nationalization must be carried out in conformity with international law. This formulation was used in General Assembly resolution 1803 (XVII). Later General Assembly resolutions, including the Charter of Economic Rights and Duties of States (Article 2, paragraph 2), refer to compensation as subject to the laws and regulations the state deems necessary. During the elaboration of the Lima Declaration and Plan of Action, serious disagreements were evident on the question of paying the compensation for nationalized assets, similar to the disagreements earlier, during the discussion of Article 2 of the Charter of the Economic Rights and Duties of States. On the whole the Western countries did not agree with the view that nationalization must conform to domestic legislation; they advocated the principle of international arbitration instead.[23]

WHAT KIND OF ORDER AND WHO
IS TO BLAME FOR FAILURES

Among the principles advanced in UNIDO's documents is control over activities of transnational corporations through the adoption of measures in the interests of the national economy on the basis of full sovereignty of states. Thus, the Lima Declaration and Plan of Action stipulated that the activity of transnational corporations must be regulated (clause 42) and that developed countries must cooperate with the governments of third world countries to ensure that activities of national and transnational corporations are consistent with the economic and social objectives of developing countries (clause 59h). The section "Survey and Appraisal" of the Delhi Declaration and Plan of Action states rather emphatically on the impermissible practice of transnational corporations in relation to the developing countries bordering on the plunder of their national riches.[24] It is not surprising that such clauses were unacceptable to Western countries, which refused to approve the document. In a broader context the problem was studied thoroughly enough by Richard Newfarmer, Raymond Vernon, and other authors.[25]

Some lawyers frequently substantiated the concept of international responsibility, foremost in connection with the willingness of the United States and West European countries to ensure protection of their interests in different regions of the world.[26] One of the long-standing motivations was the need to protect the European minority living in developing countries. Some jurists interpret this concept as the responsibility of developed countries to protect their national and transnational corporations in the third world. However, representatives of the third world countries insist this is contradictory to the right of developed countries to take actions to safeguard the interests of these corporations, because it could be an infringement of national sovereignty. This is one reason developing countries are against this interpretation of the concept of "international responsibility."[27] They readily agree that developed countries should fulfill obligations assumed by such corporations toward countries where they invest.

The principle of assisting developing countries without any political or military conditions attached found its expression in UNIDO's documents, particularly in the Lima Declaration and Plan of Action (clause 61e and f) and in the Delhi Declaration and Plan of Action (clause 59e and f). The section "Strategy of Further Industrialization of Developing Countries" in the latter document noted the need of creating without any political conditions a global North-South fund. The fund was to be administered and controlled by developing countries, while the preparation and evaluation of its annual requirements would be UNIDO's responsibility. Financing of the fund, which by the year 2000 was to reach an unrealistic level of $300 billion, owing chiefly to contributions of the developed countries, would be carried out without any political control on their part. Since this proposal totally ignored the real situation, it did not have the support of a considerable number of countries, including major Western countries, which were supposed to finance it all.

Developing countries attach great importance to linking the prices of their exports and imports and the prices of raw material and finished products; this was stated, for example, in the Lima Declaration and Plan of Action (clause 19). The Western countries took a negative stand because such a linkage would lack a real economic approach.

As representatives from many third world countries state, the economic backwardness of developing countries is the consequence of the Western countries' past colonial policy.[28] According to them, an essential condition for restoring fairness would be a compensational or preferential regime of economic relations between the West and the developing countries. The demand of unilateral concessions in economic relations and in other spheres of cooperation became one of the main demands in the policy of the Group of 77. The sixth Special Session of the General Assembly decided unilateral concessions are viewed as a temporary measure to enable developing countries to address their lag in the national product and per capita incomes.[29]

The necessity of a preferential regime for developing countries in all spheres of international economic cooperation is stated in definite terms in the Lima Declaration and Plan of Action, in particular in clause 41 and clause 61a and b. From this, the world share of developing countries' industrial production is to reach at least 25 percent by the end of the century, rising by 8 percent per year on the average in this group of countries (clause 28). The United States and Sweden and the World Bank delegation at the second UNIDO General Conference expressed the well-founded view that 25 percent was not based on any satisfactory economic estimates. No special vote was taken on clause 28.

UNIDO's decisions envisioned reshaping the international monetary system to encourage development and flow of resources to developing countries. Thus, the Lima Declaration and Plan of Action noted a desirable participation of developing countries in decision making on international monetary questions (clause 43), a need to improve the international monetary system (clause 44), and urgent rescheduling for repaying long-standing debts and the interest on them (clause 61d). The Western countries objected to the clause concerning direct special participation of developing countries in solving these questions. They believed such institutions as the

International Monetary Fund and the World Bank were capable of handling those matters on a balanced global basis.

Western countries strongly objected to assisting producers of particular commodities among developing countries (clause 47). The Western countries' interests were at loggerheads with the activities of such organizations as the Organization of Petroleum Exporting Countries.[30]

The principle of ensuring access for developing countries to the achievements of modern science and technology (clauses 53–55 and 61j of the Lima Declaration and Plan of Action) was adopted without dissension. Similarly the need for negotiations on the elaboration of an international code of conduct for the transfer of technology (clause 61g) was recognized by all parties concerned.

An important principle in developing a new international economic order was a special attitude to the least-developed and land-locked countries in the programs of assistance,[31] referred to in resolution 2768 (XXVI) of the UN General Assembly of November 1971. Twenty-five countries met the criteria of per capita income of less than $100, the share of industrial output in the GDP of less than 10 percent, and national illiteracy higher than 80 percent. Guidelines for UNIDO were laid down by General Assembly resolution 3201 (S-VI), which included a chapter devoted to a special program of assistance to countries hit hardest by the economic crisis. Among such countries it listed the group of least-developed countries and land-locked and island states. Due to factors including a considerable growth of prices for imported oil and oil products, the economic position of these countries drastically deteriorated. General Assembly resolution 3338 (XXIX) of December 1974 also drew attention to island countries.

Issues of special assistance to the least-developed countries were first discussed in UNIDO at the sixth and seventh sessions of the IDB in June 1972 and May 1973, respectively. Their resolutions 31 (VI) and 37 (VII) reproduced the provisions of the indicated General Assembly resolutions with reference to UNIDO's technical assistance.[32]

The UNIDO Constitution considered a number of decisions on this question adopted by the UN General Assembly in the early and mid 1970s. Article 2 (i) of the Constitution states that UNIDO devotes particular attention to the adoption of special measures aimed at assisting the least-developed, land-locked, and island countries most seriously affected by economic crises and natural calamities. Paragraphs 35–37 and 62 of the Lima Declaration and Plan of Action envisaged the creation of conditions essential for industrialization in the least-developed, land-locked, and island countries, the provision of special assistance to them, and urgent measures for the expansion of their export and import facilities, including establishing a special trade regime, granting favorable loans, deferring old debts, and increasing the volume of technical assistance. The clauses in question listed additional criteria for states requiring special assistance, such as high growth of import prices compared with export prices, increase of external debt, and adverse consequences of the growth of charges for transportation services. These provisions were approved by Western countries without reservations. Subsequently the fourth UNIDO General Conference adopted the resolution "The Least-Developed Countries: Implementation of the New Basic Programme of Action," which essentially reproduced decisions adopted on this theme by other UN forums.[33] This was one of the rare cases where discussions brought consequences: most of UNIDO's programs were slightly diverted to favor the least-developed countries.

ATTEMPTS TO REGULATE INTERNATIONAL INDUSTRIAL COOPERATION

UNIDO's norm-setting capacity could be valuable for international cooperation in the field of industrial development, which is its primary object. No other organ in the UN system has the mandate of elaborating in detail normative provisions relating to international industrial cooperation. Thus, UNIDO's role might be relevant.

Creating new branches of international law is not a new venture. In particular, some researchers from the third world proposed to identify a so-called law of international development.[34] Those attempts were not rejected in the West. For instance, Guy Feur and Jacques Bouveresse made a substantial contribution to this concept.[35]

M. Bouhassian stressed the importance of international regulation of industrial cooperation. He wrote, "Industrial cooperation is ever more clearly and in different aspects assuming the form of new juridical relations. . . . Industrial cooperation, it seems, may embrace the complexity of large-scale operations and become an instrument of deep-going reshaping of international economic relations. The novelty of this institution has not yet been manifested in all possible forms in practice and its theory remains fragmentary and requires large efforts."[36] I do not think that regulation of industrial cooperation should lead to any reshaping of international economic relations, which is favored by researchers from the third world countries.

UNIDO could so far hardly fulfill such a task of regulating industrial cooperation and has not helped much in creating useful norms. Nevertheless, some provisions of UNIDO's documents could be interpreted as addressing such problems.

A major principle of international economic relations could be, according to UNIDO's documents, the sovereign right of each state to industrialization and an equitable share in world industrial production. This was reflected in the Preamble to the UNIDO Constitution, which states, "It is the sovereign right of all countries to achieve their industrialization, and any process of such industrialization must conform to the broad objectives of self-sustaining and integrated socio-economic development, and should include the appropriate changes which would ensure the just and effective participation of all peoples in the industrialization of their countries. . . . All countries, irrespective of their social and economic systems, are determined to promote the common welfare of their peoples by individual and collective actions aimed at . . . securing their equitable share in total world industrial production. . . ."

Though this principle is formulated in the most general way, the recognition of the inalienable sovereign right of developing countries to secure their equitable share in global industrial production is not well grounded. Not every country in the world provides favorable conditions for international development, thus advocating such principle as a general rule could be counterproductive. For some countries, for example, agriculture would produce the best results. I am not inclined to advocate elaborating common, universal efforts in tackling the problems of industrial development in third world countries whose precarious economic situation is a major handicap for achieving prosperity for mankind at large. At the same time, this aim should not be interpreted as a need for immediate increase of technical assistance, which in itself is not a viable solution and which was an implied interpretation by the developing countries.

The majority of third world countries face a common problem, weakness of national capital, which is insufficient to stimulate industrial development. Apart from foreign capital, that might be the state that can become an important investor, if its activities do not cross a dangerous line when it starts to press on private initiative. The state could indeed play a certain role in the strategy of industrial development when private sources are insufficient for necessary investments. However, this role would be very limited so as not to impede private initiative.

In a number of documents, UNIDO expressed a position that the state has the mission of mobilizing internal resources for the needs of industrial development. This argument was backed by the Eastern bloc countries with centrally planned economies. The Western countries were reserved toward this issue, so this provision was not included in the UNIDO Constitution. However, among the measures of the national scale proposed, for example, in the Lima Declaration and Plan of Action, there was emphasis laid on the role of the state in pushing forward industrial development (clause 58n). The introduction of the Delhi Declaration and Plan of Action drew special attention to the importance of using the state sector with reference to the transfer of industry to developing countries, which was even less realistic.

The Eastern bloc countries insisted that the formulation of development strategy should emphasize the "principle" of planned management by the state of the economic policies. UNIDO was at an impasse in view of sharp discussions on this question in various organs of the organization; the Western countries disputed the need for mentioning this provision. Article 2(d) of the UNIDO Constitution states that this organization "shall promote and encourage the development and use of planning techniques, and assist in the formulation of development, scientific and technological programmes and plans for industrialization. . . ." This approach is stated even more definitely in the Lima Declaration and Plan of Action (clause 58a), which emphasizes the need to elaborate a long-term strategy of industrialization. That provision was never applied to economically detrimental central planning in the Soviet Union and East European countries.

UNIDO's documents, the Lima Declaration and Plan of Action (clause 58c) among them, advanced a broad principle of social justice in implementing industrial development policy in the third world countries. The Eastern bloc attached particular importance to this principle, routinely observing that industrialization must not lead to enrichment of the propertied groups of the population in developing countries to the detriment of others. Even if such an interpretation seems poorly supported, there is much sense in that industrial development must secure a gradual rise of the welfare of industrial workers and, consequently, the least-provided-for strata of the population. Those should be the tasks of industrial development, which could be well used to reduce poverty.

A substantial problem in the developing countries is the imbalance of their economic systems, caused among other things, by bad management. Some sectors, exports, for example, develop at a faster pace, while most others are stagnant or not developed at all. The resulting imbalances in the economic system reach dangerous limits, restraining economic progress.

Those factors might be a natural consequence of free-market economics, which encourage the sectors most fit for competition. However, some of UNIDO's documents imply this should be eliminated. According to this interpretation, all the more important is the principle of comprehensive development of industry consistent with the interests of developing countries.[37] Article 2(e) of the UNIDO Constitution stipulates that the organization "shall encourage and assist in the development of an integrated and interdisciplinary approach towards the accelerated industrialization of the developing countries." The Lima Declaration and Plan of Action (clause 58f) state that it is necessary to create production facilities in developing countries embracing "all branches of industry and, first and foremost, the steel and metallurgical industry," to strengthen ties between branches, and to create manufacturing and processing capacities. Although identifying priority branches was typical for the majority of developing countries and the Soviet Union with its Eastern European allies, it is not always a necessary prerequisite for economic success. As the recent economic history showed convincingly, such huge projects as steel and metallurgical enterprises are not profitable and not necessary in many developing countries.

According to some of UNIDO's decisions, mobilization for the needs of industrial development of the cooperative movement is of primary importance for developing countries. Cooperative entities possess great economic reserves and help solve problems of employment. The Lima Declaration and Plan of Action stresses the importance of giving an increased role to industrial cooperatives as a means of mobilizing manpower and other resources. In conditions of enormous unemployment in the third world, growth of such cooperatives could indeed be economically viable at a certain stage. Cooperation of individual producers is an effective lever to accelerate economic growth as well.

Difficulties experienced by developing countries in marketing their industrial output in Western countries are sometimes, as some UNIDO papers pointed out, compounded by measures aimed at limiting the access of manufactured goods of these countries to their markets. Such trade policy of Western countries manifested, especially in the late 1970s and the first half of the 1980s, not as a growth of customs barriers, but as the introduction of quotas and restrictions in the form of special criteria for the characteristics and specifications of commodities. However, in some cases it was an unavoidable practice, to withdraw national producers from the jeopardy of cheap import inflow and to observe environment, medical, and other standards. The preamble to the Delhi Declaration and Plan of Action called for the impermissibility of additional restrictions on the access of manufactured goods and semi-finished products from developing countries, but without going into details. Industrial exports of developing countries later became a matter of special discussion in the framework of the General Agreement on Tariffs and Trade (GATT), especially at the Uruguay round.

Key groups of UNIDO member countries have, in the main, come to agree on the transfer of some industrial capacities from the North to developing countries in connection with the world industrial growth, but on different premises. This principle is seen by third world representatives as an element of the struggle for the policy of industrialization. According to this principle, in view of deep structural changes in the world industry, a part of these industrial capacities must be shifted to the developing countries. Since this provision was very general, the Western countries did not oppose it. At the same time, the draft of the relevant resolution, "World Industrial Reshaping and the Transfer of Industrial Capacities," discussed at the fourth UNIDO General Conference, was not adopted because the Western countries could not accept clause 4. In this clause the developed countries were invited to support the efforts of developing countries to achieve full utilization of the industrial potential, to honor their pledges, and to "put an end to protectionism" through full implementation and strict observance of regulations, especially for imports from developing countries.[38] If developing countries had not insisted on such strong terms, the resolution would probably have been adopted.

In general, UNIDO has made rather modest and not necessarily very valuable progress so far in formulating principles of international cooperation in industrial development.[39] Apart from diverging positions on this issue of different groups of countries, which in many concrete matters are potentially reconcilable, there are organizational obstacles. UNIDO does not have a single department, including within the secretariat, that would deal specifically with elaborating legal issues of international industrial cooperation and their codification. In this respect there are many other fields of cooperation in the system of international economic, scientific, and technical relations in which the norm-setting process has advanced much farther owing to the activities of international organizations.

The principles of international industrial cooperation, in my mind, require further substantial development and codification in the form of an international treaty (a multilateral convention), though not necessarily to be negotiated only under UNIDO's aegis. This would help, for example, to bypass defects of the two Declarations and Plans of Action adopted by the UNIDO General Conferences. This convention could support nondiscrimination in interna-tional industrial cooperation and other principles. Organizationally, UNIDO hypothetically offers opportunities for drafting the convention on the principles of cooperation of states in industrial development, which could make a definite contribution to further developing mutually beneficial economic relations between different groups of countries. However, there are no other international bodies that possess a negotiating mechanism, for instance, the World Bank group.

A convention on the principles of international industrial cooperation could become a contribution to the formulation of international law principles regarding economic relations between states that the earlier UNIDO's documents mostly ignore.

The convention could include a preamble with the following provisions, which, I believe, are mostly within an area of potential consensus of key groups of countries concerned:

Industrial cooperation on the global scale is impossible without a lasting and stable peace and requires active collective efforts of all states to lower the level of military potentials and to reduce armaments, their production, and defense expenditures.

Industrial development of third world countries lays the foundation of their economic independence and is an important factor in the exercise of their sovereignty.

International industrial cooperation is affected adversely by the problem of the critical and self-augmenting debt of developing countries to the developed countries. Mutually acceptable settlement is essential for the improvement of international economic and political relations.

Promoting international industrial cooperation on a global basis corresponds to the interests of all member states of the world community, regardless of the level of their economic development.

Member countries proceed from substantial contribution made by the UN system to the elaboration of the principles of international industrial cooperation and take cognizance of the UNIDO Constitution.

The convention proper could contain the following provisions:

Each state, regardless of its economic regime and level of development, has the indisputable right to further industrial development as an important component of its sovereignty and economic independence and to achieve an equitable share in world economic production.

Each state has the right to regulate industrial property on its territory regardless of whether it is national or foreign and to establish its legal status, including the profit and other remittances taking into account its economic interests.

In the event of nationalizing industrial property on its territory, including foreign industrial property, the state fixes the amount and conditions of material compensation in cooperation with proprietors and according to international law principles.

International industrial cooperation is built on a nondiscriminatory basis and implies refusal to create obstacles to any country's access to advanced technology, with the exception of the areas determining the interests of national security of the respective states.

The states must strive for the broadest exchange of technical information on mutually beneficial terms in areas connected with scientific and technical progress and reduce restrictions imposed in view of military-political considerations.

While conducting international exchanges of industrial products, the developed countries abstain from customs duties on the imports of respective commodities from developing countries without obligatory observance of the principle of reciprocity.

While engaging in international exchange of industrial goods, the developed countries refrain from setting quotas, licensing, and imposing other nontariff restrictions on the import of respective commodities from developing countries without an obligatory reciprocity.

With the aim of settling disputes in industrial cooperation, member countries may resort to international judicial and arbitration procedures. For this purpose an international judicial and arbitration service on questions of international industrial cooperation is set up (possibly within the UNIDO organizational structure).

With a view to developing an appropriate area of international economic law, a permanently functioning commission of international industrial cooperation law shall be set up (also possibly in the UNIDO framework).

NOTES

1. W. Koo, Jr., *Voting Procedures*; E. Yemin, *Legislative Powers*.

2. M. Abraham, *Perspectives on Modernization*; O. Asamoah, *The Legal Significance of the Decisions of the General Assembly of the United Nations*, 1966; H. Chin, *The Capacity of International Organizations to Conclude Treaties and the Special Legal Aspects of the Treaties So Concluded*, 1966.

3. J. Castaneda, *Legal Effects of United Nations Resolutions*, 1970.

4. W. Meng, *Das Recht der internationalen Organisationen — eine Entwicklungsstufe des Völksrechts*, 1979; G. Addicks and H. Bünning, *Ökonomische Strategien der Entwicklungspolitik*, 1979.

5. G. Tunkin, *Pravo i sila*, p. 76.

6. M. Lachs, *Le rôle des organizations internationales dans la formation du droit international*, 1964.

7. E. Yemin, *Legislative Powers*.

8. O. Asamoah, *Legal Significance*.

9. ID/SCN/Res. I.

10. C. Ferguson in *The Changing United Nations: Options for the United Nations*, ed. by D. Key, 1977, p. 143.

11. F. Kratochwil and J. Ruggie, "International Organization: a State of the Art and an Art of the State," *International Organization*, 1986, p. 767.

12. K. Köppinger, *Der Weg der UNIDO*, pp. 131–38; critical assessment of the position of Western countries is found in the work of A. Remuli, *Tiers-Monde et émergence d'un nouvel ordre économique international*, 1975.

13. The reasoning for this position is related in S. Kim, *The Quest for a Just World Order*, 1984.

14. W. Meng, *Das Recht der internationalen Organisationen*; R. Bermejo, *Vers un nouvel ordre économique international: Étude centrée sur les aspects juridiques*, 1982, pp. 181–86.

15. A. Benancheon, "L'industrialisation des pays du Tiers Monde et égalité souveraine," *Annuaire du Tiers Monde*, 1975, pp. 40–58.

16. H. Shamsul, *International Politics: A Third World Perspective*, 1987.

17. This thesis is routinely referred to in the works of researchers from developing countries. See for instance R. Hingorani, *International Law Through the United Nations*, 1972; R. Bermejo, *Vers un nouvel ordre*, pp. 197–202.

18. P. Vellas, *Aspects du droit international économique*, 1989; A. Cassese, *Il diritto internazionale nel mondo contemporaneo*, 1984.

19. J. Duffar, *Contribution à l'étude des privilèges et immunités des organisations internationales*, 1982; H. Schermers, *International Institutional Law*, 1972.

20. M. Abraham, *Perspectives of Modernization*; G. Addicks and H. Bünning, *Strategien der Entwicklungspolitik*.

21. P. Bermejo, *Vers un nouvel ordre*, pp. 197–202.

22. M. Bedjaoui, *Pour un nouvel ordre économique international*.

23. J. Tumblir, *Weltwirtschaftsordnung: Regeln, Kooperation und Soveranität*, 1979; G. Gallais-Hamonno, *Les nationalisations ... a quél prix? Pourguoi taire?* 1977.

24. The opposite view of Western jurists is set out in L. Wildhaber, *Internationalrechtliche Probleme multinationaler Korporationen*, 1978.

25. R. Newfarmer, ed., *Profits, Progress and Poverty: Case Studies of International Industries in Latin America*, 1985; R. Vernon, *Sovereignty at Bay*, 1971; R. Vernon, *Storm over the Multinationals*, 1977.

26. H. Schermers, *Structure*, 1972.

27. A. Benancheon, "L'industrialsation des pays."

28. For more information about this thesis see M. Bedjaoui, *Pour un nouvel ordre*.

29. The related problems were examined in particular by D. Carreau et al., *Droit international économique*, 1990.

30. See L. Wildhaber, *Internationalrechtliche Probleme*.

31. The issue was reflected in J. Ahmed, "The Least Developed Among the Developing Countries," *JWLL*, 1974, pp. 201–09. See a much different view on the necessity of such special assistance in T. Weiss and A. Jennings, *More for the Least? Prospects for Poorest Countries in the Eighties*, 1983.

32. ID/B/Res. 31(VI), 37(VII).

33. ID/CONF. S/Res. 6.

34. M. Bennouna, *Droit international du dévelopment: Tier-Monde et interpretation du droit international*, 1983.

35. G. Feur, *Droit international du développement*, 1985; J. Bouveresse, *Droit et politique du developpement et de la coopération*, 1990.

36. M. Bouhassin, *Droit international de la coopération industrielle*, 1980, pp. 450–51.

37. This is discussed in R. Bermejo, *Vers un nouvel ordre*.

38. ID/CONF. 5/46.

39. This is recognized by M. Bouhassin, *Droit international*, pp. 6–9.

9

International Political
Issues on Agenda

INDEBTEDNESS OF THE THIRD WORLD,
OTHER GLOBAL ECONOMIC ISSUES

The United Nations Industrial Development Organization (UNIDO) became a specialized agency in a period characterized by an aggravation of economic problems in most developing countries. In essence, the goals and objectives of the Lima and Delhi Declarations and Plans of Action, as well as the UN International Development Decade strategy for the 1980s regarding the developing countries, have remained on paper. Industrial production growth rates in those countries fell in the 1980s. In 1982–1984, for the first time since World War II, most developing countries experienced an absolute reduction in industrial production.

The foreign debt of the developing countries has grown to an enormous size, exceeding $1.4 trillion. The developing countries often took new loans merely to repay previous loans. The problem was becoming chronic.

These phenomena are partially explained by the inability of the third world countries to remain competitive in international economic relations. This is exacerbated further by unfavorable terms on international commodity markets, especially raw materials markets, by increasing difficulties staying on the market in the developed capitalist countries; by a growth of interest rates on credits; and even by subsequent outflow of a part of profits of transnational corporations. As a result, developing countries incur losses, although apparently it is not the only reason that counts.

Many developing countries are ready to provide new advantages and concessions to transnational companies creating favorable regimes for investments. Yet they keep accusing the latter of disorganizing international economic relations. In violation of generally accepted international norms, as the developing countries' leaders insist, the transnational corporations "organize trading, lending or technological blockades" and use different methods of exerting pressure and sanctions against some developing countries. This rhetoric, however, is not economically substantiated.

In the meantime, it is not a totally unfounded viewpoint that creditors from the Western countries are to be partially blamed for the increased indebtedness of the third world and for the debt crisis. They could have stopped offering credit once it started to be increasingly insecure. It is clear that all parties concerned are to make maximum efforts to eliminate the grave consequences of this problem, now of a global nature.

Within the framework of general debate at different UNIDO forums, starting with the Lima General Conference, the issue of the growing debt of the developing countries has been discussed many times. At the same time, the Western countries reasonably argued that this problem should not be discussed separately at the UNIDO forums because it is not exactly its mandate. The second session of the UNIDO General Conference in 1987, however, adopted the resolution "Foreign Debt and Industrial Development," which, in particular, added to the respective decisions of the seventh United Nations Conference on Trade and Development session held the same year. The resolution states that the indebtedness and servicing of the debt "are a heavy constant burden restricting the economic and social development of many developing countries." The General Conference requested UNIDO's General-Director to ensure preparing proposals in the field of industrial development to alleviate the consequences of foreign debt for the developing countries.[1] Proposals regarding the ways to eliminate the developing countries' foreign debt, made by Mikhail Gorbachev in his statement at the UN General Assembly session in December 1988, also provided an impetus to discussions and an adequate solution of this problem.

The working documents of UNIDO point out to a major problem in attaining progress in industrializing a large number of third world countries, identifying it as an external debt. For instance, in the report by the Director-General on this issue to the Industrial Development Board (IDB) in 1989, it was indicated that industrial development was closely interwoven with external debt problems. The external debt of developing countries rose by the beginning of the 1990s to $1,320 billion, or about half of their combined gross national products. Due to increasing interest payments, the record net negative resource transfer of $43 billion occurred in 1988.[2] A large part of this debt was caused by financing large-scale industrialization projects that turned out to be mismanaged and became unprofitable, therefore not allowing payment of the debts.

The report concluded finding a follow-up in subsequent decisions of the organization, as the Director-General proposed applying a selective geographical focus for UNIDO's operations along the mentioned debt problem: Africa and Latin America. On a conceptual level, this issue was raised in UNIDO's yearly publication, "Industry and Development Global Report," which addressed overcoming the debt problem. On the level of the General Conference, the problem was tackled by the resolution "External Debt and Industrial Development," which was adopted by the second and third sessions. Apart from the organization's general approach to the problem, resolutions had some impact on UNIDO's concrete operations. Yet I believe that the debt problem is unlikely to be solved by adopting resolutions. For the organization's programs, however, it is rather important to identify the problem and to take it into account in the operational activities.

Some Western economists justify the growing use of foreign private capital for industrial development purposes with the assumption that with adequate control the excessive influence of this capital on the developing economies can be avoided. This assumption is usually disputed by researchers from the third world countries. In any case, an important prerequisite for the government of a developing country wishing to reap benefits from cooperation with transnational corporations is a clearly formulated national industrial development strategy. This would precisely specify the role of foreign private investments, in what sectors and on what terms they would be welcome. Apparently, foreign private investments can play basically an auxiliary role in the industrial development of the third world countries.

The activities of UNIDO's secretariat have shown a trend in the 1980s to coordinate certain practical activities of the organization with those of private companies. At the beginning it was criticized by the USSR and the East European countries that insisted that such "deviations" do not fully conform with UNIDO's objectives and can undermine its operating efficiency and the role of the Industrial Development Board. This argument was later dropped.

The rhetoric regarding transnational corporations' activities was seldom included in UNIDO's resolutions. There are few references to the transnational corporations' "destructive role" in the third world in the Lima and Delhi Declarations and Plans of Action. Yet, UNIDO failed to constructively address this problem. UNIDO's adoption of a balanced position on this issue would be significant for considering the industrial development strategy in the developing countries.

A promising activity for UNIDO could be preparing a draft standard code on industrial investments to be used by a developing country as a basis for enacting an appropriate domestic legislation. Such a legislative act governing industrial investments in the country, including foreign investments, could be useful for many developing countries that do not have adequately developed normative material. A standard industrial development code could take into account the experience accumulated by different countries and could be based on democratic principles elaborated in different sectors of international law (international private law, international economic law, and so on).

Exports of finished goods from the developing countries to the Western markets in the 1980s were considered handicapped in the conditions of the so-called new protectionism or new restriction of entry of manufactured goods from the developing countries, many of which were at dumping prices. There was quite a discussion of a presumed wave of the new protectionism in the West toward the industrial imports from the developing countries of both traditionally labor-intensive industrial products (textile, clothing, shoes) and products of new manufacturing industries (metals and transportation equipment, certain types of machines, electric devices). According to some third world countries, it contradicts the Lima decisions that stressed the need for additional advantages of international trade for the developing countries. Growing protection measures took the form of bilateral export restriction agreements or marketing regulation agreements used to exert pressure on the exporting countries. However, the assessment of those phenomena in UNIDO's documents was seldom balanced and reflected the position of the developing countries.

Generally, the difficult economic situation for most developing countries and worldwide make it imperative for UNIDO to take an active part in developing and implementing measures for improving international economic relations, especially on the South-North axis. This would include eliminating any methods of economic aggression contradicting the generally recognized norms of international law and the UN charter, such as the use or threat of use of embargoes, boycotts, technological blockades, and dumping. It is also important to assist the third world countries in identifying and implementing effective measures conducive to relieving their crises and ensuring an industrial development responding to their national interests.

INTERNATIONAL GEO-POLITICAL
ISSUES PULLED ON AGENDA

Issues of international cooperation and promotion of the third world's industrial development relate to the general problems of international relations. Evidently, an international organization such as UNIDO, where the developing countries are in large majority, cannot completely avoid reflecting the process of world politics. Yet, excessive politicization of the organization's agenda and activities becomes an issue when the UN system already has plenty of other bodies, particularly the Security Council, specifically dedicated to problems of peace and security.

A provision has been included in some UNIDO documents concerning the need to use international industrial cooperation in the interests of strengthening international peace and security on the basis of peaceful coexistence of states with different social and political regimes. This provision did not have a direct relationship with the organization's activities. However, the Eastern bloc countries, supported by the developing countries, proposed including this provision in the charter of UNIDO: "all countries regardless of their social and economic systems are decided to promote the general well-being of their peoples by . . . actions aimed at . . . contributing to the cause of international peace and security and prosperity of all nations."

After efforts of third world countries, mainly supported by the Eastern bloc, the general political debate at UNIDO forums in the 1970s touched upon problems including the maintenance of peace, relaxation of international tensions, and cessation of the arms race. Economic development at large was interpreted as directly dependent on the solution of those problems. One of the arguments was that funds spent on armaments in different countries of the world represented gigantic potential for the increase of resources for industrial development and promotion of international industrial cooperation in the interests of all countries and peoples.

Practical measures to curb the arms race have been discussed many times following the decisions of the UN bodies. Sometimes those proposals were void of concrete plans of action. Thus, the delegations of the USSR usually suggested that all countries with significant economic and military potential, as well as the permanent members of the Security Council, should cut their military budgets to an extent agreed in absolute terms. In the meantime, specific amounts could be agreed upon to be additionally allocated for assistance to the developing countries. Establishing a special mechanism to distribute that assistance within the framework of the UN was proposed. The UNIDO forums agreed on projects of international industrial development, which could become possible if this and other similar proposals in the field of disarmament were adopted. However, apart from general discussions, no specific agreements have been reached apart from propaganda. Real issues were addressed on a bilateral basis between the United States and the Soviet Union (until its role was taken over by Russia).

Acute political problems emerged due to the positions of parties in some regional conflicts. A pretext was a consideration of assistance to certain developing countries or peoples that were in the process of forming their states.

A gradual bias toward a closer relationship between UNIDO's decisions and world policy problems took place in the 1970s and in the early 1980s. While in the past such issues were only implicit, for example, at the General Conference and IDB sessions and in the adoption of assistance programs to certain states and territories, subsequently world political problems began to be considered as a separate subject. Yet, the rationale of this was often put into question.

In this regard, the discussion of the situation in the Middle East at the fourth General Conference of UNIDO in 1984 was very characteristic. During the consideration of the draft resolution "Cessation of War in the Persian Gulf," notwithstanding the objections of Western countries, it was decided by thirty-seven for to twenty against with twenty-five abstaining that the issue falls under the jurisdiction of the Conference. The draft implored member states to exert every effort to put an end to the war and the governments of the appropriate states "to come to a just and equitable settlement of the conflict either through negotiations, or through intermediaries." The resolution was adopted by forty-four votes for, one against, and forty-three abstaining.[3] The Western countries took the stand that the issue had no relation to UNIDO's mandate.

The issue of the situation in South Africa has been raised at UNIDO forums many times at the insistence of the developing countries, as they chose to use as many UN bodies in their campaign against Pretoria as possible. The eighteenth and nineteenth IDB sessions adopted conclusions 1984/11 and 1985/14, respectively, on the issue of technical assistance to the national liberation movements in South Africa recognized by the Organization of African Unity (OAU). The United States, Great Britain, Japan, Sweden, and Belgium voted against; Western countries and Chile in the first case and Western countries, Chile, and Malawi in the second case abstained. The same IDB sessions adopted decisions on technical assistance to the people of Namibia, conclusions 1984/10 and 1985/12, respectively. The United States voted against; eight Western countries abstained in the first case; the same eight Western countries and Malawi abstained in the second case. Namibia joined UNIDO with a special status at the second General Conference session in 1987. A resolution on technical aid to Namibia was adopted at the same session by seventy-six votes in favor, with two against and sixteen abstentions (without a roll-call vote).[4]

The fourth General Conference voted on the resolution "Technical Assistance to the National Liberation Movements in South Africa Recognized by the Organization of African Unity." It was adopted by sixty-six votes for to six against with twenty-one abstentions. A similar resolution was adopted at the nineteenth IDB session in 1985 by eighty-three votes in favor with two against and fifteen abstentions.[5] UNIDO's resolutions proposed to increase technical assistance to the national liberation movements in South Africa. Furthermore, all member states, the UN system, and intergovernmental and nongovernmental organizations were called to render assistance to the national liberation movements in South Africa, recognized by the OAU, "aiming at the social and economic development of the oppressed majority in the South of Africa."[6]

Another problem discussed at UNIDO forums was the Israeli policy toward the Palestinian people and neighboring countries. The eighteenth and nineteenth IDB sessions adopted conclusions 1984/12 and 1985/13, respectively, regarding assistance to the Palestinian people. The United States voted against in both cases; ten Western countries abstained in the first case; ten Western countries and Malawi abstained in the second case. A similar resolution, adopted by the fourth General Conference, "Technical Assistance to the Palestinian People," proposed to promote technical assistance to the Palestinian people and to "immediately lift the restrictions imposed by the Israeli occupation authorities and impeding the development of the economy of the occupied Palestine territories." The Conference urged the "Israeli occupation authorities to give to UNIDO's personnel and experts access to the occupied Palestine territories in order to implement industrial development projects there." The resolution was adopted by roll-call vote with seventy votes in favor, two votes against (the United States and Israel), and twenty-three abstentions (twenty-one Western countries, Guatemala, and Uruguay). A similar resolution was adopted at the second General Conference session in 1987 by seventy-nine to two votes with sixteen abstentions.[7] The fourth General Conference adopted by consensus the politically oriented resolution "Urgent Assistance to Lebanon Aimed at the Restoration of its Industrial Sector."[8]

Decisions of a political nature were adopted by the UNIDO forums similarly to the related decisions of other UN bodies, including the General Assembly and the Economic and Social Council (ECOSOC). This does not prove the necessity of UNIDO's decisions themselves, even if they reflected positions on a number of international issues maintained by key groups of countries.

Consideration of international political problems in the framework of UNIDO and decisions on them reflected the desire of the third world countries to contribute by all means, even surpassing the scope of the organization's mandate, to their position on international problems facing the international community. To a large extent this related to the willingness of the developing countries to involve UNIDO in the political process characteristic of the leading UN bodies.

U.S. ATTITUDE TOWARD UNIDO

The position of the United States on UNIDO matters should be considered in the context of its policy toward the UN and specialized agencies providing technical assistance. The attitude was rather reserved, if not negative, especially starting in the early 1970s.

The United States clearly had reasons to be rather disappointed. The largest contributor to UNIDO's budget and program of work, it enjoyed only one vote at the General Conference. In terms of the decision-making process within a membership of 151 states, the United States commands only about 0.7 percent of votes at the UNIDO General Conference and could be and was routinely outvoted by the third world countries, despite an unstable coalition with other Western countries.

Altogether slightly more than 100 member countries pay between 0.01 percent and 0.09 percent each, their total share being less than 2 percent of UNIDO's regular budget. More than seventy countries of UNIDO are required to pay only 0.01 percent (or about $10,000 in the early 1990s). The difference between the United States and the smallest contributor (25 percent and 0.01 percent) is enormous. In terms of geo-political groups, the belligerent Group of 77 pays only 9.7 percent (of which OPEC members pay 3.7 percent). The votes of the USSR and East European countries did not make much difference at the UNIDO plenary organ as they command only about 5 percent of the votes.

From that prospective the calls in the United States for weighted voting had definite logic, because the discrepancy between the country's contribution and its voting power is striking. Indeed, the strongest economy in the world commands the same voting power at the UNIDO General Conference as each of a number of small island developing countries with populations less than one million people and no manufacturing. However, the demand for weighted voting has not been so far considered as a realistic option as it would mean changing the total UN arrangement as agreed upon by fifty-one founding states in 1945. Once the voting procedure is under revision, the whole UN structure might be jeopardized. This does not appear to correspond to the interests of the United States or of any other great powers.

Apart from the drive of third world countries with their ever-growing economic demands, several more factors contributed to the United States' mistrust of many UN agencies, UNIDO included. The USSR, usually rather reserved toward UN machinery, found it appropriate to back calls for a new international economic order as a means to deepen the division between the West and the third world. It was coupled with demagoguery about the vestiges of colonialism and the dangers of imperialism and neo-colonialism, which were readily adapted by most radical regimes in the third world and had a serious impact on the Group of 77 policy in general.

Thus, the huge blow to the UN system, UNIDO included, came in August 1985 with the amendment by Senator Nancy Kassebaum to the Foreign Relations Authorization Act. According to the amendment, the United States should pay no more than 20 percent of the assessed annual budget of the UN or any of the specialized agencies that do not adopt weighted voting procedures on matters of budgetary consequence. The second step in the same direction, the Gramm-Rudman-Hollings Act in December 1985, provided for a program of reduced federal deficits over the following five years. Thus, if the deficits were expected higher than those specified, then funds would be cut automatically. This reflected on the U.S. commitments to the UN system, UNIDO included. Some other minor Congressional acts involved across-the-board reductions that further cut U.S. payments to less than 15 percent of the total assessments of member states in the UN and specialized agencies.

However, UNIDO was evidently considered not the worst case from the U.S. perspective. The policy of the United States was never directed against UNIDO; the latter was not singled out in public statements and was spared criticism at the governmental level. While identifying its position toward UNIDO, the U.S. representatives have never advocated the disbanding of that organization or threatened to leave it.

If hypothetically the United States (or any other major Western power) judged its participation in UNIDO useless, it has had at least two easy and appropriate opportunities to leave this organization without a cumbersome procedure of withdrawal, even without explanations of motives. Those situations occurred in 1979 and in 1985.

The UNIDO Constitution was signed April 9, 1979 by eighty-one states. The United States was certainly free not to sign the Constitution and stay out of the new organization, which would not therefore become universal and would be doomed from the very beginning. There could be probably no easier way to part from an agency. However, the U.S. administration acted otherwise, authorizing signing the UNIDO Constitution and never publicly expressing doubts about joining the new UNIDO.

The second opportunity to part from UNIDO was envisaged by the Constitution, which provided for a step-by-step creation of the organization. The crucial point was notification of the depositary of the UNIDO Constitution (UN Secretary-General) that this document became obligatory for this particular country. As a special provision of the Constitution, any signatory of the constituent act was free to refrain from notifying the depository without any explanation and just stay away from the organization. However, the United States notified the UN Secretary-General in June 1985 that it considered the UNIDO Constitution the document that "enters into force for this country."

Thus, the United States at least twice explicitly chose to participate in the new UNIDO. Apart from those two self-explanatory acts, there were more than enough opportunities to block negotiations on matters vital for UNIDO at any point between 1975 and 1979 when the Constitution was being negotiated or between 1979 and 1985 when the conditions of enforcing the creation of the organization were being discussed. However, the United States did not do that and participated actively in the negotiations at all stages, leaving a strong impact on the final agreement.

It should be stressed that the United States reconfirmed its participation in UNIDO notwithstanding the mounting wave against the UN system in Congress, only three months before adopting Kassebaum's amendment. Thus, in the view of the U.S. government, the arguments in favor of participating in UNIDO clearly outweighed arguments against it.

NOTES

1. GC. 2/INF.4
2. IDB. 5/14.
3. ID/CONF. 5/Res.13.
4. GC. 2/SR.10.
5. Ibid.
6. ID/CONF. 5/Res.15.
7. ID/CONF. 5/Res.14, GC. 2/SR.10.
8. ID/CONF. 5/Res.12.

10

Moving into the 1990s

TOWARD A NEW PROFILE OF
THE GENERAL CONFERENCE

The late 1980s and the early 1990s have not been very successful for global industrial growth on the whole. The growth rate for developing countries in 1990 stood at 6.1 percent, slightly less than before, and for developed countries, 3.3 percent, which was less than an average in the 1980s. The overall share of developing countries in 1990 was marginally higher than before, 14.2 percent, and is expected to rise to 17 percent by the year 2000.[1] It is, nevertheless, far below the target of 25 percent suggested by the Lima Declaration and Plan of Action, a percentage that seems to be more and more unrealistic.

However, the overall more or less satisfactory results of the third world achievements in the industrial sector did not indicate the ever-increasing polarity in development of those countries. About a dozen of them had a remarkable success, precisely where market economies developed unrestricted and were propped by Western expertise, including transnational concerns. However, it was not the rule, as the vast majority of countries were worse off then before.

The worst predictable scenarios had occurred in African countries. According to the United Nations Industrial Development Organization (UNIDO) research papers, the manufacturing sector in sub–Saharan Africa underwent an absolute reduction in output per worker, by about 28 percent in real terms between 1970 and 1985, from $11,200 to $8,700 (in 1980 dollars). Later figures were only slightly better.[2]

UNIDO's papers identified some of the reasons for this disastrous situation. Among these is the fact that many industrial projects in sub–Saharan Africa were either ill-conceived or apparently mismanaged, while the basic institutional framework for industrial development in the region was to be changed. However, in most documents on that topic prepared by UNIDO's secretariat there was not a hint of the possibility that the organization should share the common responsibility of the world community for a net regress of industrial production in this large part of the globe. The remedies as seen, for instance, in "Industry and Development: Global Report 1989–90" were rather old ones, which apparently did not work, for example, "immediate debt relief and increased flow of finance."[3] There was no effort to question the traditional emphasis on industry, which might be unnecessary, for instance, in many states of Africa, where it seems often that they do not provide satisfactory conditions for competitive production.

The controversial situation was reflected at the second session of the General Conference, convened in Bangkok, Thailand, on November 9–13, 1987. The session took place at a time when the difficulties associated with the transitional period connected with the transformation of the organization had been mostly overcome. One hundred nine countries took part in the session.[4]

By the time the General Conference convened, UNIDO had considerably curtailed its financial shortages, although its budgetary position was still fragile. The Conference in particular had to concentrate attention on the budgetary problems and to adopt decision N-20, "Financial Situation of UNIDO," by which it approved a supplementary estimate of $3.1 million for the regular budget in the fiscal period 1986–1987, in accordance with Article 14.5 of the Constitution.[5] It was the amount of the net shortfall in the resources of UNIDO. As the decision indicated, the shortfall resulted from the depreciation of the dollar, though evidently it was not the only cause. The General Conference urged member states to pay the supplementary assessed contributions as soon as possible, whereas those that were in arrears were urged to pay the regular contributions without any delay.

Following the recommendations of the Programme and Budget Committee and the Industrial Development Board (IDB), the General Conference decided to terminate assessment of contributions in only one currency, the U.S. dollar.[6] As mentioned above, of particular importance was that the secretariat's expenses in Vienna were in Austrian schillings. Therefore, owing to the rise of the exchange rate of the latter, the assessments evaluated in U.S. dollars were much higher than expected. The General Conference decided to split the assessments into two parts: the one paid in U.S. dollars (28.2 percent), or equivalent at the fixed exchange rate, and the larger part in schillings (71.8 percent).

In another rather unusual decision, the General Conference authorized the continued existence of the working capital fund, which had been designed by the first session in 1985 as a temporary measure just for the period immediately after UNIDO's reorganization. The authorization of the fund pursued the task of cushioning shortfalls in regular assessments and voluntary contributions and implicitly endorsed the situation when many countries were in arrears, but those cases were not drawn to the attention of the General Conference as a separate issue on the agenda. The fund was approved in the amount of $9 million, at the same level it had existed since the reorganization of UNIDO.[7] Another purpose of the fund was to finance unforeseen and extraordinary expenditures; however, the money spent had to be reimbursed later.

At the second session of the General Conference, a considerable activity was displayed by the African countries, which succeeded in rightfully calling special attention to the disastrous situation many of them faced. As was stressed during the discussions, in Africa industrial development had not shown any substantial progress at all, as compared to a number of developing states in Asia and Latin America. In most of the African countries, the industrial sector of their economies had stagnated throughout the 1980s. It was not at all unexpected, while many African countries continued to rely on sectors of traditional exports of raw materials and agricultural production, whereas the world market for those commodities did not expand. Moreover, taking into consideration a high birth rate, quite a number of African states had a negative net economic growth in the 1980s; a small number of exceptions, such as Ghana, had successfully implemented the program of economic revival worked out by the International Monetary Fund and the World Bank group.

Therefore, the General Conference paid special attention to African countries' dissatisfaction and grievances about unfavorable terms of trade and insufficient economic assistance. As a matter of exception, the Conference singled out the Memorandum on Industrial Development in Africa, adopted by the special meeting of the conference of African ministers of industry in Addis Ababa in October 1987.

Evidently, since the adoption of the Lima and Delhi Declarations and Plans of Actions in 1975 and 1980 respectively, the position of many developing countries on issues of international economic relations had undergone very substantial changes. Gone were most of belligerent slogans and appeals putting blame on Western countries for poor economic management in the third world.

The Memorandum on Industrial Development in Africa was quite a moderate document that did not accuse the Western countries of instigating economic disarray in Africa through unjust price discrepancies or attack multinational corporations, as had been done in the Lima and Delhi Declarations and Plans of Action. Evidently, those documents in reality did not contribute to strengthening cooperation with the West, and on the contrary, a confrontational approach was counterproductive. Therefore, the memorandum was designed to find realistic ways out of the morass the African countries found themselves in.

For instance, in expressing concern about Africa's total external debt of $200 billion, the memorandum did not call for its immediate revision at the expense of the Western countries. However, the memorandum routinely accused multinational corporations, saying, "The international technological set-up, which is mainly controlled by multinational companies, impedes a speedy and adequate acquisition and development of technology in Africa."[8]

The General Conference took "note with interest" of the memorandum by its resolution N-3. As a matter of concrete action, the Conference adopted both provisions of resolution 5 on institutional arrangements.[9] The Director-General was requested to study the feasibility of establishing a special UNIDO regional office for Africa to coordinate all activities of this organization on that continent. Secondly, it was recommended to increase the number of senior industrial development field advisers in Africa, particularly in the least-developed countries (so far their number did not exceed thirty experts).

Although the provision of establishing a regional office did not meet serious objections of member states, it seems hardly convincing that such a measure, which provided for further administrative expenditures but did not change the methods of providing assistance, could really improve realization of projects in African countries.

With a more general profile, the General Conference addressed the plight of many third world countries that face difficult economic situations by adopting resolution N-1, "Strengthening of Economic and Technical Cooperation among Developing Countries." The sense of the resolution was that third world countries should not rely solely on assistance from the North but should cooperate among themselves to alleviate many of their urgent problems related to industrial development, including mutual participation in financial matters. By virtue of this resolution, the General Conference recommended that "UNIDO strengthen the exchange of information among developing countries on their need for and offer of economic and technical cooperation with a view to intensifying their mutual cooperation in the industrial sphere."[10]

I pointed out differences of approaches, which concerned a surprisingly small number of resolutions; consensus was much more typical. On the whole, the second session of the General Conference addressed, in a business-like manner, most of the issues that the organization was facing and resolved them to the satisfaction of almost all countries.

In my opinion the second session in the whole could be assessed as a moderate success of the organization. There was practically no bitter confrontation, which took place in the 1970s on a wide range of issues, and with a few exceptions decisions and resolutions were adopted by consensus, which pointed to a certain level of preparedness of proposed drafts. A business-like approach was more or less characteristic for this session. It certainly helped heal the old wounds left after a controversial third General Conference in New Delhi that helped to identify the matters on which the major groups of countries disagreed.

AIMING AT "DEPOLITICIZING" THE AGENDA

The third regular session of the General Conference took place in Vienna from November 20 to 24, 1989. This session was a step toward maximizing UNIDO's activities without wasting effort on controversial political issues dividing different groups of countries. In comparison with the Bangkok session, the number of states actually represented grew by about 25 percent and was well over 100. This time not all the decisions of the General Conference were adopted by consensus, which had happened in Bangkok two years earlier. Of twenty-two resolutions, two were not adopted by consensus. However, even that was a rather good achievement. At the previous session out of twelve resolutions that the General Conference adopted, three were not adopted by consensus. I shall address the cases of the lack of consensus below.

The Conference discussed once again the financial difficulties of the organization, although they had slightly lessened by that time. Both major financial innovations introduced earlier, regarding a split-currency system of assessments and the working capital fund, were reconfirmed. The Conference decided to continue the application of the split-currency system, which helped alleviate the monetary shortages that the organization had experienced after its transformation into a specialized agency. The working fund, too, was left at the same level of $9 million and with the same purposes.[11] Probably those were rather reasonable decisions while thanks to the working capital the organization had survived in the worst times in terms of its budgetary situation.

The issue of appointing a new Director-General of UNIDO aroused no confrontation. The General Conference adopted the recommendation of the IDB and reappointed by acclamation the then Director-General, Domingo Siazon, Jr. (Philippines), for a new term of four years. This appointment differed from what had happened in UNIDO's past in similar situations when the election of an executive head for the new term was becoming a rather complicated and controversial issue. Both previous heads of the secretariat, Rahman Khan (Algeria) and Abdel-Rahman (Egypt), had aroused more than enough dissatisfaction on the part of Western countries and even the Eastern bloc countries because of their alleged backing of third world countries' unbalanced demands and rather authoritarian styles of managing administrative issues.

The new head of UNIDO's secretariat had displayed a more balanced approach toward positions of all major groups of countries, leaving less dissatisfaction and complaints regarding the role of the Director-General. As it had been demonstrated in many other specialized agencies, the overall positive attitude of member states to the accomplishment of the executive head contributes a lot to the confidence in an international organization.

The General Conference adopted a number of resolutions that had been basically already approved in a slightly different version at the preceding sessions and that became a kind of routine confirmation of the stand taken earlier. Among them were resolutions on "Economic and Technical Cooperation Among Developing Countries," "Development and Transfer of Technology," "Mobilization of Financial Resources for Industrial Development," "Industrial Development Decade for Africa," and "Industrialization of Least Developed Countries."

A breakthrough was achieved on two issues that had been tabled at two previous sessions of the General Conference: the Namibian problem and the South African Liberation movements recognized by the Organization of African Unity (OAU), as they were touched upon by UNIDO's assistance.

The resolution "Technical Assistance to the Namibian People" was adopted by consensus this time, although two years earlier in Bangkok, a similar resolution was voted for by seventy-six states with one against (the United States) and sixteen abstaining (Western countries). The text of the resolution was remarkably identical, but for a provision which concerned who had the right to represent Namibia. In the resolution adopted in Bangkok, the General Conference stressed that "the formulation and execution of technical assistance to the Namibian people should be undertaken in close cooperation with the South West Africa People's Organization [SWAPO], the sole and authentic representative of the Namibian people," which evidently was not an indisputable assertion from the point of view of many Western countries. In the new version, adopted by consensus in 1989, any reference to SWAPO was deleted, and the addressee of the assistance was referred to as "independent Namibia."

Certainly, the change of position on the Namibian issue was not the achievement of the General Conference held in Vienna but just reflected the realities, in view of the plebiscite in Namibia and the preparation for admission of this country to the UN and specialized agencies. However, it shows how UNIDO expediently reacted to the changes, in particular admitting Namibia as a member only one month after the referendum, by a special decision relieving it from financial contributions for an unidentified period of time and adopting an unopposed resolution concerning assistance to the new state.

Another change toward a unified approach of all member states concerned the issue of assistance to the South African liberation movements recognized by the OAU; the resolution was passed by consensus. In Bangkok it had been voted for by seventy-nine states, with two against (the United States and the United Kingdom) and sixteen abstaining (Western countries). In this case the developments in South Africa had some say, but they were not very significant. The difference was in the documents. In the 1989 version, adopted by the third session, one paragraph, the most disputed one, was just deleted, as compared to the earlier version voted for at the second session.

This paragraph stated that UNIDO "strongly condemns the inhuman policies of the apartheid regime of South Africa and demands that it create a conducive situation for UNIDO technical assistance to the South African national liberation movements recognized by OAU."[12]

Evidently, the intention of avoiding counterproductive confrontation on issues that only marginally concern UNIDO's activities, but that were well in focus of a number of bodies of the UN, bore witness to increased maturity of political process in this organization.

Contrary to those two resolutions, no breakthrough progress was achieved on the issue of assistance to the Palestinian people. As had happened at the first and the second sessions of the General Conference, the resolution was not passed by consensus and was opposed by the United States and Israel. However, the number of states that abstained, all of them Western countries, decreased dramatically from fifteen to just one. It was also a consequence of changes in the wording of the resolutions.

In the version adopted in 1989, any mention of the Palestine Liberation Organization, which had usually been considered an illegal if not a criminal organization by the United States and a number of Western countries, was deleted. In the earlier versions there was the provision requesting UNIDO "to sustain and increase its technical assistance to the Palestinian people in close cooperation and coordination with the Palestine Liberation Organization."[13]

Thus, one more political dispute was slightly relieved, although in the new version there still remained a strong wording against the Israeli occupation, for instance, the General Conference "affirms that the Israeli occupation is hindering the basic requirements for the development of the economy of the occupied Palestinian territories, including the industrial sector."[14]

One more resolution was not passed by consensus at the third session of the General Assembly, that on "External Debt and Industrial Development." The United States voted against it, but there were no other objections or abstentions. A similar resolution had been passed by the second session by consensus. The main difference between the new and the previous versions of the resolution was the provision of a possible writing off of debts. The resolution in N-4 said that the General Conference "appeals to the international community to continue their efforts to bring about a substantial reduction in the external debt of the developing countries, particularly writing off the debt of the least developed among them."[15]

Such a provision, which did not arouse much doubt in principle, could not be supported by the United States, the largest supplier of development credit. The United States did not want to create precedents or to make unnecessary hints in a General Conference resolution at a possibility of writing off debts as a matter of the revised international economic order.

On the whole, the third session of the General Conference was once again quite a success; it did not lead to confrontation on major issues, as had happened in UNIDO's past. It addressed, in a business-like manner, most of the issues that the organization was facing and resolved them to the satisfaction of almost all countries. The only country that had real reasons not to be pleased with the outcome was Israel, as the General Conference once again reaffirmed its stand on the issue of the occupied territories, stressing the legitimacy of claims that the Palestinian people laid against the occupation. However, in the context of decisions made by the UN General Assembly, the Economic and Social Council (ECOSOC), the United Nations Development Programme (UNDP), and other bodies of the UN, such a position of the UNIDO conference was quite natural, if not routine.

RAISON D'ÊTRE; IS THERE A NEW IMPETUS?

There is much controversy in evaluating the accomplishments of world organizations, even with such established credentials as the UN Academic views differ not necessarily as a reflection of their governments' attitude towards a particular organization, although they are not deprived from its influence.[16]

As could be presumed from UNIDO's general mandate, the ultimate goal of the organization could be creating a regime of industrial cooperation. Using the notion of a regime proposed by John Ruggie, it should be "a set of mutual expectations, rules and regulations, plans, organizational energies and financial commitments, which have been accepted by a group of states."[17]

However, creating such a regime could be considered only as a very remote goal. The organization lacks effectiveness ("ability of the states to use the routines enshrined in principles, norms, rules and procedures") and coherence ("mutual complementarily of its principles, norms, rules and procedures") as defined by Ernst Haas to set requisites of a developed regime.[18] Evidently, UNIDO does not satisfy such requirements and has not secured a regime of industrial cooperation. All the above-described modest performance of UNIDO could raise the *raison d'étre* issue of that organization and of its usefulness.

As a complex matter there is probably no one-sided answer to that question. It would be different if a certain approach is chosen. There is more than one viewpoint from which to evaluate the performance of the organization, depending on criteria chosen.

The technical assistance could be scrutinized as such. A purely economic approach based on Western criteria of enterprise performance would suggest that UNIDO-executed projects do not have the expected return and are not efficient enough. The ratio of supplementary expenses is rather high; the final result, especially in terms of industrial production, is not significant. However, I think that economic performance, notwithstanding how important it is, is far from being the only relevant one in this case.

There is an international agreement how to cope with some fields of activities, for instance, postal service, regulation of telecommunications and of sea and air transportation, some health problems, refugees, emergency assistance in cases of calamity, and famine. This is evidently not UNIDO's case.

UNIDO's area of cooperation does not offer easy and speedy reconciliation of diverging interests of groups of countries. This idea is well stressed by Maurice Bertrand: ". . . in areas of peace, development and international economy, there is no room for joint management, there can only be negotiations, which may, with a great deal of effort, lead to mutual concessions, but in which nothing is won in advance."[19] UNIDO cannot be an organization within areas of consensus, as it has been achieved in a number of other cases.

But should UNIDO then be abolished altogether on the grounds that it is unfortunate to deal with problems promising few chances for consensus? I think no, especially when so many countries have vested interests in that world organization. Any attempt to dismantle or weaken it would certainly meet resistance in developing countries and would be politically costly and counterproductive for the industrialized North. The conduct of the U.S. State Department is yet another confirmation of this judgment. The realistic options are how to make the organization more useful. In that respect, notwithstanding positive changes already occurred, a lot is still to be done.

Maurice Bertrand developes his view: "In the economic field, what today is really important for governments and peoples of all countries is to facilitate the establishment of the conditions of economic prosperity and to avoid the risks of unemployment, inflation, recession, and the social and political difficulties attached to their economic decreases. A better understanding of the conditions of economic cooperation through a better harmonization of national economic policies is obviously indispensable in this regard, and this is exactly the domain in which a universal organization can be effective."[20] However, that harmonization should be deprived from unnecessary politicization based on old ideological and related considerations.

Another question concerns costs. The argument that UNIDO as one of the UN-related agencies is too costly for the world community is, in my opinion, not strong. The whole UN system (voluntary and assessed contributions), with yearly costs about $7 billion in the early 1990s, even if we forget about its return in services and in kind which nevertheless exists, is only one quarter of the budget of the city of New York and only 0.004 percent of the annual world income.

Douglas Williams writes about specialized agencies on that issue: "The press often depicts both the budgets themselves and the waste as gigantic. This is untrue on both scores. The budgets represent a very small share of world public expenditure, and although waste and scandals occur and are to be entirely condemned, they probably occur less frequently than in most national administrations, — or for that matter in many private concerns."[21]

Some expenses regarding securing international stability, economic included, are necessary. In today's world, international economic stability is increasingly important for the peoples' community at large. As stressed by Stanley Hoffmann, a very real kind of crisis exists, and "that will have to be avoided: large scale economic disruptions, either in the relations between the rich and the poor. . . . Enormous progress remains to be made both in respect to the regulation of transnational activity there and in relations between advanced and underdeveloped countries. . . ."[22] Evidently, preserving global stability cannot be deprived of necessary expenses and is to be supported by the advanced industrialized nations.

Not quite surprisingly, UNIDO's technical assistance was constantly on the rise throughout its activities when it emerged in the early 1970s as another channel of technical assistance. The rate of growth was in the range of 10–20 percent, which was substantially more than the average level of inflation. In real terms the expansion was quite stable and considerable. The most spectacular single year was 1988 when the yearly increase was 22 percent, although it was partially explained by the fact that during the process of UNIDO's conversion in the mid 1980s the expansion had slowed down.[23]

The output of UNIDO's technical assistance continues to rise. The total value of projects earmarked for implementation reached an unprecedented level of $253 million in 1989, which implied that in the future the amount of UNIDO's assistance should continue to grow.[24]

All these indicators put UNIDO into the fifth position among the UN specialized agencies providing technical assistance, according to the volume of operations and of budgetary resources. The overall functioning of UNIDO permitted the Director-General to state in the 1989 yearly report: "The improved performance of the Organization was ... honored by Member States' growing trust in the ability of UNIDO to provide an innovative and effective response to the industrial problems of the developing countries."[25]

UNIDO has been increasing direct cooperation at an enterprise level, which is not quite typical for projects realized by the specialized agencies providing technical assistance. For instance, in a report by the Director-General (September 1990), this feature of UNIDO's projects was specifically stressed. "Business-oriented industrial cooperation at the enterprise level is gaining increasing importance as an effective modality of international cooperation in the field of industry. During the past 15 years UNIDO played an important pioneering role in promoting such business-oriented cooperation."[26]

Further, UNIDO has developed a network of Investment Promotion Services. As stressed in the report submitted by the Director-General on activities related to the mobilization of financial resources for industrial development, representatives of the World Bank group took part in a number of UNIDO investment forums organized in developing countries.[27]

The UNIDO program of work was strengthened as a result of the regional structure introduced in the Industrial Investment Division (with units for Africa, Asia and the Pacific, the Arab countries and Europe, and Latin America and the Caribbean). The existing network of Investment Promotion Services includes nine offices in different countries. The Director-General reiterated: "The staff of the Investment Promotion Service offices are in close touch with business communities and development agencies in their host countries, and have established data banks with information on companies interested in industrial partnerships in developing countries and the type of opportunities they are seeking."[28]

Promotion of investments is becoming an important direction of UNIDO's activities. Thus, in 1986–1987 UNIDO successfully promoted 112 industrial investment projects valued at $391 million. For 1989 alone, the achievement was 143 projects valued at $556 million.[29] It far exceeds the volume of UNIDO's proper projects.

REMOVING BOTTLENECKS: WITH A VIEW TO A BROADER INTERNATIONAL RECOGNITION

An unresolved problem still remains the relatively low level of quality and development in UNIDO's projects, according to different evaluations. This problem or the lack of significant improvement in the situation in the long run made the secretariat turn to external expertise to understand where the bottlenecks were and how to streamline technical assistance. An independent team of experts was created and presented its report in 1989.

This team of experts identified a number of problems, among them the constraints of a relatively small budget, which made it necessary to be highly selective in choosing priorities, implying that the stage of identifying and preparing the projects needed considerable improvement. The experts proposed establishing a central program analysis function and program committee to refine cost identification and improve control and flexibility of the operational budget. The report placed a special emphasis on determining the size of the regular budget subsidy to the operational budget and presenting relevant budget proposals along user-friendly lines.

In view of continuing criticism of UNIDO's performance in operational field, Director-General Domingo Siazon announced a new series of structural changes, which was the second one after a considerable reshuffle immediately after the conversion of the organization. The changes were implemented step by step in 1989–1990. Among them was the creation of the Strategy, Policy and Planning Office, the Central Reference and Monitoring Unit, and the Project Personnel Recruitment and Administration Service. The changes did not signify a breakthrough in UNIDO's performance, as evidenced by continued discussion in the secretariat of its ideal structure. Given that the structural flaws evidently were not removed, the General Conference at its third session even requested the Director-General to present a report at its next session in 1991 on his overall vision of appropriate organizational and staff structures of UNIDO.

However, in my opinion, structural changes and reshuffling of the secretariat's departments can hardly improve the performance of the organization. Since the establishment of the organization its secretariat has undergone at least six major restructurings, including two under the present Director-General. There was no clear evidence that any one of them brought about a breakthrough in the performance of the organization.

Notwithstanding some difficulties in the organization's work, its reputation, in particular in the third world, did not suffer too much. It might be evidenced by the fact that in terms of continued growth of membership, international recognition of UNIDO made further progress by the 1990s. At the third session the General Conference admitted three new members, Namibia, Vaniatu, and Tonga, increasing UNIDO's membership to 151 states. Only the UN itself and a small number of specialized agencies have more members than UNIDO, which could be to the credit of the organization. There was an exception in the sense of one voluntary withdrawal, that of Australia in 1989.

As another feature implying international recognition, the number of permanent representatives of member countries reached 120 by the 1990s, of which seventy-six are located in Vienna, twenty-one in Geneva, thirteen at Bonn, four at Brussels, two each in Paris and Rome, and one each at Bern and Bratislava.[30]

On the other hand, the number of national committees for UNIDO in member countries reached sixty-three by the 1990s. The chain of national committees for UNIDO started to get a kind of coordination. For instance, in October 1989 representatives of the national committees in European countries held a meeting in Warsaw to exchange experiences on the structure and functions of those bodies. The meeting analyzed the acquired experience and prepared recommendations for consequent coordination of action in Europe.

The secretariat marked a milestone in 1989 — the establishment of national committees for UNIDO in Moscow and Beijing. Owing to immense territorial and human resources, both the USSR (Russia from 1991) and China were important for UNIDO's activities. However, in the case of the USSR, even before its formal dissolution, the establishment of the national committee was to be developed on a republican level. Preparation was made for the creation of a similar body in Tbilissi, capital of Georgia. Hypothetically it might have aroused Moscow's objections on the premises that Georgia was then just one Union republic, but it did not happen because the central control was slipping from the Kremlin. Georgia proclaimed independence immediately after a referendum in April 1991.

As a matter of implementing Article 19.1(a) of the UNIDO Constitution, in the late 1980s as evident advance was made in developing legal links with other international organizations. UNIDO concluded a relationship agreement with the International Labor Organization (1987); International Fund for Agricultural Development, United Nations Educational, Scientific and Cultural Organization, and the World Health Organization (all three in 1989); and the Food and Agriculture Organization (1990). In compliance with Article 19.1(b) of the Constitution, UNIDO has concluded agreements with a number of nongovernmental organizations. Among those more important are the Organization of African Unity and the Latin American Economic System. By the beginning of the 1990s, UNIDO had established legal ties with seventeen nongovernmental organizations.

The fifth session of the General Conference will take place in 1993. As the agenda of the session is to be discussed by the Industrial Development Board, there might arise procedural and organizational problems, which have not been addressed or resolved by UNIDO. There are yet no sufficient precedents which leave room for different interpretations. Let me present some of arguments that might concern the forthcoming discussion of some issues in UNIDO, as well as in many other UN-related bodies.

In view of the reunification of Germany in late 1990, the German Democratic Republic (GDR) as a state ceased to exist. However, as applied to UNIDO, the GDR was included in group D of the Annex to the Constitution, which enumerated all member states. There should be a change in the list of member countries of UNIDO, which requires a special consideration of the issue and a decision by a two-thirds majority. Dividing all member states into four groups, needed for setting IDB quotas, was done in 1965 and has not been reconsidered or seriously challenged since, even during the process of UNIDO's reorganization.

Strictly speaking, the Federal Republic of Germany is the legal successor to the GDR and hypothetically could claim its place among the members of group D. But in reality at least two arguments weigh strongly against such a theoretical situation. First, Germany already has a place among the members of group B (Western countries); including the country in two groups simultaneously would be erroneous. Second, the argument of geographical distribution was from the very foundation of the organization interpreted as implying a certain pattern of social and economic system common to the countries in the same list. From this point of view also, the GDR should be deleted from group D. I believe that most probably Germany will not raise any specific claims and will let the place of the GDR be simply deleted from group D by the General Conference.

When it actually happened, as a result the number of states in group D decreased from ten to nine (Albania, Bulgaria, Belarus, Czechoslovakia, Hungary, Poland, Rumania, the Ukraine, and the USSR). However, this temporary decision became almost immediately outdated as the Soviet Union was dissolved in December 1991, and up to a dozen new states will evidently apply for membership in UNIDO.

On the other hand, Albania, which had frozen its participation in all UNIDO activities for more than twenty years, intends to revive its membership and therefore might claim its place in the electoral process for participating in the Industrial Development Board and other bodies of UNIDO. At least the assessed contribution of Albania was restored in the current program of work and budget of the organization.

As regards the future of this group itself, so far not a single one of its members has expressed a desire to leave it, even if the internal situation in Eastern Europe no longer links those countries to a centrally planned economy, which was at the origins of this group. The explanation is a pragmatic approach toward the decision-making process. Staying in group D, each of them has almost twice the probability of being a member of the Industrial Development Board and of the Programme and Budget Committee than the average member of group B (Western countries). A similar situation exists for elections of working bodies at the sessions of the General Conference, where they actually have an advantage. The same situation is true for the new states, former republics of the dissolved Soviet Union.

Notwithstanding radical changes of the political regimes in Eastern European and the Commonwealth countries, group D is about to stay, at least for the time being. There is much less certainty regarding the unanimity of this group. In the past countries of group D displayed a rare unified approach to most issues discussed in UNIDO, presented their draft documents approved by all of them, and never criticized each other. As it appears the times of such a remarkable unanimity are gone for Eastern European and Central Asian countries.

On the other hand, there is no certainty on how the unified positions of Russia, the Ukraine, Belarus, and other states — former republics of the Soviet Union — might be in the light of enforcing the right of independent foreign policy. So far, there has been no difference in their positions in UNIDO, but it is not secure in the future. Another matter that might become imminent is applications for membership in UN bodies and in specialized agencies, UNIDO included, by the republics of the Commonwealth. The republics already enforce a provision of an independent representation of its interests and missions abroad, embodied in the Commonwealth Pact. Having identified the existence of a problem involving serious legal consequences, I do not intend to address those issues here, because this is a part of a far larger topic of participation of the former Soviet Union republics and now independent countries in international organizations.

In the late 1980s and early 1990s UNIDO, as well as many other UN bodies, reached a new stage characterized by abating harsh ideological barriers that had divided the world in the past. The main division between the two opposing geo-political blocs, the one of free-market Western democracies and the other of "socialist" countries, seems to dramatically disappear.

The Eastern bloc as such does not exist any more, as in all East European countries the Communist rule has already fallen. Russia and other states formerly in the Soviet Union are no longer adversaries of the West in issues of world economic development. It might be only the beginning of a new period, which came to existence rather unexpectedly, because few people, with rare exceptions like Zbigniew Brzezinski, could foresee how quickly the Communist rule in Eastern Europe and the USSR could be scrapped; but it happened in 1989–1991.

The new situation in the world has just started to show its fruits in the political field, as evidenced by the combined efforts and almost common policy line of the West and Moscow in the Gulf War in 1991.

For the first time the Security Council, after decades of counter-productive mutual vetoing by Western countries and the USSR, started to function as it was designed to work.

In any case, the dramatic changes in the world might help depoliticize assistance to the third world provided through the UN bodies, UNIDO included, and thus make it more streamlined and efficient, aimed at addressing the global economic issues of development at large.

NOTES

1. IDB. 6/4.
2. GC. 3/26.
3. GC. 3/26.
4. Apart from decisions discussed here, it adopted thirty-four decisions dealing with the inner functioning of the organization, including the program and the budget for 1988–1989, financial and personnel regulations, and the medium-term plan for 1990–1995. Twelve resolutions on various aspects of international industrial cooperation were also adopted, among them the resolution "Mobilization of Financial Resources for Industrial Development," which was in certain respects a novelty. It dealt with the expansion of UNIDO's cooperation with international financial organizations to more actively mobilize financial resources for industrialization of developing countries. In order to further develop the provision of the legislative act of the seventh United Nations Conference on Trade and Development session a resolution, "External Debt an Industrial Development," was adopted.
5. GC. 2/Dec. 20.
6. GC. 2/Dec. 21.
7. GC. 2/Dec. 27.
8. GC. 2/Res., Annex, p. 5.
9. GC. 2/Res. 5.
10. GC. 2/Res. 1.
11. GC. 3/INF. 3, p. 1.
12. GC. 2/Res. 8.
13. GC. 2/Res. 7.
14. GC. 3/Inf. 3.
15. Ibid.
16. Maurice Bertrand writes, ". . . the intellectual confusion about world organizations is now complete: they are credited with an importance they do not possess; they are blamed for not doing what they are not given means to do; no one understands what they really do; faults are often imaginary and ascribed to them, while their real faults go unnoticed; mythical explanations are invented to explain their ineffectiveness; and finally, there is very little recognition of the few significant results they really do achieve." M. Bertrand, *The Third Generation*, p. 26.
17. J. Ruggie, "International Responses to Technology," p. 570.
18. E. Haas, "Regime Decay: Conflict Management and International Organizations," *International Organization*, 1983, pp. 192–93.

19. M. Bertrand, *The Third Generation*, pp. 29–30.
20. Ibid., p. 3.
21. D. Williams, *Specialized Agencies*, p. 239.
22. S. Hoffmann, *Janus and Minerva; Essays in the Theory and Practice of International Politics*, 1987, p. 310.
23. IDB. 6/10.
24. IDB. 6/10.
25. IDB. 6/10.
26. IDB. 6/22.
27. IDB. 7/22, p. 1.
28. IDB. 7/22.
29. IDB. 7/22, p. 2.
30. IDB. 6/10.

Conclusion

Stable functioning of an international organization is founded on observing the balance of interests between member countries. The interests of key groups of countries coincide in the field of industrial cooperation only on a rather limited scale. Overlapping interests in the United Nations Industrial Development Organization's (UNIDO) framework correspond basically to a limited assistance to industrial development in the third world countries on the part of Western and to a much lesser extent former Eastern bloc countries. The activities of UNIDO are oriented for this reason only on technical assistance to developing countries and aim to meet some of their requirements. At the same time, the Western and the former centrally planned countries had until recently different standpoints on the forms and types of assistance. As a result, international assistance reflected more or less the aims of both groups of countries. At the same time, the third world countries, due to their numerical superiority, frequently imposed their terms in UNIDO documents. The organization did not therefore display a worldwide approach to solving global problems of comprehensive industrial development at large.

In view mostly of the lack of special common interest on the part of the North in strengthening UNIDO, the place of the organization in the UN system did not in practice fully conform with the tasks set in its Constitution and earlier in General Assembly resolution 2152 (XXI). UNIDO could not in full play a key role in the efforts of the UN system in providing assistance to industrial development, and its functions are often performed by other UN organs and specialized agencies. The role of UNIDO in utilizing United Nations Development Programme resources remains relatively small.

UNIDO has had quite a persistent reputation as a rather inefficient, if not worthless, organization, unable to tackle the global problems of underdevelopment and industrial cooperation on a large scale. This poor reputation, especially among some leading Western countries, developed mostly as a result of two Declarations and Plans of Action, adopted by UNIDO's General Conferences in Lima (1975) and New Delhi (1980), as well as from a low level of project efficiency. However, in the 1980s its reputation improved slightly, which permitted finalizing UNIDO's transformation into a specialized agency. UNIDO largely put aside most of the unrealistic demands of the third world countries, aiming at imposing a controversial concept of a new international economic order. Thus, three sessions of the General Conference in the latter half of the 1980s were marked by a more unified approach of different countries to the issues on UNIDO's agenda. In particular the second session (1987) and the third session (1989) helped restore Western confidence; however, doubts regarding the overall efficiency of UNIDO's programs still remain.

The role of UNIDO in solving problems of industrial development of third world countries is rather modest. Despite the positive role of technical assistance programs, implementation of usually separate, small-scale projects by the organization having limited resources cannot have a substantial effect on the industrial development of third world countries. UNIDO's efforts thus become submerged in the multitude of other unsolved problems. Therefore, the organization should make emphasis on the types of activities its structure is most fit for: promoting investments, exchange of information on industrial matters, consulting, and preparing national engineer cadres in the third world.

I believe that the plenary organ (General Conference) is losing much of its political importance after the conversion of UNIDO. Its agenda is decided by the Industrial Development Board (IDB), most drafts, especially if they concern financial matters, are thoroughly scrutinized by the Programme and Budget Committee (PBC) and the IDB. The room for action by the General Conference is limited to introducing changes into drafts; discussions are forced to be very generalized for the mere lack of time (one-week session every two years). I think, however, that the correlation of credentials between the principal organs of UNIDO should be further reviewed with the aim of empowering the Industrial Development Board with greater functions. The General Conference should be finally stripped of unnecessary purely political issues and should only supervise the overall functioning of the organization. The concrete issues should be decided upon by the Industrial Development Board, after an advisory opinion of the Program and Budget Committee.

The conversion of UNIDO from an organ of the General Assembly into a specialized agency, which took several years and was completed in 1986, brought about serious financial problems for UNIDO. The new status of the organization terminated the reliance on the UN budgetary resources while UNIDO's own financial position was rather fragile. Inflow of both assessed and voluntary contributions did not proceed smoothly. The budgetary situation particularly deteriorated in the mid 1980s because of a drastic rise in the exchange rate of Austrian schillings to U.S. dollars. This, in practice, reduced the real volume of contributions for the Vienna-based organization. Nevertheless, in a number of decisive measures, which didn't necessarily meet consensus, the organization was able to overcome the worst of the budgetary crisis and to improve the stability of its performance. However, I do not think that UNIDO's resources should be expanded, at least for the time being, as the organization should thoroughly display the positive changes in its performance, which it has started to gradually introduce.

UNIDO's projects continue to be an object of criticism because of the relatively low level of their efficiency, slow implementation, and rigid procedures of approving and planning far in advance. Resource allocation remains dispersed and therefore is rather insignificant in terms of an overall impact. A real bottleneck continues to be the fact that most developing countries consider assistance projects as grants that do not necessarily require a high level of efficiency. Economically, UNIDO's projects are far below the performance of the World Bank group and provide one more argument against technical assistance.

In my view, the regulations of UNIDO's operational activities must be revised. The scale and significance of the operational activity of the organization and, consequently, other forms of activity will remain limited so long as this activity remains in the form of technical assistance and not linked closely with economic laws. At the same time, industrial development as the key direction of economic progress requires not so much technical assistance as large-scale promotion on easy commercial terms. UNIDO's operational activity could be transferred, even in a rather short time, to partial self-financing through crediting of projects, without interest charges or on favorable conditions, which does not contradict its constitution. In this case the overall volume of expenditures on projects could seriously increase and the level of implementation improve. I also think that UNIDO should strengthen ties with the World Bank group to cooperate in concrete projects. In particular an agreement on cooperation and coordination with those institutions would be helpful.

UNIDO lacks a sufficiently effective international mechanism for influencing (even by recommending) the policies of developing countries in the field of industrial development along the principles of free-market economics. The participation of developing countries in the elaboration of international documents on problems of industrial cooperation is expressed mainly in the declaration of general intents, but in practice this does not lead to adequate concrete actions on their part.

UNIDO operational activity, conducted on a gratuitous basis according to its legal regulations and accounting for more than a half of the expenditures of the organization, yields comparatively modest economic effects. The cost of services and commodities provided in the form of assistance is frequently not compared with economically justified expenditures, and assistance is provided at heightened prices. Developing countries do not receive enough incentives for using them with high efficiency and coordinating them with their programs of economic development.

A promising direction in the development of UNIDO's operational functions could be granting the right to member countries to make a part of voluntary contributions in kind, including deliveries of equipment and services of their specialists. In the conditions of instability in the world financial situation, and in view of disparities in foreign exchange, resources in the possession of member countries, this could lead to the expansion of the volume of assistance provided by a considerable number of countries. There could be also introduced terms of partial compensation of such expenditures in the form of deliveries of raw materials and industrial output obtained in the process of implementation of such projects, which could accrue to UNIDO and be used for promoting its subsequent projects. This could give broader scale, greater stability, and more purpose to UNIDO's operations and focus the attention of recipient countries on the economic effect of such projects.

The system of consultations within UNIDO's framework, the first of its kind in the UN system, could evolve into a unique forum where the developing countries could have broader access to technology and industrial information meeting the highest world standards. In view of a new interpretation of the respective documents, the system of consultations began to acquire the functions of mediation in establishing commercial contacts between governmental organizations of developing countries and Western industrial firms using this system to promote the movement of their commodities. However, because of the imposing expenses on the system of consultations, its further development in this direction could enter into conflict with the tasks of UNIDO and endanger its financial situation.

Thus far UNIDO has made inadequate use of important channels for giving assistance to developing countries as designated in its Constitution, such as training of national engineer personnel and elaboration, jointly with the governments of developing countries and at their request, of economically grounded models of industrial development with due regard for the local conditions and drafting of respective comprehensive programs. More efforts in this direction would be desirable.

A promising direction in international law practice could be the elaboration of a standard industrial investments code, which could be used by particular developing countries as the basis for enacting a respective internal legislative act. It could add to efforts made in this direction by the World Bank group. Such a legislative act regulating industrial investments, including foreign investments, could benefit many developing countries where the respective normative material has not yet been worked out sufficiently. A standard code of industrial investments would take into account the experience of different countries and proceed from principles worked out in different fields of international law, including international private law and international economic law.

UNIDO's regulating activity in the field of international industrial cooperation is still at its initial stage and embraces a rather limited number of general principles in this sphere of interstate relations. Even if UNIDO might not be the best mechanism for negotiating those matters and is certainly not the only option, it can contribute to such efforts. In general, it is imperative that considerable advancements in elaborating the norms of industrial cooperation and its codification be made. Such norm-setting activity of UNIDO could become a definite contribution to further development of economic ties between different groups of countries.

Notwithstanding a justified criticism of many of UNIDO's activities, it has become one of the most subscribed UN system bodies. By the early 1990s UNIDO's membership is still on the rise, surpassing 150 states and making it one of the most highly representative organizations, second only to the UN and a number of other specialized agencies. Functioning of UNIDO's organs based upon division of all members into four groups since the 1960s, according to geographic, economic, and political criteria, remain unchallenged and rather viable in principle. Although at present it is still functioning as it was conceived, the future of the group the East European countries seems to be jeopardized in the long run due to changes of political regimes in that region that occurred in the late 1980s. However, it can not reflect negatively on UNIDO's performance. The pending process of further depoliticization of that organization can offer new perspectives for UNIDO's future.

Selected Bibliography

Abi-Saab, G. Introduction, "La Notion d'organisation internationale: essai de synthèse." *Le concept d'organisation internationale.* 1980.

Abraham, M. *Perspectives on Modernization: Toward a General Theory of Third World Development.* 1980.

Abraham, N., et al. *The International Civil Service: Changing Role and Concepts.* 1980.

Addicks, G., and H. Bünning, *Ökonomische Strategien der Entwicklungspolitik.* 1979.

Ait Ouyahia, D. *Évolution de l'Organisation des Nations Unies pour le developpement industriel /ONUDI/.* 1980.

Ameri, H. *Politics and Process in the Specialized Agencies of the United Nations.* 1982.

Asher, R. *Development Assistance in the 70s, Alternatives for the United States.* 1970.

Bailey, S. *The Secretariat of the United Nations.* 1978.

Beatus, H. *Interessengruppen in internationalen Organisationen.* 1967.

Bedjaoui, M. *Pour un nouvel ordre économique international.* 1979.

Bermejo, R. *Vers un nouvel ordre économique international: Étude centrée sur les aspects juridiques.* 1982.

Bertrand, M. *The Third Generation World Organization.* 1989.

Blackmann, A. "Die Nichtrückwirkung völkerrechtlicher Verträge. Kommentar zu Article 38 der Wiener Vertragrechtskonvention." *Zeitschrift für ausländsches öffentliches Recht und Völkerrecht.* 1973.

Bouhassin, M. *Droit international de la coopération industrielle.* 1980.

Bouveresse, J. *Droit et politique du developpement et de la coopération.* 1990.

Burri, O. *Für ein Menschenheitsgewissen. UNO und Menschheit.* 1969.

Carreau, D., et al. *Droit international économique.* 1990.

Cassese, A. *Il diritto internazionale nel mondo contemporaneo.* 1984.

Chappey, J. "Les micro-états et les Nations Unies." *Annuaire français de droit international.* 1973.

Charvin, R. "L'ONUDI." *Revue générale du droit international public.* 1969, pp. 781–83.

Codding, G., Jr., and A. Rutkowski. *The International Telecommunications Union in a Changing World.* 1982.

Colard, D. *Le droit de la sécurité internationale.* 1987.

Colliard, C. *Institutions des relations internationales.* 1968.

Cox, R., et al. *The Anatomy of Influence: Decision-Making in International Organization.* 1973.

Doll, B. *Völkerrechtliche Kontinuitätsprobleme bei internationalen Organizationen.* 1967.

Drucker, P. "The Changed World Economy." *Foreign Affairs.* 1986, pp. 768–91.

Duffar, J. *Contribution à l'étude des privilèges et immunités des organizations internationales.* 1982.

Elias, T. *The Modern Law of Treaties.* 1974.

Elias, T. *The International Court of Justice and Some Contemporary Problems: Essays on International Law.* 1983.

Escher, R. *Friedliche Erledigung von Streitigkeiten nach dem System der Vereinten Nationen.* 1985.

Feur, G. *Droit international du développement.* 1985.

Franck, T. *Nation against Nation. What Happened to the UN Dream and What US Can Do about It.* 1985.

Fromuth, P., ed. *Successor Vision. The United Nations of Tomorrow.* 1988.

Galenson, W. *The International Labor Organization. An American View.* 1981.

Gallais-Hamonno, G. *Les nationalisations . . . a quél prix? Pourquoi taire?* 1977.

Gantam, S. *The Military Origins of Industrialization and International Trade Rivalry.* 1984.

Getz, H., and H. Jütterer. *Personal in internationalen Organizationen.* 1972.

Gill, G., and D. Law. *The Global Political Economy.* 1988.

Gunter, M. "The Problem of Mini-State Membership in the United Nations System." *Columbia Journal of Transnational Law.* 1977, pp. 476–77.

Haas, E. "Regime Decay: Conflict Management and International Organizations." *International Organization.* 1983, pp. 192–93.

Haggard, S., and B. Simmons. "Theories of International Regimes." *International Organization.* 1987, pp. 491–517.

Hill, M. *The United Nations System: Coordinating Its Economic and Social Work.* 1978.

Hoffmann, S. *Janus and Minerva; Essays in the Theory and Practice of International Politics.* 1987.

Ingram, J. *International Economic Problems.* 1986.

Jacobson, H. *Networks of Interdependence: International Organizations and the Global Political System.* 1986.

Keohane, R. *After Hegemony: Cooperation and Discord in the World Political Economy.* 1984.

Keohane, R., and J. Nye. "International Interdependence and Integration." *Handbook of Political Science.* 1975.

Kim, S. *The Quest for a Just World Order.* 1984.

Koo, W., Jr. *Voting Procedures in International Political Organizations.* 1947.

Köppinger, K. *Der Weg der UNIDO is die Selbständigkeit. Untersuchung zum Recht der internationalen Organisationen.* 1981.

Kratchowil, F., and J. Ruggie. "International Organization: a State of the Art and an Art of the State." *International Organization.* 1986.

Krivchikova, E. *Osnovy prava mezhdunarodnykh organizatsii* (The Basics of the Theory of Law of International Organizations). 1979.

Lachs, M. *Le rôle des organizations internationales dans la formation du droit international.* 1964.

Lauterpacht, H. *Private Law Sources and Analogies of International Law.* 1970.

Langrod, G. *The International Civil Service.* 1963.

Luard, E. *International Agencies. The Emerging Framework of Interdependence.* 1977.

Marchisio, S. *La cooperazione per lo sviluppo nel diritto delle Nazioni Unite.* 1977.

McLaren, R. *Civil Servants and Public Policy: A Comparative Study of International Secretariats.* 1980.

McNair, A. *The Law of Treaties.* 1938.

Meng, W. *Das Recht der internationalen Organisationen — eine Entwicklungsstufe des Völksrechts.* 1979.

Meron, T. *The United Nations Secretariat: The Rules and The Practice.* 1977.

Moravetsky, V. *Funkzii mezhdunarodnykh organisazii* (Functions of International Organizations). 1975.

Morse, D. *The Origin and Evolution of the ILO and Its Role in the World Community.* 1969.

Mortimore, R. *The Third World Coalition in International Politics.* 1984.

Nafziger, W. *The Economics of Developing Countries.* 1984.

Naidu, M. *Collective Security and the United Nations: A Definition of the U.N. Security System.* 1974.

Newfarmer, R., ed. *Profits, Progress and Poverty: Case Studies of International Industries in Latin America.* 1985.

Panella, L. *Gli emendementi agli atti istitutivi delle organizazzioni internazionali.* 1986.

Parry, C. *The Sources and Evidences of International Law.* 1965.

Pellet, A. *Droit international du développement.* 1978.

Pimentol, A. *Democratic World Government and the United Nations.* 1980.

Pines, D. *A World without a UN: What Would Happen if the UN Shut Down.* 1984.

Rahmatulla, K. *Implied Powers of the United Nations.* 1970.

Rajan, S. *The Expanding Jurisdiction of the United Nations.* 1982.

Remuli, A. *Tiers-Monde et émergence d'un nouvel ordre économique international.* 1975.

Reteur, P. *Introduction au droit des traités.* 1972.

Reymond, H., and S. Mailick. *International Personnel Politics and Practices.* 1985.

Riggs, R., and J. Plano. *The United Nations. International Organization and World Politics.* 1988.

Rubanik, K. *UNESCO kak spezializirovannoye uchrezhdenie OON* (UNESCO as a Specialized Agency of the UN). 1960.

Ruggie, J. "International Responses to Technology; Concepts and Trends." *International Organization.* 1975.

Sauvant, K. *The Group of 77: Evolution, Structure, Organization.* 1981.

Schermers, H. *International Institutional Law.* 1972.

Schiffer, W. *The Legal Community of Mankind.* 1954.

Sewell, J. *UNESCO and World Politics.* 1975.

Shamsul, H. *International Politics: A Third World Perspective.* 1987.

Shibayeva, E. *Spezializirovannye uchrezhdenya OON (Mezhdunarodno pravovoy aspekt)* (Specialized Agencies of the UN [International Legal Aspects]). 1966.

Sinclair, I. *The Vienna Convention on the Law of Treaties.* 1973.

Strossinger, J. *Financing the United Nations System.* 1964.

Tavernier, P. *La Charte des Nations Unies: Commentaire Article par Article.* 1970.

Tesauro, G. *Il finanziamento delle organizzazioni internazionali.* 1969.

Timmler, M. *Können und Wollen.* 1972.

Tumblir, J. *Weltwirtschaftsordnung: Regeln, Kooperation und Soveranität.* 1979.

Tunkin, G. *Pravo i sila v mezhdunarodnoy sisteme* (Law and Power in the International System). 1983.

Ungerer, W. "UNIDO." *Aussenpolitik.* 1972.

Urquhart, B. *Hammerskjöld.* 1972.

van Hoof, G. *Rethinking the Sources of International Law.* 1983.

Vellas, P. *Aspects du droit international économique.* 1989.

Verdross, A. *Universelles Völkerrecht. Theorie und Praxis.* 1984.

Vernon, R. *Les entreprises multinationales: la souveraineté en péril.* 1973.

Vernon, R. *Storm over the Multinationals.* 1977.

Weiss, T. *International Bureaucracy: An Analysis of the Operation of Fundamental and Global International Secretariats.* 1975.

Weiss, T., and A. Jennings. *More for the Least? Prospects for Poorest Countries in the Eighties.* 1983.

Wildhaber, L. *Internationalrechtliche Probleme multinationaler Korporationen.* 1978.

Williams, D. *The Specialized Agencies and the United Nations. The System in Crisis.* 1990.

Young, O. *International Cooperation: Building Regions for Natural Resources and the Environment.* 1989.

Zarb, A. *Les institutions specialisées du système des Nations Unis et leurs membres.* 1980.

Index

ABOUT THE AUTHOR

YOURY LAMBERT is presently a research associate with the Center for International Affairs at Harvard University. He is also an international lawyer. He holds degrees from Harvard, the Fletcher School of Law and Diplomacy at Tufts University, and the Academy of Diplomacy and the Academy of Science, both in Moscow. He is the author of several books, including *Ghana: In Search of Stability, 1957–1992* (Praeger, 1992).